NIHILISM
AND
NIETZSCHE

FRIEDRICH NIETZSCHE

GRAPEVINE BOOKS

Published by
GRAPEVINE BOOKS

www.grapevinebooks.com
email: contact@grapevinebooks.com

Ordering Information:
Quantity sales: Special discounts are available on quantity purchases
by corporations, associations, and others.
For details, reach out to the publisher.

First published by Grapevine Books, 2025
Copyright © Grapevine, 2025

CONTENTS

Get Your Free E-book!

Scan the QR code below to instantly access the e-book **'The Nihilist's Dictionary: Nietzsche's Most Confusing Concepts Decoded'**, absolutely free

https://bonus.grapevinebooks.com/nihilistdictionary

Preface

On Nietzsche, Nihilism, and the Path Through Collapse

Friedrich Nietzsche saw further than most. In the quiet fury of his aphorisms and the poetic violence of his vision, he anticipated something that would come to define our modern age: a creeping void where meaning once stood. He called it nihilism — not a passing mood, but a civilizational condition.

Nihilism, for Nietzsche, is what happens when the highest values humanity has built—truth, morality, religion—collapse under their own weight. We no longer believe in God, yet continue to live as though old structures still guide us. This contradiction, Nietzsche argued, leads not just to doubt but to decay: moral, psychological, and cultural.

This book is about that collapse, and about what Nietzsche believed must follow it.

But it is not simply a collection of quotes or summaries. What you hold in your hands is a carefully curated journey through Nietzsche's engagement with nihilism—from diagnosis to destruction to what he called overcoming. It begins with his sharpest analyses from The Will to Power, follows his genealogical dissections of morality and religion, then moves through cultural criticism, psychological insights, and visionary challenges posed in Zarathustra.

Why Nietzsche's Voice Still Matters

Today's world, despite its technological miracles and hyper-connectivity, trembles with the very forces Nietzsche warned of: moral confusion, political tribalism, cultural exhaustion, and a deep sense of existential drift. In such a world, Nietzsche is neither just a philosopher nor a provocateur—he is a guide to understanding the depths of our condition.

His works were not written for the faint-hearted. They confront us with discomforting truths. But in doing so, they also offer strange new tools: not to return to the past, but to move forward through the storm with clarity, courage, and creative vision.

How to Read This Book

Nietzsche did not write in the orderly format of modern philosophers. His work is fragmentary, poetic, and often contradictory by design. This book respects that spirit while offering thematic structure. The sections are not chronological. Instead, they are organized according to the progression of Nietzsche's engagement with nihilism:

Diagnosis – *What is nihilism and how has it emerged?*

Genealogy – *Where do our values come from?*

Critique – *Why modernity, Christianity, and morality are collapsing.*

Response – *What Nietzsche offers in place of the ruins: the Overman, the Will to Power, Eternal Recurrence.*

You may read this book linearly or jump to the parts that call to you. Each section stands on its own, but together they form an arc—from decay to decision. Nietzsche doesn't just ask us to understand the death of old gods—he demands we ask what comes next, and whether we are willing to become the answer.

Part I: The Diagnosis – What Is *Nihilism?*.

Introduction to European Nihilism

Part 1. Nihilism

1.

Nihilism as a Consequence of the Previous Interpretation of the Value of Existence

2

Nihilism: there is no goal, no answer to the question: why? What is the significance of nihilism? – that the highest values devalue themselves.

3

Radical nihilism is the conviction that existence itself is absolutely indefensible, in the light of the highest values we recognize; it also includes the insight that we have not the least right to assume the existence of a beyond or an intrinsic nature of things which is said to be 'divine', which is said to be morality incarnate.

This insight is a consequence of a carefully cultivated sense of 'truthfulness', which is itself a consequence of the belief in morality.

4

What advantages did the Christian hypothesis of morality offer?

(1) It conferred an absolute value on man, in contrast with the trifling and accidental role he plays in the stream of becoming and passing away.

(2) It served the advocates of God, in as much as it permitted them to characterize the world as perfect, despite all sorrow and evil, because it included 'freedom' – thus evil seemed full of meaning.

(3) It assumed that man has knowledge of absolute values, and thus adequate knowledge of precisely that which is most important.

It prevented men from feeling contempt for themselves as human beings, from siding against life and from being driven to despair by their ignorance; it was a means of self-preservation – in sum, morality was the great antidote to practical and theoretical nihilism.

5

But among the virtues cultivated by morality was truthfulness: in the end, it is this which turns us against morality, and discovers its function, its partiality. At this point, our insight acts as a stimulant to nihilism. We notice that by having interpreted the world in terms of morality for so long, we have acquired needs for what is apparently untrue, a dishonesty so inveterate that we despair of ever shaking it off. On the other hand, what makes life bearable and gives it value seems to depend on these very needs.

A conflict then arises between assigning no value to what we know, and being forbidden to assign any value to the lies we want to tell ourselves – and this antagonism results in a process of disintegration.

6

This is the antinomy: in so far as we believe in morality, we condemn existence.

7

The supreme values in whose service man is supposed to live, especially when being at their disposal is difficult and costly – these social values have been raised above man for purposes of amplification, to convey the impression that they were God's commands, or 'reality', or the world of 'truth', or the hope of a future life. Now that the base origin of these values has become obvious, everything seems to have lost its value and to have become 'meaningless' . . . but this is only an intermediate stage.

8

This nihilistic outcome (that all is worthless) is the result of a moral value judgement. We have come to find selfishness disgusting (even though we have realized that altruism is impossible). We have come to find necessity disgusting (even though we have realized that a liberum arbitrium and an 'intelligible freedom' are impossible). We see that the sphere in which we have placed our values is beyond our reach – and yet that other sphere in which we live has by no means gained value as a result: on the contrary, we have grown weary of it because we have lost the mainspring of our actions. 'Everything up to now was in vain!'

9

Pessimism as the prototype of nihilism.

10

This is our point of departure: pessimism may be regarded as a sign of strength, but in what respect? In the power of its logic and analysis, or when it takes the form of anarchistic and nihilistic tendencies. Pessimism may also be regarded as a sign of decline, but in what respect? When it seems to be the result of pampering, of cosmopolitan dilettantism, of historicism and an effort 'tout comprendre' The critical tension: the extremes appear and become predominant.

11

The logic of pessimism leads ultimately to nihilism, but what motivates it? The notion that everything is worthless, meaningless, the way that moral judgements lie behind all other high ideals. Result: moral value judgements are condemnations, repudiations; morality is the renunciation of the will to live . . .

12

Critique of nihilism

(1)

In the first place, nihilism as a psychological condition is bound to arise when we have sought a 'meaning' in all that occurs which is not to be found; so that in the end we become discouraged. Nihilism, then, is the process of becoming aware of a great waste of energy extending over a long space of time, and suffering at the thought that it was all 'in vain'; we feel unsteady, and lack

opportunities to recuperate or to regain our composure – but most of all, nihilism comes about because we are mortified by our own persistent self-deception . . . The meaning that we seek might be the existence of a moral world order, the 'compliance' of everything with a supreme canon of morality; or an increase of love and harmony in our intercourse with our fellow creatures; or something approaching a general state of happiness; or even a headlong rush into utter annihilation – aims of any kind still constitute a source of meaning. What all these notions have in common is that something is to be achieved through the world process itself; and now we grasp that the process achieves nothing, accomplishes nothing . . . That is why disappointment in regard to the alleged purpose of the process is a cause of nihilism, whether the disappointment is with respect to a very specific purpose, or is a general sense of the inadequacy of every previous hypothesis about the whole 'development' that makes use of the notion of final cause. (Man can no longer think of himself as a fellow labourer in the process, much less the centre of it.)

In the second place, nihilism as a psychological condition arises when man imagines that there is a wholeness, a system, even an organization to all that occurs, so that the mind, longing for something to admire and worship, revels in the general idea of a supreme form of governance and administration (if it is the mind of a logician, perfect consistency and objective dialectic will suffice to reconcile it to everything). When man believes in a kind of unity, in some form of 'monism', he feels a profound sense of relation to and dependence upon a whole that is infinitely superior to him, and feels himself to be a mode of the divine. 'The greater good demands the surrender of the individual . . .' but lo and behold, there is no greater good! In essence, man loses all belief in his own worth if there is no whole of infinite worth encompassing him, no power working through him; or, to put it differently, he conceived of such a whole in order to prop up his own sense of self-worth.

Nihilism as a psychological condition takes yet a third and final form. Given these two insights, that the world process accomplishes nothing, and that it has no great unity by virtue of which the individual might become a part of a larger whole, as if he were completely immersing himself in an element of supreme value, one means of evasion remains: to condemn the whole thing as an illusion, and to invent a world that lies beyond it, a world of truth. As soon as man finds out that this world was merely pieced together to meet his psychological needs, and that he has absolutely no right to it, the final form of nihilism emerges: the nihilism which involves disbelief in a metaphysical world, and which forbids itself any belief in a world of truth. From this standpoint, he must admit that process and change are the only reality, and must deny himself any short cuts to other worlds or false gods – but the world that he has no wish to deny is a world that he cannot endure . . .

What has actually happened? The sense of worthlessness arises when it is understood that the general character of existence does not admit of interpretation in terms of the notions 'purpose', 'unity' or 'truth'. Existence achieves nothing and accomplishes nothing; it lacks an overarching unity in the multiplicity of events which compose it; the character of existence is not 'true', but false; there is utterly no reason to believe in a world of truth . . .

In short, the categories 'purpose', 'unity', 'being' are no longer available to us, and since these were the categories which invested the world with value, the world now seems worthless . . .

(2)

Suppose we were to realize how impossible it is for us to interpret the world in terms of these three categories, and having gained this insight we began to find the world worthless, we would have to ask ourselves where our belief in these three categories came from in the first place – and instead of condemning everything as an illusion, we must see if it is not possible to suspend our belief in them. Once we deprive them of their value, we will no longer consider the proof of their inapplicability a reason to deprive everything else of its value.

Thus it is the belief in the categories of reason which produces nihilism – we have measured the world's worth by categories which pertain to a purely fictitious world.

Therefore, all the values which have previously rendered the world worthy of our esteem ultimately render it worthless when they prove to be inapplicable; examined psychologically, all these values are the products of specific perspectives which proved useful for maintaining and increasing the power of specific forms of domination, perspectives which we have falsely projected into the nature of things. It remains man's supreme naïveté to regard himself as the meaning and measure of all things.

* * *

13

Nihilism represents an intermediate pathological state (what is pathological is the immense generalization, the inference that life has no meaning whatsoever), whether it be that the productive forces are not yet strong enough, or that décadence still hesitates and has not yet devised its expedients.

*

The presupposition of this hypothesis is that there is no truth, no absolute nature of things, no 'thing-in-itself' – this is itself a form of nihilism, and the most extreme form at that. This latter nihilism about the value of things lies precisely in maintaining that these value judgements correspond to nothing in reality, but are instead merely symptomatic of the vigour with which such value judgements are made. They are a simplification for the sake of life.

14

A change in values is commensurate with the growth of power in the one who determines them.

The measure of disbelief, and of the 'intellectual freedom' which we allow to ourselves, may be viewed as an expression of the growth of our power.

'Nihilism' may be viewed as the ideal of the supreme intellectual power, of the superabundant life; it is partly destructive and partly ironical.

15

What is a belief? What gives rise to a belief? Every belief is an act of taking something to be true.

The most extreme form of nihilism would be to think that every belief, every act of taking something to be true, is necessarily false: because there is no world of truth at all.

Therefore, the world with which we are acquainted is an illusion seen from a particular point of view whose origin lies in ourselves, to the extent that we are always in need of a more limited, abridged and simplified world – and that it is a measure of our strength how much illusoriness, how much necessary falsehood, we are able to acknowledge without going to pieces.

From this standpoint, nihilism, as the denial of a world of truth and of being, might be a divine way of thinking . . .

16

If we are 'disillusioned', it is not with respect to life; it is rather because our eyes have been opened to all kinds of 'aspirations'. We look down in scorn and wrath at what the word 'idealism' really means; it is only in consequence of our occasional inability to suppress this perverse impulse that we truly despise ourselves. On those occasions, the wrath of our disillusionment is weaker than the force of habit . . .

17

The extent to which Schopenhauer's nihilism is still the result of the same ideal which gave rise to Christian theism. The degree of assurance in regard to the highest aspiration, the highest values and the highest perfection, was so great that the philosophers trusted it as an absolute certainty a priori, as a truth which we may take for granted, as 'God' first and foremost. 'To become like God', 'to become one with God' – for millennia people have been naïvely convinced of the desirability of these things (as a parenthetical remark for my more asinine readers, what convinces us is not therefore true: it is merely convincing).

We know better now than to take for granted this juxtaposition of ideal and personal reality: we have become atheistic. But has the ideal really been abandoned? In essence, the most recent metaphysicians still seek an underlying 'reality' for it, the 'thing-in-itself' in relation to which everything else is merely illusory. Their dogma is that because our world of illusion is so obviously not the expression of that ideal, and cannot even be traced back to that metaphysical world as its cause, it therefore cannot be 'true'. The unconditioned, so long as it is that supreme perfection, cannot possibly furnish the basis of everything conditioned. Schopenhauer, who wished it otherwise, was obliged to conceive of this metaphysical basis as the opposite of the ideal, as 'an evil, blind will', in such a way that it could be 'that which appears', that which manifests itself in the world of illusion. But even so, he did not abandon that one absolute, the ideal itself – instead, he smuggled it in . . . (Kant seemed to think that the hypothesis of 'intelligible freedom' was necessary in order to relieve God, the ens perfectum, of responsibility for this world's being such-and-such – in short, in order to explain evil and mischief: a scandalous abuse of logic for a philosopher. . .)

18

The most ubiquitous sign of modern times. Man has suffered an incredible loss of dignity in his own eyes. For a long time he thought that he played the central part and tragic hero in the drama of existence; then he made a concerted effort to prove himself at least related to the intrinsically valuable and decisive aspect of existence – as do all metaphysicians who want man to retain his dignity, in their belief that moral values are cardinal values. He who has let go of God clings all the more tenaciously to his belief in morality.

19

Every merely moral determination of values (as, e.g., that of Buddhism) ends in nihilism; the same thing awaits Europe! We think we can dispense with a religious background when we moralize, but this inevitably leads to nihilism. In religion, nothing compels us to admit that we and we alone determine what is valuable.

20

The question which nihilism poses, namely, 'To what end?', springs from the previous habit of regarding ends as set for us, given to us and required of us by something external – that is, by some supernatural authority. Although we have been weaned from believing in this sort of thing, the force of habit still leads us to look for another authority, which could speak to us in a peremptory manner, assigning to us our tasks and aims. The authority of conscience now steps into the foreground (the more we emancipate ourselves from theology, the more morality couches itself in the imperative mood), offering itself as compensation for a personal authority; and if not conscience, then the authority of reason, or the social instinct (the herd), or history with an immanent spirit, which has its own end to which we can resign ourselves. We would like to circumvent the will, its exercise in action directed towards an end and the risk involved in proposing ends to ourselves; we would like to avoid responsibility (which is why we would happily accept fatalism if we could). Finally, we allow happiness to become an obligatory end, and then, with a bit of Tartuffery,4 the greatest happiness of the greatest number.

Notice how the individual ends conflict with one another, and the collective

ends conflict with the individual ones. Everyone will become a party to this, even the philosophers. We tell ourselves (**1**) that a definite end is quite unnecessary, and (**2**) is quite unlikely in the foreseeable future in any case.

Especially now, when what is needed most is a supreme effort of will, we find ourselves weak-willed and faint-hearted.

We have no confidence whatsoever in the ability of the will to organize the whole.

21

The perfect nihilist. The eye of the nihilist, which idealizes into ugliness, is unfaithful to his memories: it discards them as a tree sheds its leaves in autumn; it does not protect them from that deathly pallor which infirmity casts over what is distant and past; the nihilist treats the whole past of mankind no better than he treats himself – he discards it.

22

It can mean two different things:

(a)   Nihilism as a sign of an increase in mental power, as active nihilism . . .

(b)   Nihilism as a decline and retrogression of mental power: passive nihilism.

23

Nihilism is the normal condition.

It may be a sign of strength: mental vigour may have grown so much that the ends which have been pursued thus far ('convictions', articles of faith) are no longer appropriate – for generally speaking, a faith is an expression of the exigencies to which a living creature is subject, the conditions under which it prospers, grows and gains power . . .

On the other hand, it may be a sign of insufficient strength to create one's own aims, purposes or beliefs.

It reaches its maximum of relative vigour as a violent and destructive force, as active nihilism. Its opposite would be a weary nihilism which no longer attacks anything, its most famous form being Buddhism, a passive nihilism as a sign of weakness. Mental vigour may become weary and exhausted, so that the previous aims and values have ceased to be appropriate and have ceased to carry conviction – so that the synthesis of values and aims (the foundation of every strong culture) dissolves, and the particular values contend with one another – disintegration – so that everything which refreshes, heals, soothes or stupefies comes into the foreground under various disguises, be they religious, moral, political, aesthetic, etc.

The Collapse of Meaning

36

The nihilistic philosopher is convinced that all that happens is gratuitous and meaningless, and that reality should not contain anything gratuitous and meaningless. But whence comes this 'should not'? But whence comes this particular 'meaning', this particular standard? In the nihilist's opinion, the sight of a world so desolate and barren leaves the philosopher dissatisfied, desolate and desperate; such a spectacle offends the philosopher's delicate sensibilities. It amounts to nothing more than a preposterous value judgement: the nature of existence is utterly inexcusable if it is not sufficiently pleasing to the philosopher.

Now it is easy to understand that the pleasure and pain occasioned by events can only serve as a means; what remains to be seen is whether we will ever be able to discern the 'meaning' and 'purpose' of things, whether the problem of meaninglessness or its opposite is not a problem which for us admits of no solution.

37

The development of nihilism from pessimism. The denaturalization of values, the Scholasticism of values. Values become detached from their natural purposes, and become mere ideals which, instead of governing and guiding conduct, turn against it and condemn it.

Diametrical opposites are introduced in lieu of natural ranks and degrees, out of hatred of that hierarchy. Opposites are better suited to a plebeian age; the plebs find them easier to comprehend.

The world is then rejected, in favour of an artificially constructed 'true and valuable' one.

Eventually we discover from what material we have constructed the 'world of truth'; now, all that we have left is what we have rejected, and we add this, our greatest disappointment, to all the other reasons for rejecting it.

Thus, we arrive at nihilism: we have retained the values by which we judge – nothing else remains!

Hence arises the problem of strength and weakness:

(1)   The weak are broken by it,

(2)   The strong destroy all that remains unbroken,

(3)   The strongest overcome the values by which we judge.

All told, this is what constitutes the tragic age.

3.   The Nihilistic Movement as an Expression of Décadence

38

There has recently been a great deal of idle talk using a loose and altogether inapplicable term: pessimism. Everywhere the talk is about pessimism, and everywhere people (occasionally even sensible people!) are wrangling over a specific question which they think admits of an answer: whether optimism or pessimism is correct. What they do not understand, although it is palpable, is that pessimism is not a problem but a symptom, that the term should be replaced by nihilism, that the question of whether it is better to be or not to be, is itself an illness, a decline in strength, a kind of hypersensitivity.

The pessimistic movement is only an expression of physiological décadence .. .

39

We need to understand that every kind of disease and decay is constantly making some contribution to the common fund of our value judgements, and that décadence even constitutes the bulk of the prevailing value judgements. Not only do we have to combat the present misery which is the consequence of this degeneration, we also have to combat all the previous décadence that remains behind, i.e. that remains virulent. How such a total aberration of human instinct is even possible, how value judgements could come to be so thoroughly affected by décadence remains the question mark par excellence, the real enigma which the animal 'man' presents to all philosophers.

40

The notion 'décadence'. Degeneration, decay and waste are not to be condemned per se: they are the natural consequences of life and growth. The phenomenon of décadence is just as necessary to life as its progress and ascent, and we are in no position to eliminate it. On the contrary, it is only reasonable to give décadence its due.

It is disgraceful that all the advocates of Socialist theories believe that there could be circumstances and social arrangements which would no longer promote vice, disease, crime, prostitution and even poverty . . . But that amounts to a condemnation of life itself . . . A society is not at liberty to remain young, and even at the height of its powers a society still produces refuse and waste. The more bold and energetic its progress, the more prolific it is in failures and defectives – and the nearer its destruction. One cannot ward off decrepitude, or disease, or vice with better institutions; it is folly to think otherwise.

41

Fundamental insight into the nature of décadence: what have been considered its causes are in fact its consequences, and that entirely alters our perspective on the problems of morality. Vice, luxury, crime, disease even: the whole moral struggle against vice, luxury, etc. seems naïve and superfluous . . . There is no such thing as 'betterment' – against remorse.

Décadence itself is not to be resisted: it is absolutely necessary, and is found in every age and people. What ought to be resisted with all our might is the contagion spreading to the healthy parts of the organism. Is that being done? No, on the contrary, precisely the opposite is being done, on behalf of mankind. How do the previous supreme values of philosophy, religion, morality, art, etc. stand in relation to this fundamental question in biology?

Ever since Napoleon (a man who regarded civilization as his natural enemy), the remedy for all this has been militarism . . .

42

The consequences of décadence include: vice, viciousness; sickness, sickliness; wrongdoing, criminality; celibacy, sterility; hysteria, weakness of will; alcoholism; pessimism; anarchism.

Regarding degeneracy, the first principle is that everything which has previously been regarded as a cause of degeneration is really its consequence.

Vice as a consequence. Sickness, sterility. Wrongdoing: slanderers, subversives, unbelievers, destroyers; scepticism, asceticism, nihilism, otherworldliness. Libertinage (including the intellectual kind) as well as celibacy. Weakness of will, pessimism, anarchism.

But even those things which have been regarded as the remedies of fatigue are only palliatives of some of its effects; the 'cured' are merely degenerate types.

55

However, an extreme position is not supplanted by a more moderate one, but by its opposite extreme. Thus the belief that nature is utterly immoral, that everything is purposeless and meaningless, is a psychologically inevitable sentiment, when belief in God and in an essentially moral world order is no longer tenable. Nihilism appears at this point, not because the pain of existence is greater than formerly, but because the idea that evil, or for that matter existence itself, has a 'meaning' is regarded with the utmost suspicion. One interpretation has failed, but since it was considered the interpretation, it now seems as if there is no meaning in existence at all, as if all is in vain.

It remains to be seen whether this sense of futility characteristic of our current nihilism is warranted. We have become so suspicious of our former value judgements that we are apt to ask, 'are all "values" nothing but plot devices, whose sole purpose is to prolong the farce without bringing it any nearer to a conclusion?' The thought that existence goes on and on, gratuitously, without aim or purpose, paralyses us more than any other, especially when we grasp that we are being played for fools, yet powerless to prevent it.

Let us pursue this thought in its most terrible form: existence as it is, without meaning or aim, but ineluctably recurring, without ending in nothingness: 'the eternal recurrence'.

This is the most extreme form of nihilism: nothingness (that is, 'meaninglessness') for ever!

It is a European form of Buddhism; the energy of matter and of force requires such a belief. It is the most scientific of all possible hypotheses. We deny that there is any ultimate aim of existence; if there were one, it would necessarily have been reached.

It should be understood that what we envisage here is the opposite of pantheism; for the belief that 'everything is perfect, divine, eternal' also requires belief in the 'eternal recurrence'. The question is: is this pantheistic affirmation of all things also rendered impossible along with morality? Strictly speaking, we have only overcome the notion of a moral God. Is there any sense in the notion of a God who is beyond 'good and evil'? Is pantheism in this sense possible? If we remove the idea of purpose from the process, can we still affirm the process? We could if something were accomplished at every moment of the process – and it was always the same thing.

Spinoza came to occupy just such a position, in as much as he considered every moment logically necessary; and his instincts, which were fundamentally logical, gloried in such a world.

However, this is but a single case. If an individual were to see himself in the fundamental characteristic that underlies and finds expression in every event, it would also necessarily impel him to accept, approve and glory in every moment of existence in general. What matters is that the fundamental characteristic be experienced as commendable, valuable and enjoyable.

It is powerlessness against men, not powerlessness against nature, that engenders the most desperate bitterness towards existence. It is abuse and oppression that drive whole classes of men to the brink of despair and suicide, and it is morality that protects them from this. Morality treated despots, tyrants and 'masters' in general as enemies against whom the common man must be protected, i.e. first of all, encouraged and strengthened. Morality has therefore always taught the most profound hatred and contempt for the fundamental characteristic of all rulers: their will to power. To deny, subvert and suppress this morality would mean to feel differently about this most hated of all impulses, and to provide it with an assessment that is quite the reverse. If the suffering and the oppressed no longer believed that they were justified in their contempt for the will to power, they would proceed to the next stage of their condition: hopeless desperation. This would be the case if this characteristic were essential to life, if it could be shown that even the 'will to be moral' was merely the 'will to power' in disguise, and that even the hatred and contempt they feel for the will to power is itself a form of power-seeking. The oppressed would then see that they were on an equal footing with their oppressors, and that they have no special privileges or superiority in this respect.

On the contrary! Nothing in life has any value apart from the degree of power it represents – assuming, of course, that life itself is the will to power. Morality protected these unfortunates from nihilism, in that it attributed to each and every one of them an infinite value, a metaphysical value, and assigned them a place in a hierarchy which did not correspond with that of the secular power and hierarchy: it taught submission, humility, etc. Suppose that belief in this morality were to disintegrate, well then, these unfortunates would no longer have their consolation – and they too would disintegrate.

This disintegration presents itself as a slow suicide, as an instinctive tendency to select that which is inevitably destructive. The symptoms of these unfortunates' self-destruction are self-vivisection, poisoning, intoxication, Romanticism and, above all, the instinctive compulsion to act in ways that make mortal enemies of the powerful (grooming one's own executioner, so to speak), the will to destroy as the will of a still deeper instinct, of the instinct to destroy oneself, of the will to embrace nothingness.

Nihilism is a symptom of the fact that these unfortunates no longer have any consolation. They destroy in order to be destroyed. Having been relieved of morality, they no longer have any reason for 'submission' – they establish themselves on the basis of the opposite principle, and want power for themselves by compelling the powerful to become their executioners. This is the European form of Buddhism, the active negation that comes after life has lost all 'meaning'.

It is not that they endure greater 'hardships' now; on the contrary! 'God, morality and submission' were remedies prescribed for people in terrible depths of misery; the circumstances under which active nihilism arises are comparatively more favourable. Already, the fact that morality is regarded as conquered presupposes a high degree of intellectual culture; this, in turn, presupposes living in comparative luxuriousness. The sophistication of these nihilists is also indicated by their irredeemable scepticism towards philosophers, the symptom of a certain intellectual fatigue brought about by the long conflict of philosophical opinions; their position is by no means that of the commoners. Think of the situation in which the Buddha appeared. The teaching of the eternal recurrence would rest upon learned assumptions (such as those Buddha the teacher had, e.g. the notion of causality, etc.).

What is here meant by the expression 'unfortunates? Above all, it is being used in a physiological (?) and not in a political sense. The most unhealthy kind of men in Europe (in all classes) form the basis of this nihilism. They will experience belief in the eternal recurrence as a curse, and men who are stricken with this curse will not be content to wait patiently for their own annihilation; on the contrary, they will not hesitate to bring about the annihilation of all that is aimless and meaningless, though this is only a paroxysm of blind rage at the thought that all things have existed from eternity, including this period of nihilism and its appetite for destruction.

The value of such a crisis is that it purifies, that it forces together related elements to their mutual destruction, that it assigns common tasks to men of opposite ways of thinking – bringing to light the weaker and more insecure among them, thus giving impetus to the establishment of a hierarchy of forces with respect to health: recognizing commanders as commanders, subordinates as subordinates, though not within the existing social order, it goes without saying.

Who will prove to be the strongest in this situation? The most moderate, those who have no need of extreme beliefs; those who not only accept but embrace a great deal of contingency and absurdity; those who can contemplate a significant reduction in man's value, but without thereby becoming weak and petty; who are richest in health, who are able to cope with misfortune, and therefore do not fear misfortune – men who are sure of their power, and who with conscious pride represent the accumulated strength of the whole human race.

What would such a man think of the eternal recurrence?

56

On the history of European nihilism. In the period of confusion, there are all sorts of attempts to conserve the old without abandoning the new. In the period of clarity, it becomes apparent that the old and the new are fundamentally opposed; that the old values are born of declining life, and that the new ones are born of ascending life; that knowledge of nature and history no longer allowed us such 'hopes'; that all old ideals are deadly (born of décadence and constitutive of it, however much they may come to us splendidly clad in morality like a suit of Sunday's best). We understand the old, but are not nearly strong enough for the new. The period of the three great passions: contempt, compassion and destructiveness. The period of catastrophe: the rise of a doctrine which will sift men . . . by which both weak and strong are driven to extremities and forced to a decision.

Part 2. On the History of European Nihilism

1.Modern Gloom

57

My friends, we had a hard time when we were young: we even suffered from youth itself as from a severe illness. This is due to the times into which we were thrown – a period of great, ever-worsening decline and disintegration, which, in all its weaknesses, and even in its greatest strength, is inimical to the spirit of youth. Disintegration, and thus uncertainty, is peculiar to this age: nothing stands on a firm footing or rests on an unwavering faith: men live for tomorrow, as the day after tomorrow has become doubtful. Everything on our way is slippery and dangerous, and while we have not yet fallen through the ice, it is getting very thin: we feel the baleful breath of the warm, thawing wind – where we tread, soon no one will be able to follow

58

If this is not an age of decline and diminishing vitality, an age rife with melancholy, then it is at the least one of reckless, indiscriminate experimentation which may give rise to a general impression of decline, and perhaps even decline itself, given its profusion of failed experiments.

59

On the history of modern gloom

The nomads of the state (officials, etc.) have no sense of 'homeland' – the family is in decline.

'The good man' is a symptom of exhaustion. Justice is the will to power (cultivation).

Lasciviousness and neurosis.

Sombre music – where has the refreshing music gone?

The anarchist. Misanthropy. Disgust.

The most profound distinction is whether hunger or abundance has become creative? It is the former that creates the ideals of Romanticism. Nordic unnaturalness.

The need for alcoholic beverages in the worker – 'hardship'.

Philosophical nihilism.

60

NB. The slow emergence and rise of the middle and lower classes (including those intellectually and physically inferior) was already abundantly foreshadowed prior to the French Revolution and would have gone forwards just as well without it. As a whole, then, the preponderance of the herd over all shepherds and bellwethers brings in its train:

(1) A melancholy disposition: that Stoicism which accompanies a frivolous appearance of happiness peculiar to noble cultures is on the decline; much that was once suffered in silence is now allowed to be seen and heard.

(2) Moral hypocrisy, a way of trying to distinguish oneself through morality, but

by means of the virtues of the herd (sympathy, solicitude, good deeds),

which are recognized and honoured only to the extent that the herd is capable of them.

(3) The very great deal of sympathy and conviviality, the satisfaction of great fellowship which is peculiar to all herds – 'public spirit', 'patriotism', everything in which the individual is immaterial.

61

Our age, in its endeavour to alleviate misfortune and wage pre-emptive war against every unpleasant eventuality, is an age of the poor. Our 'rich' – they are the poorest of all! The real purpose of all wealth has been forgotten!

62

Critique of modern man (and of his moralistic dishonesty). The idea that 'the good man' has merely been corrupted and led astray by bad institutions (by tyrants and priests). The elevation of 'reason' to a position of authority, with history regarded as the overcoming of error, the future regarded as progress. The Christian state, 'the Lord of hosts'. Christian sexual relations, or marriage. The realm of 'justice', the cult of 'humanity', 'freedom'.

The Romantic posturing of modern man: the noble (Byron, V. Hugo, G. Sand), and their noble indignation, their sanctification by passion (as one's true 'nature').

The espousal of the oppressed and unfortunate becoming a motto for historians and romanciers. Modern Stoics and their 'duty'. The value placed on 'selflessness' in art and knowledge. Altruism as the most mendacious form of egoism (utilitarianism), the most sentimental form of egoism.

All this smacks of the eighteenth century. But there are other qualities of that age which we have not inherited: insouciance, cheerfulness, elegance, clearness of intellect; the intellectual tempo has changed; the enjoyment of intellectual subtlety and lucidity has given way to the enjoyment of colour, harmony, composition, realism, etc. Empiricism in the intellectual realm. In short, it is the eighteenth century of Rousseau.

63

Broadly speaking, modern man has become exceedingly humane. That this is not generally perceived demonstrates that we are now so sensitive to petty hardships that we unreasonably disregard what has been achieved. Here we must make allowances for the fact that our world is rife with décadence, and seen from that point of view would have to seem corrupt and miserable. But from a decadent point of view, the world has always seemed that way . . .

Two things taken together have aided this impression: a certain oversensitiveness, even of the moral sentiments, and a measure of bitterness and gloom with which pessimism colours judgements. As a result, the opposite idea prevails that morality is in a very bad way.

Also contributing to this impression is the disentanglement of science from moral and religious intentions; as a matter of fact, this is a very good sign, though it is for the most part misunderstood.

In support of the proposition that we have become more humane, I would mention the fact of credit, international commerce and transportation, all of which are expressions of an extraordinary degree of genial trust among men . . .

In my own way, I am attempting a justification of history.

Part II: The Roots of *Nihilism*

The Roots of Nihilism [The Improvers of Mankind]
"GUILT," "BAD CONSCIENCE," AND THE LIKE.

1.

The breeding of an animal that can promise—is not this just that very paradox of a task which nature has set itself in regard to man? Is not this the very problem of man? The fact that this problem has been to a great extent solved, must appear all the more phenomenal to one who can estimate at its full value that force of forgetfulness which works in opposition to it. Forgetfulness is no mere vis inertiæ, as the superficial believe, rather is it a power of obstruction, active and, in the strictest sense of the word, positive—a power responsible for the fact that what we have lived, experienced, taken into ourselves, no more enters into consciousness during the process of digestion (it might be called psychic absorption) than all the whole manifold process by which our physical nutrition, the so-called "incorporation," is carried on. The temporary shutting of the doors and windows of consciousness, the relief from the clamant alarums and excursions, with which our subconscious world of servant organs works in mutual co-operation and antagonism; a little quietude, a little tabula rasa of the consciousness, so as to make room again for the new, and above all for the more noble functions and functionaries, room for government, foresight, predetermination (for our organism is on an oligarchic model)—this is the utility, as I have said, of the active forgetfulness, which is a very sentinel and nurse of psychic order, repose, etiquette; and this shows at once why it is that there can exist no happiness, no gladness, no hope, no pride, no real present, without forgetfulness. The man in whom this preventative apparatus is damaged and discarded, is to be compared to a dyspeptic, and it is something more than a comparison—he can "get rid of" nothing. But this very animal who finds it necessary to be forgetful, in whom, in fact, forgetfulness represents a force and a form of robust health, has reared for himself an opposition-power, a memory, with whose help forgetfulness is, in certain instances, kept in check—in the cases, namely, where promises have to be made;—so that it is by no means a mere passive inability to get rid of a once indented impression, not merely the indigestion occasioned by a once pledged word, which one cannot dispose of, but an active refusal to get rid of it, a continuing and a wish to continue what has once been willed, an actual memory of the will; so that between the original "I will," "I shall do," and the actual discharge of the will, its act, we can easily interpose a world of new strange phenomena, circumstances, veritable volitions, without the snapping of this long chain of the will. But what is the underlying hypothesis of all this? How thoroughly, in order to be able to regulate the future in this way, must man have first learnt to distinguish between necessitated and accidental phenomena, to think causally, to see the distant as present and to anticipate it, to fix with certainty what is the end, and what is the means to that end; above all, to reckon, to have power to calculate—how thoroughly must man have first become calculable, disciplined, necessitated even for himself and his own conception of himself, that, like a man entering into a promise, he could guarantee himself as a future.

<h1 style="text-align:center">2.</h1>

This is simply the long history of the origin of responsibility. That task of breeding an animal which can make promises, includes, as we have already grasped, as its condition and preliminary, the more immediate task of first making man to a certain extent, necessitated, uniform, like among his like, regular, and consequently calculable. The immense work of what I have called, "morality of custom"[1] (cp. Dawn of Day, Aphs. **9**, **14**, and **16**), the actual work of man on himself during the longest period of the human race, his whole prehistoric work, finds its meaning, its great justification (in spite of all its innate hardness, despotism, stupidity, and idiocy) in this fact: man, with the help of the morality of customs and of social strait-waistcoats, was made genuinely calculable. If, however, we place ourselves at the end of this colossal process, at the point where the tree finally matures its fruits, when society and its morality of custom finally bring to light that to which it was only the means, then do we find as the ripest fruit on its tree the sovereign individual, that resembles only himself, that has got loose from the morality of custom, the autonomous "super-moral" individual (for "autonomous" and "moral" are mutually-exclusive terms),—in short, the man of the personal, long, and independent will, competent to promise, and we find in him a proud consciousness (vibrating in every fibre), of what has been at last achieved and become vivified in him, a genuine consciousness of power and freedom, a feeling of human perfection in general. And this man who has grown to freedom, who is really competent to promise, this lord of the free will, this sovereign—how is it possible for him not to know how great is his superiority over everything incapable of binding itself by promises, or of being its own security, how great is the trust, the awe, the reverence that he awakes—he "deserves" all three—not to know that with this mastery over himself he is necessarily also given the mastery over circumstances, over nature, over all creatures with shorter wills, less reliable characters? The "free" man, the owner of a long unbreakable will, finds in this possession his standard of value: looking out from himself upon the others, he honours or he despises, and just as necessarily as he honours his peers, the strong and the reliable (those who can bind themselves by promises),—that is, every one who promises like a sovereign, with difficulty, rarely and slowly, who is sparing with his trusts but confers honour by the very fact of trusting, who gives his word as something that can be relied on, because he knows himself strong enough to keep it even in the teeth of disasters, even in the "teeth of fate,"—so with equal necessity will he have the heel of his foot ready for the lean and empty jackasses, who promise when they have no business to do so, and his rod of chastisement ready for the liar, who already breaks his word at the very minute when it is on his lips. The proud knowledge of the extraordinary privilege of responsibility, the consciousness of this rare freedom, of this power over himself and over fate, has sunk right down to his innermost depths, and has become an instinct, a dominating instinct—what name will he give to it, to this dominating instinct, if he needs to have a word for it? But there is no doubt about it—the sovereign man calls it his conscience.

<h1 style="text-align:center">3.</h1>

His conscience?—One apprehends at once that the idea "conscience," which is here seen in its supreme manifestation, supreme in fact to almost the point of strangeness, should already have behind it a long history and evolution. The ability to guarantee one's self with all due pride, and also at the same time to say yes to one's self—that is, as has been said, a ripe fruit, but also a late fruit:——How long must needs this fruit hang sour and bitter on the tree! And for an even longer period there was not a glimpse of such a fruit to to be had—no one had taken it on himself to promise it, although everything on the tree was quite ready for it, and everything was maturing for that very consummation. "How is a memory to be made for the man-animal? How is an impression to be so deeply fixed upon this ephemeral understanding, half dense, and half silly, upon this incarnate forgetfulness, that it will be permanently present?" As one may imagine, this primeval problem was not solved by exactly gentle answers and gentle means; perhaps there is nothing more awful and more sinister in the early history of man than his system of mnemonics. "Something is burnt in so as to remain in his memory: only that which never stops hurting remains in his memory." This is an axiom of the oldest (unfortunately also the longest) psychology in the world. It might even be said that wherever solemnity, seriousness, mystery, and gloomy colours are now found in the life of the men and of nations of the world, there is some survival of that horror which was once the universal concomitant of all promises, pledges, and obligations. The past, the past with all its length, depth, and hardness, wafts to us its breath, and bubbles up in us again, when we become "serious." When man thinks it necessary to make for himself a memory, he never accomplishes it without blood, tortures, and sacrifice; the most dreadful sacrifices and forfeitures (among them the sacrifice of the first-born), the most loathsome mutilation (for instance, castration), the most cruel rituals of all the religious cults (for all religions are really at bottom systems of cruelty)——all these things originate from that instinct which found in pain its most potent mnemonic. In a certain sense the whole of asceticism is to be ascribed to this: certain ideas have got to be made inextinguishable, omnipresent, "fixed," with the object of hypnotising the whole nervous and intellectual system through these "fixed ideas"—and the ascetic methods and modes of life are the means of freeing those ideas from the competition of all other ideas so as to make them "unforgettable." The worse memory man had, the ghastlier the signs presented by his customs; the severity of the penal laws affords in particular a gauge of the extent of man's difficulty in conquering forgetfulness, and in keeping a few primal postulates of social intercourse ever present to the minds of those who were the slaves of every momentary emotion and every momentary desire. We Germans do certainly not regard ourselves as an especially cruel and hard-hearted nation, still less as an especially casual and happy-go-lucky one; but one has only to look at our old penal ordinances in order to realise what a lot of trouble it takes in the world to evolve a "nation of thinkers" (I mean: the European nation which exhibits at this very day the maximum of reliability, seriousness, bad taste, and positiveness, which has on the strength of these qualities a right to train every kind of European mandarin). These Germans employed terrible means to make for themselves a memory, to enable them to master their rooted plebeian instincts and the brutal crudity of those instincts: think of the old German punishments, for instance, stoning (as far back as the legend, the millstone falls on the head of the guilty man), breaking on the wheel (the most original invention and speciality of the German genius in the sphere of punishment), dart-throwing, tearing, or trampling by horses ("quartering"), boiling the criminal in oil or wine (still prevalent in the fourteenth and fifteenth centuries), the highly popular flaying ("slicing into strips"), cutting the flesh out of the breast; think also of the evil-doer being besmeared with honey, and then exposed to the flies in a blazing sun. It was by the help of such images and precedents that man eventually kept in his memory five or six "I will nots" with regard to which he had already given his promise, so as to be able to enjoy the advantages of society—and verily with the help of this kind of memory man eventually attained "reason"! Alas! reason, seriousness, mastery over the emotions, all these gloomy, dismal things which are called reflection, all these privileges and pageantries of humanity: how dear is the price that they have exacted! How much blood and cruelty is the foundation of all "good things"!

4.

But how is it that that other melancholy object, the consciousness of sin, the whole "bad conscience," came into the world? And it is here that we turn back to our genealogists of morals. For the second time I say—or have I not said it yet?—that they are worth nothing. Just their own five-spans-long limited modern experience; no knowledge of the past, and no wish to know it; still less a historic instinct, a power of "second sight" (which is what is really required in this case)—and despite this to go in for the history of morals. It stands to reason that this must needs produce results which are removed from the truth by something more than a respectful distance.

Have these current genealogists of morals ever allowed themselves to have even the vaguest notion, for instance, that the cardinal moral idea of "ought"[2] originates from the very material idea of "owe"? Or that punishment developed as a retaliation absolutely independently of any preliminary hypothesis of the freedom or determination of the will?—And this to such an extent, that a high degree of civilisation was always first necessary for the animal man to begin to make those much more primitive distinctions of "intentional," "negligent," "accidental," "responsible," and their contraries, and apply them in the assessing of punishment. That idea—"the wrong-doer deserves punishment because he might have acted otherwise," in spite of the fact that it is nowadays so cheap, obvious, natural, and inevitable, and that it has had to serve as an illustration of the way in which the sentiment of justice appeared on earth, is in point of fact an exceedingly late, and even refined form of human judgment and inference; the placing of this idea back at the beginning of the world is simply a clumsy violation of the principles of primitive psychology. Throughout the longest period of human history punishment was never based on the responsibility of the evil-doer for his action, and was consequently not based on the hypothesis that only the guilty should be punished;—on the contrary, punishment was inflicted in those days for the same reason that parents punish their children even nowadays, out of anger at an injury that they have suffered, an anger which vents itself mechanically on the author of the injury—but this anger is kept in bounds and modified through the idea that every injury has somewhere or other its equivalent price, and can really be paid off, even though it be by means of pain to the author. Whence is it that this ancient deep-rooted and now perhaps ineradicable idea has drawn its strength, this idea of an equivalency between injury and pain? I have already revealed its origin, in the contractual relationship between creditor and ower, that is as old as the existence of legal rights at all, and in its turn points back to the primary forms of purchase, sale, barter, and trade.

5.

The realisation of these contractual relations excites, of course (as would be already expected from our previous observations), a great deal of suspicion and opposition towards the primitive society which made or sanctioned them. In this society promises will be made; in this society the object is to provide the promiser with a memory; in this society, so may we suspect, there will be full scope for hardness, cruelty, and pain: the "ower," in order to induce credit in his promise of repayment, in order to give a guarantee of the earnestness and sanctity of his promise, in order to drill into his own conscience the duty, the solemn duty, of repayment, will, by virtue of a contract with his creditor to meet the contingency of his not paying, pledge something that he still possesses, something that he still has in his power, for instance, his life or his wife, or his freedom or his body (or under certain religious conditions even his salvation, his soul's welfare, even his peace in the grave; so in Egypt, where the corpse of the ower found even in the grave no rest from the creditor—of course, from the Egyptian standpoint, this peace was a matter of particular importance). But especially has the creditor the power of inflicting on the body of the ower all kinds of pain and torture— the power, for instance, of cutting off from it an amount that appeared proportionate to the greatness of the debt;—this point of view resulted in the universal prevalence at an early date of precise schemes of valuation, frequently horrible in the minuteness and meticulosity of their application, legally sanctioned schemes of valuation for individual limbs and parts of the body. I consider it as already a progress, as a proof of a freer, less petty, and more Roman conception of law, when the Roman Code of the Twelve Tables decreed that it was immaterial how much or how little the creditors in such a contingency cut off, "si plus minusve secuerunt, ne fraude esto." Let us make the logic of the whole of this equalisation process clear; it is strange enough. The equivalence consists in this: instead of an advantage directly compensatory of his injury (that is, instead of an equalisation in money, lands, or some kind of chattel), the creditor is granted by way of repayment and compensation a certain sensation of satisfaction—the satisfaction of being able to vent, without any trouble, his power on one who is powerless, the delight "de faire le mal pour le plaisir de le faire," the joy in sheer violence: and this joy will be relished in proportion to the lowness and humbleness of the creditor in the social scale, and is quite apt to have the effect of the most delicious dainty, and even seem the foretaste of a higher social position. Thanks to the punishment of the "ower," the creditor participates in the rights of the masters. At last he too, for once in a way, attains the edifying consciousness of being able to despise and ill-treat a creature—as an "inferior"—or at any rate of seeing him being despised and ill-treated, in case the actual power of punishment, the administration of punishment, has already become transferred to the "authorities." The compensation consequently consists in a claim on cruelty and a right to draw thereon.

6.

It is then in this sphere of the law of contract that we find the cradle of the whole moral world of the ideas of "guilt," "conscience," "duty," the "sacredness of duty,"—their commencement, like the commencement of all great things in the world, is thoroughly and continuously saturated with blood. And should we not add that this world has never really lost a certain savour of blood and torture (not even in old Kant; the categorical imperative reeks of cruelty). It was in this sphere likewise that there first became formed that sinister and perhaps now indissoluble association of the ideas of "guilt" and "suffering." To put the question yet again, why can suffering be a compensation for "owing"?—Because the infliction of suffering produces the highest degree of happiness, because the injured party will get in exchange for his loss (including his vexation at his loss) an extraordinary counter-pleasure: the infliction of suffering—a real feast, something that, as I have said, was all the more appreciated the greater the paradox created by the rank and social status of the creditor. These observations are purely conjectural; for, apart from the painful nature of the task, it is hard to plumb such profound depths: the clumsy introduction of the idea of "revenge" as a connecting-link simply hides and obscures the view instead of rendering it clearer (revenge itself simply leads back again to the identical problem—"How can the infliction of suffering be a satisfaction?"). In my opinion it is repugnant to the delicacy, and still more to the hypocrisy of tame domestic animals (that is, modern men; that is, ourselves), to realise with all their energy the extent to which cruelty constituted the great joy and delight of ancient man, was an ingredient which seasoned nearly all his pleasures, and conversely the extent of the naïveté and innocence with which he manifested his need for cruelty, when he actually made as a matter of principle "disinterested malice" (or, to use Spinoza's expression, the sympathia malevolens) into a normal characteristic of man—as consequently something to which the conscience says a hearty yes. The more profound observer has perhaps already had sufficient opportunity for noticing this most ancient and radical joy and delight of mankind; in Beyond Good and Evil, Aph. **188** (and even earlier, in The Dawn of Day, Aphs. **18, 77, 113**), I have cautiously indicated the continually growing spiritualisation and "deification" of cruelty, which pervades the whole history of the higher civilisation (and in the larger sense even constitutes it). At any rate the time is not so long past when it was impossible to conceive of royal weddings and national festivals on a grand scale, without executions, tortures, or perhaps an auto-da-fé", or similarly to conceive of an aristocratic household, without a creature to serve as a butt for the cruel and malicious baiting of the inmates. (The reader will perhaps remember Don Quixote at the court of the Duchess: we read nowadays the whole of Don Quixote with a bitter taste in the mouth, almost with a sensation of torture, a fact which would appear very strange and very incomprehensible to the author and his contemporaries—they read it with the best conscience in the world as the gayest of books; they almost died with laughing at it.) The sight of suffering does one good, the infliction of suffering does one more good—this is a hard maxim, but none the less a fundamental maxim, old, powerful, and "human, all-too-human"; one, moreover, to which perhaps even the apes as well would subscribe: for it is said that in inventing bizarre cruelties they are giving abundant proof of their future humanity, to which, as it were, they are playing the prelude. Without cruelty, no feast: so teaches the oldest and longest history of man—and in punishment too is there so much of the festive.

7.

Entertaining, as I do, these thoughts, I am, let me say in parenthesis, fundamentally opposed to helping our pessimists to new water for the discordant and groaning mills of their disgust with life; on the contrary, it should be shown specifically that, at the time when mankind was not yet ashamed of its cruelty, life in the world was brighter than it is nowadays when there are pessimists. The darkening of the heavens over man has always increased in proportion to the growth of man's shame before man. The tired pessimistic outlook, the mistrust of the riddle of life, the icy negation of disgusted ennui, all those are not the signs of the most evil age of the human race: much rather do they come first to the light of day, as the swamp-flowers, which they are, when the swamp to which they belong, comes into existence—I mean the diseased refinement and moralisation, thanks to which the "animal man" has at last learnt to be ashamed of all his instincts. On the road to angelhood (not to use in this context a harder word) man has developed that dyspeptic stomach and coated tongue, which have made not only the joy and innocence of the animal repulsive to him, but also life itself:—so that sometimes he stands with stopped nostrils before his own self, and, like Pope Innocent the Third, makes a black list of his own horrors ("unclean generation, loathsome nutrition when in the maternal body, badness of the matter out of which man develops, awful stench, secretion of saliva, urine, and excrement"). Nowadays, when suffering is always trotted out as the first argument against existence, as its most sinister query, it is well to remember the times when men judged on converse principles because they could not dispense with the infliction of suffering, and saw therein a magic of the first order, a veritable bait of seduction to life.

Perhaps in those days (this is to solace the weaklings) pain did not hurt so much as it does nowadays: any physician who has treated negroes (granted that these are taken as representative of the prehistoric man) suffering from severe internal inflammations which would bring a European, even though he had the soundest constitution, almost to despair, would be in a position to come to this conclusion. Pain has not the same effect with negroes. (The curve of human sensibilities to pain seems indeed to sink in an extraordinary and almost sudden fashion, as soon as one has passed the upper ten thousand or ten millions of over-civilised humanity, and I personally have no doubt that, by comparison with one painful night passed by one single hysterical chit of a cultured woman, the suffering of all the animals taken together who have been put to the question of the knife, so as to give scientific answers, are simply negligible.) We may perhaps be allowed to admit the possibility of the craving for cruelty not necessarily having become really extinct: it only requires, in view of the fact that pain hurts more nowadays, a certain sublimation and subtilisation, it must especially be translated to the imaginative and psychic plane, and be adorned with such smug euphemisms, that even the most fastidious and hypocritical conscience could never grow suspicious of their real nature ("Tragic pity" is one of these euphemisms: another is "les nostalgies de la croix"). What really raises one's indignation against suffering is not suffering intrinsically, but the senselessness of suffering; such a senselessness, however, existed neither in Christianity, which interpreted suffering into a whole mysterious salvation-apparatus, nor in the beliefs of the naive ancient man, who only knew how to find a meaning in suffering from the standpoint of the spectator, or the inflictor of the suffering. In order to get the secret, undiscovered, and unwitnessed suffering out of the world it was almost compulsory to invent gods and a hierarchy of intermediate beings, in short, something which wanders even among secret places, sees even in the dark, and makes a point of never missing an interesting and painful spectacle. It was with the help of such inventions that life got to learn the tour de force, which has become part of its stock-in-trade, the tour de force of self-justification, of the justification of evil; nowadays this would perhaps require other auxiliary devices (for instance, life as a riddle, life as a problem of knowledge). "Every evil is justified in the sight of which a god finds edification," so rang the logic of primitive sentiment—and, indeed, was it only of primitive? The gods conceived as friends of spectacles of cruelty—oh how far does this primeval conception extend even nowadays into our European civilisation!

One would perhaps like in this context to consult Luther and Calvin. It is at any rate certain that even the Greeks knew no more piquant seasoning for the happiness of their gods than the joys of cruelty. What, do you think, was the mood with which Homer makes his gods look down upon the fates of men? What final meaning have at bottom the Trojan War and similar tragic horrors? It is impossible to entertain any doubt on the point: they were intended as festival games for the gods, and, in so far as the poet is of a more godlike breed than other men, as festival games also for the poets. It was in just this spirit and no other, that at a later date the moral philosophers of Greece conceived the eyes of God as still looking down on the moral struggle, the heroism, and the self-torture of the virtuous; the Heracles of duty was on a stage, and was conscious of the fact; virtue without witnesses was something quite unthinkable for this nation of actors. Must not that philosophic invention, so audacious and so fatal, which was then absolutely new to Europe, the invention of "free will," of the absolute spontaneity of man in good and evil, simply have been made for the specific purpose of justifying the idea, that the interest of the gods in humanity and human virtue was inexhaustible?

There would never on the stage of this free-will world be a dearth of really new, really novel and exciting situations, plots, catastrophes. A world thought out on completely deterministic lines would be easily guessed by the gods, and would consequently soon bore them—sufficient reason for these friends of the gods, the philosophers, not to ascribe to their gods such a deterministic world. The whole of ancient humanity is full of delicate consideration for the spectator, being as it is a world of thorough publicity and theatricality, which could not conceive of happiness without spectacles and festivals.—And, as has already been said, even in great punishment there is so much which is festive.

8.

The feeling of "ought," of personal obligation (to take up again the train of our inquiry), has had, as we saw, its origin in the oldest and most original personal relationship that there is, the relationship between buyer and seller, creditor and ower: here it was that individual confronted individual, and that individual matched himself against individual. There has not yet been found a grade of civilisation so low, as not to manifest some trace of this relationship. Making prices, assessing values, thinking out equivalents, exchanging—all this preoccupied the primal thoughts of man to such an extent that in a certain sense it constituted thinking itself: it was here that was trained the oldest form of sagacity, it was here in this sphere that we can perhaps trace the first commencement of man's pride, of his feeling of superiority over other animals. Perhaps our word "Mensch" (manas) still expresses just something of this self-pride: man denoted himself as the being who measures values, who values and measures, as the "assessing" animal par excellence. Sale and purchase, together with their psychological concomitants, are older than the origins of any form of social organisation and union: it is rather from the most rudimentary form of individual right that the budding consciousness of exchange, commerce, debt, right, obligation, compensation was first transferred to the rudest and most elementary of the social complexes (in their relation to similar complexes), the habit of comparing force with force, together with that of measuring, of calculating. His eye was now focussed to this perspective; and with that ponderous consistency characteristic of ancient thought, which, though set in motion with difficulty, yet proceeds inflexibly along the line on which it has started, man soon arrived at the great generalisation, "everything has its price, all can be paid for," the oldest and most naive moral canon of justice, the beginning of all "kindness," of all "equity," of all "goodwill," of all "objectivity" in the world. Justice in this initial phase is the goodwill among people of about equal power to come to terms with each other, to come to an understanding again by means of a settlement, and with regard to the less powerful, to compel them to agree among themselves to a settlement.

9.

Measured always by the standard of antiquity (this antiquity, moreover, is present or again possible at all periods), the community stands to its members in that important and radical relationship of creditor to his "owers." Man lives in a community, man enjoys the advantages of a community (and what advantages! we occasionally underestimate them nowadays), man lives protected, spared, in peace and trust, secure from certain injuries and enmities, to which the man outside the community, the "peaceless" man, is exposed,—a German understands the original meaning of "Elend" (êlend),—secure because he has entered into pledges and obligations to the community in respect of these very injuries and enmities. What happens when this is not the case? The community, the defrauded creditor, will get itself paid, as well as it can, one can reckon on that. In this case the question of the direct damage done by the offender is quite subsidiary: quite apart from this the criminal[3] is above all a breaker, a breaker of word and covenant to the whole, as regards all the advantages and amenities of the communal life in which up to that time he had participated. The criminal is an "ower" who not only fails to repay the advances and advantages that have been given to him, but even sets out to attack his creditor: consequently he is in the future not only, as is fair, deprived of all these advantages and amenities—he is in addition reminded of the importance of those advantages. The wrath of the injured creditor, of the community, puts him back in the wild and outlawed status from which he was previously protected: the community repudiates him—and now every kind of enmity can vent itself on him. Punishment is in this stage of civilisation simply the copy, the mimic, of the normal treatment of the hated, disdained, and conquered enemy, who is not only deprived of every right and protection but of every mercy; so we have the martial law and triumphant festival of the væ victis! in all its mercilessness and cruelty. This shows why war itself (counting the sacrificial cult of war) has produced all the forms under which punishment has manifested itself in history.

10.

As it grows more powerful, the community tends to take the offences of the individual less seriously, because they are now regarded as being much less revolutionary and dangerous to the corporate existence: the evil-doer is no more outlawed and put outside the pale, the common wrath can no longer vent itself upon him with its old licence,— on the contrary, from this very time it is against this wrath, and particularly against the wrath of those directly injured, that the evil-doer is carefully shielded and protected by the community. As, in fact, the penal law develops, the following characteristics become more and more clearly marked: compromise with the wrath of those directly affected by the misdeed; a consequent endeavour to localise the matter and to prevent a further, or indeed a general spread of the disturbance; attempts to find equivalents and to settle the whole matter (compositio); above all, the will, which manifests itself with increasing definiteness, to treat every offence as in a certain degree capable of being paid off, and consequently, at any rate up to a certain point, to isolate the offender from his act. As the power and the self-consciousness of a community increases, so proportionately does the penal law become mitigated; conversely every weakening and jeopardising of the community revives the harshest forms of that law. The creditor has always grown more humane proportionately as he has grown more rich; finally the amount of injury he can endure without really suffering becomes the criterion of his wealth. It is possible to conceive of a society blessed with so great a consciousness of its own power as to indulge in the most aristocratic luxury of letting its wrong-doers go scot-free.—"What do my parasites matter to me?" might society say. "Let them live and flourish! I am strong enough for it."—The justice which began with the maxim, "Everything can be paid off, everything must be paid off," ends with connivance at the escape of those who cannot pay to escape—it ends, like every good thing on earth, by destroying itself.—The self-destruction of Justice! we know the pretty name it calls itself—Grace! it remains, as is obvious, the privilege of the strongest, better still, their super-law.

11.

A deprecatory word here against the attempts, that have lately been made, to find the origin of justice on quite another basis—namely, on that of resentment. Let me whisper a word in the ear of the psychologists, if they would fain study revenge itself at close quarters: this plant blooms its prettiest at present among Anarchists and anti-Semites, a hidden flower, as it has ever been, like the violet, though, forsooth, with another perfume. And as like must necessarily emanate from like, it will not be a matter for surprise that it is just in such circles that we see the birth of endeavours (it is their old birthplace—compare above, First Essay, paragraph **14**), to sanctify revenge under the name of justice (as though Justice were at bottom merely a development of the consciousness of injury), and thus with the rehabilitation of revenge to reinstate generally and collectively all the reactive emotions. I object to this last point least of all. It even seems meritorious when regarded from the standpoint of the whole problem of biology (from which standpoint the value of these emotions has up to the present been underestimated). And that to which I alone call attention, is the circumstance that it is the spirit of revenge itself, from which develops this new nuance of scientific equity (for the benefit of hate, envy, mistrust, jealousy, suspicion, rancour, revenge). This scientific "equity" stops immediately and makes way for the accents of deadly enmity and prejudice, so soon as another group of emotions comes on the scene, which in my opinion are of a much higher biological value than these reactions, and consequently have a paramount claim to the valuation and appreciation of science: I mean the really active emotions, such as personal and material ambition, and so forth. (E. Dühring, Value of Life; Course of Philosophy, and passim.) So much against this tendency in general: but as for the particular maxim of Dühring's, that the home of Justice is to be found in the sphere of the reactive feelings, our love of truth compels us drastically to invert his own proposition and to oppose to him this other maxim: the last sphere conquered by the spirit of justice is the sphere of the feeling of reaction! When it really comes about that the just man remains just even as regards his injurer (and not merely cold, moderate, reserved, indifferent: being just is always a positive state); when, in spite of the strong provocation of personal insult, contempt, and calumny, the lofty and clear objectivity of the just and judging eye (whose glance is as profound as it is gentle) is untroubled, why then we have a piece of perfection, a past master of the world—something, in fact, which it would not be wise to expect, and which should not at any rate be too easily believed. Speaking generally, there is no doubt but that even the justest individual only requires a little dose of hostility, malice, or innuendo to drive the blood into his brain and the fairness from it. The active man, the attacking, aggressive man is always a hundred degrees nearer to justice than the man who merely reacts; he certainly has no need to adopt the tactics, necessary in the case of the reacting man, of making false and biassed valuations of his object. It is, in point of fact, for this reason that the aggressive man has at all times enjoyed the stronger, bolder, more aristocratic, and also freer outlook, the better conscience. On the other hand, we already surmise who it really is that has on his conscience the invention of the "bad conscience,"—the resentful man! Finally, let man look at himself in history. In what sphere up to the present has the whole administration of law, the actual need of law, found its earthly home? Perchance in the sphere of the reacting man? Not for a minute: rather in that of the active, strong, spontaneous, aggressive man? I deliberately defy the above-mentioned agitator (who himself makes this self-confession, "the creed of revenge has run through all my works and endeavours like the red thread of Justice"), and say, that judged historically law in the world represents the very war against the reactive feelings, the very war waged on those feelings by the powers of activity and aggression, which devote some of their strength to damming and keeping within bounds this effervescence of hysterical reactivity, and to forcing it to some compromise. Everywhere where justice is practised and justice is maintained, it is to be observed that the stronger power, when confronted with the weaker powers which are inferior to it (whether they be groups, or individuals), searches for weapons to put an end to the senseless fury of resentment, while it carries on its object, partly by taking the victim of resentment out of the clutches of revenge, partly by substituting for revenge a campaign of its own against the enemies of peace and order, partly by finding, suggesting, and occasionally enforcing settlements, partly by standardising certain equivalents for injuries, to which equivalents the element of resentment is henceforth finally referred. The most drastic measure, however, taken and effectuated by the supreme power, to combat the preponderance of the feelings of spite and vindictiveness—it takes this measure as soon as it is at all strong enough to do so—is the foundation of law, the imperative declaration of what in its eyes is to be regarded as just and lawful, and what unjust and unlawful: and while, after the foundation of law, the supreme power treats the aggressive and arbitrary acts of individuals, or of whole groups, as a violation of law, and a revolt against itself, it distracts the feelings of its subjects from the immediate injury inflicted by such a violation, and thus eventually attains the very opposite result to that always desired by revenge, which sees and recognises nothing but the standpoint of the injured party. From henceforth the eye becomes trained to a more and more impersonal valuation of the deed, even the eye of the injured party himself (though this is in the final stage of all, as has been previously remarked)—on this principle "right" and "wrong" first manifest themselves after the foundation of law (and not, as Dühring maintains, only after the act of violation). To talk of intrinsic right and intrinsic wrong is absolutely non-sensical; intrinsically, an injury, an oppression, an exploitation, an annihilation can be nothing wrong, inasmuch as life is essentially (that is, in its cardinal functions) something which functions by injuring, oppressing, exploiting, and annihilating, and is absolutely inconceivable without such a character. It is necessary to make an even more serious confession:—viewed from the most advanced biological standpoint, conditions of legality can be only exceptional conditions, in that they are partial restrictions of the real life-will, which makes for power, and in that they are subordinated to the life-will's general end as particular means, that is, as means to create larger units of strength. A legal organisation, conceived of as sovereign and universal, not as a weapon in a fight of complexes of power, but as a weapon against fighting, generally something after the style of Dühring's communistic model of treating every will as equal with every other will, would be a principle hostile to life, a destroyer and dissolver of man, an outrage on the future of man, a symptom of fatigue, a secret cut to Nothingness.—

12.

A word more on the origin and end of punishment—two problems which are or ought to be kept distinct, but which unfortunately are usually lumped into one. And what tactics have our moral genealogists employed up to the present in these cases? Their inveterate naïveté. They find out some "end" in the punishment, for instance, revenge and deterrence, and then in all their innocence set this end at the beginning, as the causa fiendi of the punishment, and—they have done the trick. But the patching up of a history of the origin of law is the last use to which the "End in Law"[4] ought to be put. Perhaps there is no more pregnant principle for any kind of history than the following, which, difficult though it is to master, should none the less be mastered in every detail.—The origin of the existence of a thing and its final utility, its practical application and incorporation in a system of ends, are toto cœlo opposed to each other—everything, anything, which exists and which prevails anywhere, will always be put to new purposes by a force superior to itself, will be commandeered afresh, will be turned and transformed to new uses; all "happening" in the organic world consists of overpowering and dominating, and again all overpowering and domination is a new interpretation and adjustment, which must necessarily obscure or absolutely extinguish the subsisting "meaning" and "end." The most perfect comprehension of the utility of any physiological organ (or also of a legal institution, social custom, political habit, form in art or in religious worship) does not for a minute imply any simultaneous comprehension of its origin: this may seem uncomfortable and unpalatable to the older men,—for it has been the immemorial belief that understanding the final cause or the utility of a thing, a form, an institution, means also understanding the reason for its origin: to give an example of this logic, the eye was made to see, the hand was made to grasp. So even punishment was conceived as invented with a view to punishing. But all ends and all utilities are only signs that a Will to Power has mastered a less powerful force, has impressed thereon out of its own self the meaning of a function; and the whole history of a "Thing," an organ, a custom, can on the same principle be regarded as a continuous "sign-chain" of perpetually new interpretations and adjustments, whose causes, so far from needing to have even a mutual connection, sometimes follow and alternate with each other absolutely haphazard. Similarly, the evolution of a "thing," of a custom, is anything but its progressus to an end, still less a logical and direct progressus attained with the minimum expenditure of energy and cost: it is rather the succession of processes of subjugation, more or less profound, more or less mutually independent, which operate on the thing itself; it is, further, the resistance which in each case invariably displayed this subjugation, the Protean wriggles by way of defence and reaction, and, further, the results of successful counter-efforts. The form is fluid, but the meaning is even more so—even inside every individual organism the case is the same: with every genuine growth of the whole, the "function" of the individual organs becomes shifted,—in certain cases a partial perishing of these organs, a diminution of their numbers (for instance, through annihilation of the connecting members), can be a symptom of growing strength and perfection. What I mean is this: even partial loss of utility, decay, and degeneration, loss of function and purpose, in a word, death, appertain to the conditions of the genuine progressus; which always appears in the shape of a will and way to greater power, and is always realised at the expense of innumerable smaller powers. The magnitude of a "progress" is gauged by the greatness of the sacrifice that it requires: humanity as a mass sacrificed to the prosperity of the one stronger species of Man—that would be a progress. I emphasise all the more this cardinal characteristic of the historic method, for the reason that in its essence it runs counter to predominant instincts and prevailing taste, which much prefer to put up with absolute casualness, even with the mechanical senselessness of all phenomena, than with the theory of a power-will, in exhaustive play throughout all phenomena. The democratic idiosyncrasy against everything which rules and wishes to rule, the modern misarchism (to coin a bad word for a bad thing), has gradually but so thoroughly transformed itself into the guise of intellectualism, the most abstract intellectualism, that even nowadays it penetrates and has the right to penetrate step by step into the most exact and apparently the most objective sciences: this tendency has, in fact, in my view already dominated the whole of physiology and biology, and to their detriment, as is obvious, in so far as it has spirited away a radical idea, the idea of true activity. The tyranny of this idiosyncrasy, however, results in the theory of "adaptation" being pushed forward into the van of the argument, exploited; adaptation—that means to say, a second-class activity, a mere capacity for "reacting"; in fact, life itself has been defined (by Herbert Spencer) as an increasingly effective internal adaptation to external circumstances. This definition, however, fails to realise the real essence of life, its will to power. It fails to appreciate the paramount superiority enjoyed by those plastic forces of spontaneity, aggression, and encroachment with their new interpretations and tendencies, to the operation of which adaptation is only a natural corollary: consequently the sovereign office of the highest functionaries in the organism itself (among which the life-will appears as an active and formative principle) is repudiated. One remembers Huxley's reproach to Spencer of his "administrative Nihilism": but it is a case of something much more than "administration."

13.

To return to our subject, namely punishment, we must make consequently a double distinction: first, the relatively permanent element, the custom, the act, the "drama," a certain rigid sequence of methods of procedure; on the other hand, the fluid element, the meaning, the end, the expectation which is attached to the operation of such procedure. At this point we immediately assume, per analogiam (in accordance with the theory of the historic method, which we have elaborated above), that the procedure itself is something older and earlier than its utilisation in punishment, that this utilisation was introduced and interpreted into the procedure (which had existed for a long time, but whose employment had another meaning), in short, that the case is different from that hitherto supposed by our naïf genealogists of morals and of law, who thought that the procedure was invented for the purpose of punishment, in the same way that the hand had been previously thought to have been invented for the purpose of grasping. With regard to the other element in punishment, its fluid element, its meaning, the idea of punishment in a very late stage of civilisation (for instance, contemporary Europe) is not content with manifesting merely one meaning, but manifests a whole synthesis "of meanings." The past general history of punishment, the history of its employment for the most diverse ends, crystallises eventually into a kind of unity, which is difficult to analyse into its parts, and which, it is necessary to emphasise, absolutely defies definition. (It is nowadays impossible to say definitely the precise reason for punishment: all ideas, in which a whole process is promiscuously comprehended, elude definition; it is only that which has no history, which can be defined.) At an earlier stage, on the contrary, that synthesis of meanings appears much less rigid and much more elastic; we can realise how in each individual case the elements of the synthesis change their value and their position, so that now one element and now another stands out and predominates over the others, nay, in certain cases one element (perhaps the end of deterrence) seems to eliminate all the rest. At any rate, so as to give some idea of the uncertain, supplementary, and accidental nature of the meaning of punishment and of the manner in which one identical procedure can be employed and adapted for the most diametrically opposed objects, I will at this point give a scheme that has suggested itself to me, a scheme itself based on comparatively small and accidental material.—Punishment, as rendering the criminal harmless and incapable of further injury.—Punishment, as compensation for the injury sustained by the injured party, in any form whatsoever (including the form of sentimental compensation).—Punishment, as an isolation of that which disturbs the equilibrium, so as to prevent the further spreading of the disturbance.—Punishment as a means of inspiring fear of those who determine and execute the punishment.—Punishment as a kind of compensation for advantages which the wrong-doer has up to that time enjoyed (for example, when he is utilised as a slave in the mines).—Punishment, as the elimination of an element of decay (sometimes of a whole branch, as according to the Chinese laws, consequently as a means to the purification of the race, or the preservation of a social type).—Punishment as a festival, as the violent oppression and humiliation of an enemy that has at last been subdued.—Punishment as a mnemonic, whether for him who suffers the punishment—the so-called "correction," or for the witnesses of its administration. Punishment, as the payment of a fee stipulated for by the power which protects the evil-doer from the excesses of revenge.—Punishment, as a compromise with the natural phenomenon of revenge, in so far as revenge is still maintained and claimed as a privilege by the stronger races.—Punishment as a declaration and measure of war against an enemy of peace, of law, of order, of authority, who is fought by society with the weapons which war provides, as a spirit dangerous to the community, as a breaker of the contract on which the community is based, as a rebel, a traitor, and a breaker of the peace.

14.

This list is certainly not complete; it is obvious that punishment is overloaded with utilities of all kinds. This makes it all the more permissible to eliminate one supposed utility, which passes, at any rate in the popular mind, for its most essential utility, and which is just what even now provides the strongest support for that faith in punishment which is nowadays for many reasons tottering. Punishment is supposed to have the value of exciting in the guilty the consciousness of guilt; in punishment is sought the proper *instrumentum* of that psychic reaction which becomes known as a "bad conscience," "remorse." But this theory is even, from the point of view of the present, a violation of reality and psychology: and how much more so is the case when we have to deal with the longest period of man's history, his primitive history! Genuine remorse is certainly extremely rare among wrong-doers and the victims of punishment; prisons and houses of correction are not the soil on which this worm of remorse pullulates for choice—this is the unanimous opinion of all conscientious observers, who in many cases arrive at such a judgment with enough reluctance and against their own personal wishes. Speaking generally, punishment hardens and numbs, it produces concentration, it sharpens the consciousness of alienation, it strengthens the power of resistance. When it happens that it breaks the man's energy and brings about a piteous prostration and abjectness, such a result is certainly even less salutary than the average effect of punishment, which is characterised by a harsh and sinister doggedness. The thought of those prehistoric millennia brings us to the unhesitating conclusion, that it was simply through punishment that the evolution of the consciousness of guilt was most forcibly retarded—at any rate in the victims of the punishing power. In particular, let us not underestimate the extent to which, by the very sight of the judicial and executive procedure, the wrong-doer is himself prevented from feeling that his deed, the character of his act, is intrinsically reprehensible: for he sees clearly the same kind of acts practised in the service of justice, and then called good, and practised with a good conscience; acts such as espionage, trickery, bribery, trapping, the whole intriguing and insidious art of the policeman and the informer— the whole system, in fact, manifested in the different kinds of punishment (a system not excused by passion, but based on principle), of robbing, oppressing, insulting, imprisoning, racking, murdering.—All this he sees treated by his judges, not as acts meriting censure and condemnation in themselves, but only in a particular context and application. It was not on this soil that grew the "bad conscience," that most sinister and interesting plant of our earthly vegetation— in point of fact, throughout a most lengthy period, no suggestion of having to do with a "guilty man" manifested itself in the consciousness of the man who judged and punished. One had merely to deal with an author of an injury, an irresponsible piece of fate. And the man himself, on whom the punishment subsequently fell like a piece of fate, was occasioned no more of an "inner pain" than would be occasioned by the sudden approach of some uncalculated event, some terrible natural catastrophe, a rushing, crushing avalanche against which there is no resistance.

15.

This truth came insidiously enough to the consciousness of Spinoza (to the disgust of his commentators, who (like Kuno Fischer, for instance) give themselves no end of trouble to misunderstand him on this point), when one afternoon (as he sat raking up who knows what memory) he indulged in the question of what was really left for him personally of the celebrated *morsus conscientiæ*—Spinoza, who had relegated "good and evil" to the sphere of human imagination, and indignantly defended the honour of his "free" God against those blasphemers who affirmed that God did everything sub ratione boni ("but this was tantamount to subordinating God to fate, and would really be the greatest of all absurdities"). For Spinoza the world had returned again to that innocence in which it lay before the discovery of the bad conscience: what, then, had happened to the morsus conscientiæ? "The antithesis of gaudium," said he at last to himself,—"A sadness accompanied by the recollection of a past event which has turned out contrary to all expectation" (Eth. III., Propos. XVIII. Schol. i. ii.). Evil-doers have throughout thousands of years felt when overtaken by punishment exactly like Spinoza, on the subject of their "offence": "here is something which went wrong contrary to my anticipation," not "I ought not to have done this."—They submitted themselves to punishment, just as one submits one's self to a disease, to a misfortune, or to death, with that stubborn and resigned fatalism which gives the Russians, for instance, even nowadays, the advantage over us Westerners, in the handling of life. If at that period there was a critique of action, the criterion was prudence: the real effect of punishment is unquestionably chiefly to be found in a sharpening of the sense of prudence, in a lengthening of the memory, in a will to adopt more of a policy of caution, suspicion, and secrecy; in the recognition that there are many things which are unquestionably beyond one's capacity; in a kind of improvement in self-criticism. The broad effects which can be obtained by punishment in man and beast, are the increase of fear, the sharpening of the sense of cunning, the mastery of the desires: so it is that punishment tames man, but does not make him "better"—it would be more correct even to go so far as to assert the contrary ("Injury makes a man cunning," says a popular proverb: so far as it makes him cunning, it makes him also bad. Fortunately, it often enough makes him stupid).

16.

At this juncture I cannot avoid trying to give a tentative and provisional expression to my own hypothesis concerning the origin of the bad conscience: it is difficult to make it fully appreciated, and it requires continuous meditation, attention, and digestion. I regard the bad conscience as the serious illness which man was bound to contract under the stress of the most radical change which he has ever experienced—that change, when he found himself finally imprisoned within the pale of society and of peace.

Just like the plight of the water-animals, when they were compelled either to become land-animals or to perish, so was the plight of these half-animals, perfectly adapted as they were to the savage life of war, prowling, and adventure—suddenly all their instincts were rendered worthless and "switched off." Henceforward they had to walk on their feet—"carry themselves," whereas heretofore they had been carried by the water: a terrible heaviness oppressed them. They found themselves clumsy in obeying the simplest directions, confronted with this new and unknown world they had no longer their old guides—the regulative instincts that had led them unconsciously to safety—they were reduced, were those unhappy creatures, to thinking, inferring, calculating, putting together causes and results, reduced to that poorest and most erratic organ of theirs, their "consciousness." I do not believe there was ever in the world such a feeling of misery, such a leaden discomfort—further, those old instincts had not immediately ceased their demands! Only it was difficult and rarely possible to gratify them: speaking broadly, they were compelled to satisfy themselves by new and, as it were, hole-and-corner methods. All instincts which do not find a vent without, turn inwards—this is what I mean by the growing "internalisation" of man: consequently we have the first growth in man, of what subsequently was called his soul. The whole inner world, originally as thin as if it had been stretched between two layers of skin, burst apart and expanded proportionately, and obtained depth, breadth, and height, when man's external outlet became obstructed. These terrible bulwarks, with which the social organisation protected itself against the old instincts of freedom (punishments belong pre-eminently to these bulwarks), brought it about that all those instincts of wild, free, prowling man became turned backwards against man himself. Enmity, cruelty, the delight in persecution, in surprises, change, destruction—the turning all these instincts against their own possessors: this is the origin of the "bad conscience." It was man, who, lacking external enemies and obstacles, and imprisoned as he was in the oppressive narrowness and monotony of custom, in his own impatience lacerated, persecuted, gnawed, frightened, and ill-treated himself; it was this animal in the hands of the tamer, which beat itself against the bars of its cage; it was this being who, pining and yearning for that desert home of which it had been deprived, was compelled to create out of its own self, an adventure, a torture-chamber, a hazardous and perilous desert—it was this fool, this homesick and desperate prisoner—who invented the "bad conscience." But thereby he introduced that most grave and sinister illness, from which mankind has not yet recovered, the suffering of man from the disease called man, as the result of a violent breaking from his animal past, the result, as it were, of a spasmodic plunge into a new environment and new conditions of existence, the result of a declaration of war against the old instincts, which up to that time had been the staple of his power, his joy, his formidableness. Let us immediately add that this fact of an animal ego turning against itself, taking part against itself, produced in the world so novel, profound, unheard-of, problematic, inconsistent, and pregnant a phenomenon, that the aspect of the world was radically altered thereby. In sooth, only divine spectators could have appreciated the drama that then began, and whose end baffles conjecture as yet—a drama too subtle, too wonderful, too paradoxical to warrant its undergoing a non-sensical and unheeded performance on some random grotesque planet! Henceforth man is to be counted as one of the most unexpected and sensational lucky shots in the game of the "big baby" of Heracleitus, whether he be called Zeus or Chance—he awakens on his behalf the interest, excitement, hope, almost the confidence, of his being the harbinger and forerunner of something, of man being no end, but only a stage, an interlude, a bridge, a great promise.

17.

It is primarily involved in this hypothesis of the origin of the bad conscience, that that alteration was no gradual and no voluntary alteration, and that it did not manifest itself as an organic adaptation to new conditions, but as a break, a jump, a necessity, an inevitable fate, against which there was no resistance and never a spark of resentment. And secondarily, that the fitting of a hitherto unchecked and amorphous population into a fixed form, starting as it had done in an act of violence, could only be accomplished by acts of violence and nothing else—that the oldest "State" appeared consequently as a ghastly tyranny, a grinding ruthless piece of machinery, which went on working, till this raw material of a semi-animal populace was not only thoroughly kneaded and elastic, but also moulded. I used the word "State": my meaning is self-evident, namely, a herd of blonde beasts of prey, a race of conquerors and masters, which with all its warlike organisation and all its organising power pounces with its terrible claws on a population, in numbers possibly tremendously superior, but as yet formless, as yet nomad. Such is the origin of the "State." That fantastic theory that makes it begin with a contract is, I think, disposed of. He who can command, he who is a master by "nature," he who comes on the scene forceful in deed and gesture—what has he to do with contracts? Such beings defy calculation, they come like fate, without cause, reason, notice, excuse, they are there like the lightning is there, too terrible, too sudden, too convincing, too "different," to be personally even hated. Their work is an instinctive creating and impressing of forms, they are the most involuntary, unconscious artists that there are:—their appearance produces instantaneously a scheme of sovereignty which is live, in which the functions are partitioned and apportioned, in which above all no part is received or finds a place, until pregnant with a "meaning" in regard to the whole. They are ignorant of the meaning of guilt, responsibility, consideration, are these born organisers; in them predominates that terrible artist-egoism, that gleams like brass, and that knows itself justified to all eternity, in its work, even as a mother in her child. It is not in them that there grew the bad conscience, that is elementary—but it would not have grown without them, repulsive growth as it was, it would be missing, had not a tremendous quantity of freedom been expelled from the world by the stress of their hammer-strokes, their artist violence, or been at any rate made invisible and, as it were, latent. This instinct of freedom forced into being latent—it is already clear— this instinct of freedom forced back, trodden back, imprisoned within itself, and finally only able to find vent and relief in itself; this, only this, is the beginning of the "bad conscience."

18.

Beware of thinking lightly of this phenomenon, by reason of its initial painful ugliness. At bottom it is the same active force which is at work on a more grandiose scale in those potent artists and organisers, and builds states, which here, internally, on a smaller and pettier scale and with a retrogressive tendency, makes itself a bad science in the "labyrinth of the breast," to use Goethe's phrase, and which builds negative ideals; it is, I repeat, that identical instinct of freedom (to use my own language, the will to power): only the material, on which this force with all its constructive and tyrannous nature is let loose, is here man himself, his whole old animal self—and not as in the case of that more grandiose and sensational phenomenon, the other man, other men. This secret self-tyranny, this cruelty of the artist, this delight in giving a form to one's self as a piece of difficult, refractory, and suffering material, in burning in a will, a critique, a contradiction, a contempt, a negation; this sinister and ghastly labour of love on the part of a soul, whose will is cloven in two within itself, which makes itself suffer from delight in the infliction of suffering; this wholly active bad conscience has finally (as one already anticipates)—true fountainhead as it is of idealism and imagination— produced an abundance of novel and amazing beauty and affirmation, and perhaps has really been the first to give birth to beauty at all. What would beauty be, forsooth, if its contradiction had not first been presented to consciousness, if the ugly had not first said to itself, "I am ugly"? At any rate, after this hint the problem of how far idealism and beauty can be traced in such opposite ideas as "selflessness," self-denial, self-sacrifice, becomes less problematical; and indubitably in future we shall certainly know the real and original character of the delight experienced by the self-less, the self-denying, the self-sacrificing: this delight is a phase of cruelty.—So much provisionally for the origin of "altruism" as a moral value, and the marking out the ground from which this value has grown: it is only the bad conscience, only the will for self-abuse, that provides the necessary conditions for the existence of altruism as a value.

19.

Undoubtedly the bad conscience is an illness, but an illness like pregnancy is an illness. If we search out the conditions under which this illness reaches its most terrible and sublime zenith, we shall see what really first brought about its entry into the world. But to do this we must take a long breath, and we must first of all go back once again to an earlier point of view. The relation at civil law of the ower to his creditor (which has already been discussed in detail), has been interpreted once again (and indeed in a manner which historically is exceedingly remarkable and suspicious) into a relationship, which is perhaps more incomprehensible to us moderns than to any other era; that is, into the relationship of the existing generation to its ancestors. Within the original tribal association—we are talking of primitive times—each living generation recognises a legal obligation towards the earlier generation, and particularly towards the earliest, which founded the family (and this is something much more than a mere sentimental obligation, the existence of which, during the longest period of man's history, is by no means indisputable). There prevails in them the conviction that it is only thanks to sacrifices and efforts of their ancestors, that the race persists at all—and that this has to be paid back to them by sacrifices and services. Thus is recognised the owing of a debt, which accumulates continually by reason of these ancestors never ceasing in their subsequent life as potent spirits to secure by their power new privileges and advantages to the race. Gratis, perchance? But there is no gratis for that raw and "mean-souled" age. What return can be made?—Sacrifice (at first, nourishment, in its crudest sense), festivals, temples, tributes of veneration, above all, obedience—since all customs are, quâ works of the ancestors, equally their precepts and commands—are the ancestors ever given enough? This suspicion remains and grows: from time to time it extorts a great wholesale ransom, something monstrous in the way of repayment of the creditor (the notorious sacrifice of the first-born, for example, blood, human blood in any case). The fear of ancestors and their power, the consciousness of owing debts to them, necessarily increases, according to this kind of logic, in the exact proportion that the race itself increases, that the race itself becomes more victorious, more independent, more honoured, more feared. This, and not the contrary, is the fact. Each step towards race decay, all disastrous events, all symptoms of degeneration, of approaching disintegration, always diminish the fear of the founders' spirit, and whittle away the idea of his sagacity, providence, and potent presence. Conceive this crude kind of logic carried to its climax: it follows that the ancestors of the most powerful races must, through the growing fear that they exercise on the imaginations, grow themselves into monstrous dimensions, and become relegated to the gloom of a divine mystery that transcends imagination—the ancestor becomes at last necessarily transfigured into a god. Perhaps this is the very origin of the gods, that is, an origin from fear! And those who feel bound to add, "but from piety also," will have difficulty in maintaining this theory, with regard to the primeval and longest period of the human race. And of course this is even more the case as regards the middle period, the formative period of the aristocratic races—the aristocratic races which have given back with interest to their founders, the ancestors (heroes, gods), all those qualities which in the meanwhile have appeared in themselves, that is, the aristocratic qualities. We will later on glance again at the ennobling and promotion of the gods (which of course is totally distinct from their "sanctification"): let us now provisionally follow to its end the course of the whole of this development of the consciousness of "owing."

20.

According to the teaching of history, the consciousness of owing debts to the deity by no means came to an end with the decay of the clan organisation of society; just as mankind has inherited the ideas of "good" and "bad" from the race-nobility (together with its fundamental tendency towards establishing social distinctions), so with the heritage of the racial and tribal gods it has also inherited the incubus of debts as yet unpaid and the desire to discharge them. The transition is effected by those large populations of slaves and bondsmen, who, whether through compulsion or through submission and "mimicry," have accommodated themselves to the religion of their masters; through this channel these inherited tendencies inundate the world. The feeling of owing a debt to the deity has grown continuously for several centuries, always in the same proportion in which the idea of God and the consciousness of God have grown and become exalted among mankind. (The whole history of ethnic fights, victories, reconciliations, amalgamations, everything, in fact, which precedes the eventual classing of all the social elements in each great race-synthesis, are mirrored in the hotch-potch genealogy of their gods, in the legends of their fights, victories, and reconciliations. Progress towards universal empires invariably means progress towards universal deities; despotism, with its subjugation of the independent nobility, always paves the way for some system or other of monotheism.) The appearance of the Christian god, as the record god up to this time, has for that very reason brought equally into the world the record amount of guilt consciousness. Granted that we have gradually started on the reverse movement, there is no little probability in the deduction, based on the continuous decay in the belief in the Christian god, to the effect that there also already exists a considerable decay in the human consciousness of owing (ought); in fact, we cannot shut our eyes to the prospect of the complete and eventual triumph of atheism freeing mankind from all this feeling of obligation to their origin, their causa prima. Atheism and a kind of second innocence complement and supplement each other.

21.

So much for my rough and preliminary sketch of the interrelation of the ideas "ought" (owe) and "duty" with the postulates of religion. I have intentionally shelved up to the present the actual moralisation of these ideas (their being pushed back into the conscience, or more precisely the interweaving of the bad conscience with the idea of God), and at the end of the last paragraph used language to the effect that this moralisation did not exist, and that consequently these ideas had necessarily come to an end, by reason of what had happened to their hypothesis, the credence in our "creditor," in God. The actual facts differ terribly from this theory. It is with the moralisation of the ideas "ought" and "duty," and with their being pushed back into the bad conscience, that comes the first actual attempt to reverse the direction of the development we have just described, or at any rate to arrest its evolution; it is just at this juncture that the very hope of an eventual redemption has to put itself once for all into the prison of pessimism, it is at this juncture that the eye has to recoil and rebound in despair from off an adamantine impossibility, it is at this juncture that the ideas "guilt" and "duty" have to turn backwards—turn backwards against whom? There is no doubt about it; primarily against the "ower," in whom the bad conscience now establishes itself, eats, extends, and grows like a polypus throughout its length and breadth, all with such virulence, that at last, with the impossibility of paying the debt, there becomes conceived the idea of the impossibility of paying the penalty, the thought of its inexpiability (the idea of "eternal punishment")—finally, too, it turns against the "creditor," whether found in the causa prima of man, the origin of the human race, its sire, who henceforth becomes burdened with a curse ("Adam," "original sin," "determination of the will"), or in Nature from whose womb man springs, and on whom the responsibility for the principle of evil is now cast ("Diabolisation of Nature"), or in existence generally, on this logic an absolute white elephant, with which mankind is landed (the Nihilistic flight from life, the demand for Nothingness, or for the opposite of existence, for some other existence, Buddhism and the like)—till suddenly we stand before that paradoxical and awful expedient, through which a tortured humanity has found a temporary alleviation, that stroke of genius called Christianity:—God personally immolating himself for the debt of man, God paying himself personally out of a pound of his own flesh, God as the one being who can deliver man from what man had become unable to deliver himself—the creditor playing scapegoat for his debtor, from love (can you believe it?), from love of his debtor!...

22.

The reader will already have conjectured what took place on the stage and behind the scenes of this drama. That will for self-torture, that inverted cruelty of the animal man, who, turned subjective and scared into introspection (encaged as he was in "the State," as part of his taming process), invented the bad conscience so as to hurt himself, after the natural outlet for this will to hurt, became blocked—in other words, this man of the bad conscience exploited the religious hypothesis so as to carry his martyrdom to the ghastliest pitch of agonised intensity. Owing something to God: this thought becomes his instrument of torture. He apprehends in God the most extreme antitheses that he can find to his own characteristic and ineradicable animal instincts, he himself gives a new interpretation to these animal instincts as being against what he "owes" to God (as enmity, rebellion, and revolt against the "Lord," the "Father," the "Sire," the "Beginning of the world"), he places himself between the horns of the dilemma, "God" and "Devil." Every negation which he is inclined to utter to himself, to the nature, naturalness, and reality of his being, he whips into an ejaculation of "yes," uttering it as something existing, living, efficient, as being God, as the holiness of God, the judgment of God, as the hangmanship of God, as transcendence, as eternity, as unending torment, as hell, as infinity of punishment and guilt. This is a kind of madness of the will in the sphere of psychological cruelty which is absolutely unparalleled:—man's will to find himself guilty and blameworthy to the point of inexpiability, his will to think of himself as punished, without the punishment ever being able to balance the guilt, his will to infect and to poison the fundamental basis of the universe with the problem of punishment and guilt, in order to cut off once and for all any escape out of this labyrinth of "fixed ideas," his will for rearing an ideal—that of the "holy God"—face to face with which he can have tangible proof of his own un-worthiness. Alas for this mad melancholy beast man! What phantasies invade it, what paroxysms of perversity, hysterical senselessness, and mental bestiality break out immediately, at the very slightest check on its being the beast of action. All this is excessively interesting, but at the same time tainted with a black, gloomy, enervating melancholy, so that a forcible veto must be invoked against looking too long into these abysses. Here is disease, undubitably, the most ghastly disease that has as yet played havoc among men: and he who can still hear (but man turns now deaf ears to such sounds), how in this night of torment and nonsense there has rung out the cry of love, the cry of the most passionate ecstasy, of redemption in love, he turns away gripped by an invincible horror—in man there is so much that is ghastly—too long has the world been a mad-house.

23.

Let this suffice once for all concerning the origin of the "holy God." The fact that in itself the conception of gods is not bound to lead necessarily to this degradation of the imagination (a temporary representation of whose vagaries we felt bound give), the fact that there exist nobler methods of utilising the invention of gods than in this self-crucifixion and self-degradation of man, in which the last two thousand years of Europe have been past masters—these facts can fortunately be still perceived from every glance that we cast at the Grecian gods, these mirrors of noble and grandiose men, in which the animal in man felt itself deified, and did not devour itself in subjective frenzy. These Greeks long utilised their gods as simple buffers against the "bad conscience"—so that they could continue to enjoy their freedom of soul: this, of course, is diametrically opposed to Christianity's theory of its god. They went very far on this principle, did these splendid and lion-hearted children; and there is no lesser authority than that of the Homeric Zeus for making them realise occasionally that they are taking life too casually. "Wonderful," says he on one occasion—it has to do with the case of Ægistheus, a very bad case indeed—

"Wonderful how they grumble, the mortals against the immortals,
Only from us, they presume, comes evil, but in their folly,
Fashion they, spite of fate, the doom of their own disaster."

Yet the reader will note and observe that this Olympian spectator and judge is far from being angry with them and thinking evil of them on this score. "How foolish they are," so thinks he of the misdeeds of mortals—and "folly," "imprudence," "a little brain disturbance," and nothing more, are what the Greeks, even of the strongest, bravest period, have admitted to be the ground of much that is evil and fatal.—Folly, not sin, do you understand?... But even this brain disturbance was a problem—"Come, how is it even possible? How could it have really got in brains like ours, the brains of men of aristocratic ancestry, of men of fortune, of men of good natural endowments, of men of the best society, of men of nobility and virtue?" This was the question that for century on century the aristocratic Greek put to himself when confronted with every (to him incomprehensible) outrage and sacrilege with which one of his peers had polluted himself. "It must be that a god had infatuated him," he would say at last, nodding his head.—This solution is typical of the Greeks, ... accordingly the gods in those times subserved the functions of justifying man to a certain extent even in evil—in those days they took upon themselves not the punishment, but, what is more noble, the guilt.

[47] NIHILISM AND NIETZSCHE

I conclude with three queries, as you will see. "Is an ideal actually set up here, or is one pulled down?" I am perhaps asked.... But have ye sufficiently asked yourselves how dear a payment has the setting up of every ideal in the world exacted? To achieve that consummation how much truth must always be traduced and misunderstood, how many lies must be sanctified, how much conscience has got to be disturbed, how many pounds of "God" have got to be sacrificed every time? To enable a sanctuary to be set up a sanctuary has got to be destroyed: that is a law—show me an instance where it has not been fulfilled!... We modern men, we inherit the immemorial tradition of vivisecting the conscience, and practising cruelty to our animal selves. That is the sphere of our most protracted training, perhaps of our artistic prowess, at any rate of our dilettantism and our perverted taste. Man has for too long regarded his natural proclivities with an "evil eye," so that eventually they have become in his system affiliated to a bad conscience. A converse endeavour would be intrinsically feasible— but who is strong enough to attempt it?—namely, to affiliate to the "bad conscience" all those unnatural proclivities, all those transcendental aspirations, contrary to sense, instinct, nature, and animalism—in short, all past and present ideals, which are all ideals opposed to life, and traducing the world. To whom is one to turn nowadays with such hopes and pretensions?—It is just the good men that we should thus bring about our ears; and in addition, as stands to reason, the indolent, the hedgers, the vain, the hysterical, the tired.... What is more offensive or more thoroughly calculated to alienate, than giving any hint of the exalted severity with which we treat ourselves? And again how conciliatory, how full of love does all the world show itself towards us so soon as we do as all the world docs, and "let ourselves go" like all the world. For such a consummation we need spirits of different calibre than seems really feasible in this age; spirits rendered potent through wars and victories, to whom conquest, adventure, danger, even pain, have become a need; for such a consummation we need habituation to sharp, rare air, to winter wanderings, to literal and metaphorical ice and mountains; we even need a kind of sublime malice, a supreme and most self-conscious insolence of knowledge, which is the appanage of great health; we need (to summarise the awful truth) just this great health!

Is this even feasible to-day?... But some day, in a stronger age than this rotting and introspective present, must he in sooth come to us, even the redeemer of great love and scorn, the creative spirit, rebounding by the impetus of his own force back again away from every transcendental plane and dimension, he whose solitude is misunderstanded (sic) of the people, as though it were a flight from reality;—while actually it is only his diving, burrowing, and penetrating into reality, so that when he comes again to the light he can at once bring about by these means the redemption of this reality; its redemption from the curse which the old ideal has laid upon it. This man of the future, who in this wise will redeem us from the old ideal, as he will from that ideal's necessary corollary of great nausea, will to nothingness, and Nihilism; this tocsin of noon and of the great verdict, which renders the will again free, who gives back to the world its goal and to man his hope, this Antichrist and Antinihilist, this conqueror of God and of Nothingness—he must one day come.

But what am I talking of? Enough! Enough? At this juncture I have only one proper course, silence: otherwise tresspass on a domain open alone to one who is younger than I, one stronger, more "future" than I—open alone to Zarathustra, Zarathustra the godless.

[1]The German is: "Sittlichkeit der Sitte." H. B. S.

[2]The German world "schuld" means both debt and guilt. Cp. the English "owe" and "ought," by which I occasionally render the double meaning.—H. B. S.

[3]German: "Verbrecher."—H.B.S.

[4]An allusion to Der Zweck im Recht, by the great German jurist, Professor Ihering.

PREJUDICES OF PHILOSOPHERS

1. The Will to Truth, which is to tempt us to many a hazardous enterprise, the famous Truthfulness of which all philosophers have hitherto spoken with respect, what questions has this Will to Truth not laid before us! What strange, perplexing, questionable questions! It is already a long story; yet it seems as if it were hardly commenced. Is it any wonder if we at last grow distrustful, lose patience, and turn impatiently away? That this Sphinx teaches us at last to ask questions ourselves? WHO is it really that puts questions to us here? WHAT really is this "Will to Truth" in us? In fact we made a long halt at the question as to the origin of this Will—until at last we came to an absolute standstill before a yet more fundamental question. We inquired about the VALUE of this Will. Granted that we want the truth: WHY NOT RATHER untruth? And uncertainty? Even ignorance? The problem of the value of truth presented itself before us—or was it we who presented ourselves before the problem? Which of us is the Oedipus here? Which the Sphinx? It would seem to be a rendezvous of questions and notes of interrogation. And could it be believed that it at last seems to us as if the problem had never been propounded before, as if we were the first to discern it, get a sight of it, and RISK RAISING it? For there is risk in raising it, perhaps there is no greater risk.

2. "HOW COULD anything originate out of its opposite? For example, truth out of error? or the Will to Truth out of the will to deception? or the generous deed out of selfishness? or the pure sun-bright vision of the wise man out of covetousness? Such genesis is impossible; whoever dreams of it is a fool, nay, worse than a fool; things of the highest value must have a different origin, an origin of THEIR own—in this transitory, seductive, illusory, paltry world, in this turmoil of delusion and cupidity, they cannot have their source. But rather in the lap of Being, in the intransitory, in the concealed God, in the 'Thing-in-itself—THERE must be their source, and nowhere else!"—This mode of reasoning discloses the typical prejudice by which metaphysicians of all times can be recognized, this mode of valuation is at the back of all their logical procedure; through this "belief" of theirs, they exert themselves for their "knowledge," for something that is in the end solemnly christened "the Truth." The fundamental

belief of metaphysicians is THE BELIEF IN ANTITHESES OF VALUES. It never occurred even to the wariest of them to doubt here on the very threshold (where doubt, however, was most necessary); though they had made a solemn vow, "DE OMNIBUS DUBITANDUM." For it may be doubted, firstly, whether antitheses exist at all; and secondly, whether the popular valuations and antitheses of value upon which metaphysicians have set their seal, are not perhaps merely superficial estimates, merely provisional perspectives, besides being probably made from some corner, perhaps from below—"frog perspectives," as it were, to borrow an expression current among painters. In spite of all the value which may belong to the true, the positive, and the unselfish, it might be possible that a higher and more fundamental value for life generally should be assigned to pretence, to the will to delusion, to selfishness, and cupidity. It might even be possible that WHAT constitutes the value of those good and respected things, consists precisely in their being insidiously related, knotted, and crocheted to these evil and apparently opposed things—perhaps even in being essentially identical with them. Perhaps! But who wishes to concern himself with such dangerous "Perhapses"! For that investigation one must await the advent of a new order of philosophers, such as will have other tastes and inclinations, the reverse of those hitherto prevalent—philosophers of the dangerous "Perhaps" in every sense of the term. And to speak in all seriousness, I see such new philosophers beginning to appear.

3. Having kept a sharp eye on philosophers, and having read between their lines long enough, I now say to myself that the greater part of conscious thinking must be counted among the instinctive functions, and it is so even in the case of philosophical thinking; one has here to learn anew, as one learned anew about heredity and "innateness." As little as the act of birth comes into consideration in the whole process and procedure of heredity, just as little is "being-conscious" OPPOSED to the instinctive in any decisive sense; the greater part of the conscious thinking of a philosopher is secretly influenced by his instincts, and forced into definite channels. And behind all logic and its seeming sovereignty of movement, there are valuations, or to speak more plainly, physiological demands, for the maintenance of a definite mode of life For example, that the certain is worth more than the uncertain, that illusion is less valuable than "truth" such valuations, in spite of their regulative importance for US, might notwithstanding be only superficial valuations, special kinds of niaiserie, such as may be necessary for the maintenance of beings such as ourselves. Supposing, in effect, that man is not just the "measure of things."

4. The falseness of an opinion is not for us any objection to it: it is here, perhaps, that our new language sounds most strangely. The question is, how far an opinion is life-furthering, life-preserving, species-preserving, perhaps species-rearing, and we are fundamentally inclined to maintain that the falsest opinions (to which the synthetic judgments a priori belong), are the most indispensable to us, that without a recognition of logical fictions, without a comparison of reality with the purely IMAGINED world of the absolute and immutable, without a constant counterfeiting of the world by means of numbers, man could not live—that the renunciation of false opinions would be a renunciation of life, a negation of life. TO RECOGNISE UNTRUTH AS A CONDITION OF LIFE; that is certainly to impugn the traditional ideas of value in a dangerous manner, and a philosophy which ventures to do so, has thereby alone placed itself beyond good and evil.

5. That which causes philosophers to be regarded half-distrustfully and half-mockingly, is not the oft-repeated discovery how innocent they are—how often and easily they make mistakes and lose their way, in short, how childish and childlike they are,—but that there is not enough honest dealing with them, whereas they all raise a loud and virtuous outcry when the problem of truthfulness is even hinted at in the remotest manner. They all pose as though their real opinions had been discovered and attained through the self-evolving of a cold, pure, divinely indifferent dialectic (in contrast to all sorts of mystics, who, fairer and foolisher, talk of "inspiration"), whereas, in fact, a prejudiced proposition, idea, or "suggestion," which is generally their heart's desire abstracted and refined, is defended by them with arguments sought out after the event. They are all advocates who do not wish to be regarded as such, generally astute defenders, also, of their prejudices, which they dub "truths,"—and VERY far from having the conscience which bravely admits this to itself, very far from having the good taste of the courage which goes so far as to let this be understood, perhaps to warn friend or foe, or in cheerful confidence and self-ridicule. The spectacle of the Tartuffery of old Kant, equally stiff and decent, with which he entices us into the dialectic by-ways that lead (more correctly mislead) to his "categorical imperative"— makes us fastidious ones smile, we who find no small amusement in spying out the subtle tricks of old moralists and ethical preachers. Or, still more so, the hocus-pocus in mathematical form, by means of which Spinoza has, as it were, clad his philosophy in mail and mask—in fact, the "love of HIS wisdom," to translate the term fairly and squarely—in order thereby to strike terror at once into the heart of the assailant who should dare to cast a glance on that invincible maiden, that Pallas Athene:—how much of personal timidity and vulnerability does this masquerade of a sickly recluse betray!

6. It has gradually become clear to me what every great philosophy up till now has consisted of—namely, the confession of its originator, and a species of involuntary and unconscious auto-biography; and moreover that the moral (or immoral) purpose in every philosophy has constituted the true vital germ out of which the entire plant has always grown. Indeed, to understand how the abstrusest metaphysical assertions of a philosopher have been arrived at, it is always well (and wise) to first ask oneself: "What morality do they (or does he) aim at?" Accordingly, I do not believe that an "impulse to knowledge" is the father of philosophy; but that another impulse, here as elsewhere, has only made use of knowledge (and mistaken knowledge!) as an instrument. But whoever considers the fundamental impulses of man with a view to determining how far they may have here acted as INSPIRING GENII (or as demons and cobolds), will find that they have all practiced philosophy at one time or another, and that each one of them would have been only too glad to look upon itself as the ultimate end of existence and the legitimate LORD over all the other impulses. For every impulse is imperious, and as SUCH, attempts to philosophize. To be sure, in the case of scholars, in the case of really scientific men, it may be otherwise—"better," if you will; there there may really be such a thing as an "impulse to knowledge," some kind of small, independent clock-work, which, when well wound up, works away industriously to that end, WITHOUT the rest of the scholarly impulses taking any material part therein. The actual "interests" of the scholar, therefore, are generally in quite another direction—in the family, perhaps, or in money-making, or in politics; it is, in fact, almost indifferent at what point of research his little machine is placed, and whether the hopeful young worker becomes a good philologist, a mushroom specialist, or a chemist; he is not CHARACTERISED by becoming this or that. In the philosopher, on the contrary, there is absolutely nothing impersonal; and above all, his morality furnishes a decided and decisive testimony as to WHO HE IS,—that is to say, in what order the deepest impulses of his nature stand to each other.

7. How malicious philosophers can be! I know of nothing more stinging than the joke Epicurus took the liberty of making on Plato and the Platonists; he called them Dionysiokolakes. In its original sense, and on the face of it, the word signifies "Flatterers of Dionysius"—consequently, tyrants' accessories and lick-spittles; besides this, however, it is as much as to say, "They are all ACTORS, there is nothing genuine about them" (for Dionysiokolax was a popular name for an actor). And the latter is really the malignant reproach that Epicurus cast upon Plato: he was annoyed by the grandiose manner, the mise en scene style of which Plato and his scholars were masters—of which Epicurus was not a master! He, the old school-teacher of Samos, who sat concealed in his little garden at Athens, and wrote three hundred books, perhaps out of rage and ambitious envy of Plato, who knows! Greece took a hundred years to find out who the garden-god Epicurus really was. Did she ever find out?

8. There is a point in every philosophy at which the "conviction" of the philosopher appears on the scene; or, to put it in the words of an ancient mystery:

Adventavit asinus, Pulcher et fortissimus.

9. You desire to LIVE "according to Nature"? Oh, you noble Stoics, what fraud of words! Imagine to yourselves a being like Nature, boundlessly extravagant, boundlessly indifferent, without purpose or consideration, without pity or justice, at once fruitful and barren and uncertain: imagine to yourselves INDIFFERENCE as a power—how COULD you live in accordance with such indifference? To live—is not that just endeavouring to be otherwise than this Nature? Is not living valuing, preferring, being unjust, being limited, endeavouring to be different? And granted that your imperative, "living according to Nature," means actually the same as "living according to life"—how could you do DIFFERENTLY? Why should you make a principle out of what you yourselves are, and must be? In reality, however, it is quite otherwise with you: while you pretend to read with rapture the canon of your law in Nature, you want something quite the contrary, you extraordinary stage-players and self-deluders! In your pride you wish to dictate your morals and ideals to Nature, to Nature herself, and to incorporate them therein; you insist that it shall be Nature "according to the Stoa," and would like everything to be made after your own image, as a vast, eternal glorification and generalism of Stoicism! With all your love for truth, you have forced yourselves so long, so persistently, and with such hypnotic rigidity to see Nature FALSELY, that is to say, Stoically, that you are no longer able to see it otherwise—and to crown all, some unfathomable superciliousness gives you the Bedlamite hope that BECAUSE you are able to tyrannize over yourselves—Stoicism is self-tyranny—Nature will also allow herself to be tyrannized over: is not the Stoic a PART of Nature?... But this is an old and everlasting story: what happened in old times with the Stoics still happens today, as soon as ever a philosophy begins to believe in itself. It always creates the world in its own image; it cannot do otherwise; philosophy is this tyrannical impulse

itself, the most spiritual Will to Power, the will to "creation of the world," the will to the causa prima.

10. The eagerness and subtlety, I should even say craftiness, with which the problem of "the real and the apparent world" is dealt with at present throughout Europe, furnishes food for thought and attention; and he who hears only a "Will to Truth" in the background, and nothing else, cannot certainly boast of the sharpest ears. In rare and isolated cases, it may really have happened that such a Will to Truth—a certain extravagant and adventurous pluck, a metaphysician's ambition of the forlorn hope—has participated therein: that which in the end always prefers a handful of "certainty" to a whole cartload of beautiful possibilities; there may even be puritanical fanatics of conscience, who prefer to put their last trust in a sure nothing, rather than in an uncertain something. But that is Nihilism, and the sign of a despairing, mortally wearied soul, notwithstanding the courageous bearing such a virtue may display. It seems, however, to be otherwise with stronger and livelier thinkers who are still eager for life. In that they side AGAINST appearance, and speak superciliously of "perspective," in that they rank the credibility of their own bodies about as low as the credibility of the ocular evidence that "the earth stands still," and thus, apparently, allowing with complacency their securest possession to escape (for what does one at present believe in more firmly than in one's body?),—who knows if they are not really trying to win back something which was formerly an even securer possession, something of the old domain of the faith of former times, perhaps the "immortal soul," perhaps "the old God," in short, ideas by which they could live better, that is to say, more vigorously and more joyously, than by "modern ideas"? There is DISTRUST of these modern ideas in this mode of looking at things, a disbelief in all that has been constructed yesterday and today; there is perhaps some slight admixture of satiety and scorn, which can no longer endure the BRIC-A-BRAC of ideas of the most varied origin, such as so-called Positivism at present throws on the market; a disgust of the more refined taste at the village-fair motleyness and patchiness of all these reality-philosophasters, in whom there is nothing either new or true, except this motleyness. Therein it seems to me that we should agree with those skeptical anti-realists and knowledge-microscopists of the present day; their instinct, which repels them from MODERN reality, is unrefuted... what do their retrograde by-paths concern us! The main thing about them is NOT that they wish to go "back," but that they wish to get AWAY therefrom. A little MORE strength, swing, courage, and artistic power, and they would be OFF—and not back!

11. It seems to me that there is everywhere an attempt at present to divert attention from the actual influence which Kant exercised on German philosophy, and especially to ignore prudently the value which he set upon himself. Kant was first and foremost proud of his Table of Categories; with it in his hand he said: "This is the most difficult thing that could ever be undertaken on behalf of metaphysics." Let us only understand this "could be"! He was proud of having DISCOVERED a new faculty in man, the faculty of synthetic judgment a priori. Granting that he deceived himself in this matter; the development and rapid flourishing of German philosophy depended nevertheless on his pride, and on the eager rivalry of the younger generation to discover if possible something—at all events "new faculties"—of which to be still prouder!—But let us reflect for a moment—it is high time to do so. "How are synthetic judgments a priori

POSSIBLE?" Kant asks himself—and what is really his answer? "BY MEANS OF A MEANS (faculty)"—but unfortunately not in five words, but so circumstantially, imposingly, and with such display of German profundity and verbal flourishes, that one altogether loses sight of the comical *niaiserie allemande* involved in such an answer. People were beside themselves with delight over this new faculty, and the jubilation reached its climax when Kant further discovered a moral faculty in man—for at that time Germans were still moral, not yet dabbling in the "Politics of hard fact." Then came the honeymoon of German philosophy. All the young theologians of the Tubingen institution went immediately into the groves—all seeking for "faculties." And what did they not find—in that innocent, rich, and still youthful period of the German spirit, to which Romanticism, the malicious fairy, piped and sang, when one could not yet distinguish between "finding" and "inventing"! Above all a faculty for the "transcendental"; Schelling christened it, intellectual intuition, and thereby gratified the most earnest longings of the naturally pious-inclined Germans. One can do no greater wrong to the whole of this exuberant and eccentric movement (which was really youthfulness, notwithstanding that it disguised itself so boldly, in hoary and senile conceptions), than to take it seriously, or even treat it with moral indignation. Enough, however—the world grew older, and the dream vanished. A time came when people rubbed their foreheads, and they still rub them today. People had been dreaming, and first and foremost—old Kant. "By means of a means (faculty)"—he had said, or at least meant to say. But, is that—an answer? An explanation? Or is it not rather merely a repetition of the question? How does opium induce sleep? "By means of a means (faculty)," namely the *virtus dormitiva*, replies the doctor in Moliere,

Quia est in eo virtus dormitiva,

Cujus est natura sensus assoupire.

But such replies belong to the realm of comedy, and it is high time to replace the Kantian question, "How are synthetic judgments a PRIORI possible?" by another question, "Why is belief in such judgments necessary?"—in effect, it is high time that we should understand that such judgments must be believed to be true, for the sake of the preservation of creatures like ourselves; though they still might naturally be false judgments! Or, more plainly spoken, and roughly and readily—synthetic judgments a priori should not "be possible" at all; we have no right to them; in our mouths they are nothing but false judgments. Only, of course, the belief in their truth is necessary, as plausible belief and ocular evidence belonging to the perspective view of life. And finally, to call to mind the enormous influence which "German philosophy"—I hope you understand its right to inverted commas (goosefeet)?—has exercised throughout the whole of Europe, there is no doubt that a certain VIRTUS DORMITIVA had a share in it; thanks to German philosophy, it was a delight to the noble idlers, the virtuous, the mystics, the artiste, the three-fourths Christians, and the political obscurantists of all nations, to find an antidote to the still overwhelming sensualism which overflowed from the last century into this, in short—"sensus assoupire."...

12. As regards materialistic atomism, it is one of the best-refuted theories that have been advanced, and in Europe there is now perhaps no one in the learned world so unscholarly as to attach serious signification to it, except for convenient everyday use (as an abbreviation of the means of expression)—thanks chiefly to the Pole Boscovich: he and the Pole Copernicus have hitherto been the greatest and most successful opponents of ocular evidence. For while Copernicus has persuaded us to believe, contrary to all the senses, that the earth does NOT stand fast, Boscovich has taught us to abjure the belief in the last thing that "stood fast" of the earth—the belief in "substance," in "matter," in the earth-residuum, and particle-atom: it is the greatest triumph over the senses that has hitherto been gained on earth. One must, however, go still further, and also declare war, relentless war to the knife, against the "atomistic requirements" which still lead a dangerous after-life in places where no one suspects them, like the more celebrated "metaphysical requirements": one must also above all give the finishing stroke to that other and more portentous atomism which Christianity has taught best and longest, the SOUL-ATOMISM. Let it be permitted to designate by this expression the belief which regards the soul as something indestructible, eternal, indivisible, as a monad, as an atomon: this belief ought to be expelled from science! Between ourselves, it is not at all necessary to get rid of "the soul" thereby, and thus renounce one of the oldest and most venerated hypotheses—as happens frequently to the clumsiness of naturalists, who can hardly touch on the soul without immediately losing it. But the way is open for new acceptations and refinements of the soul-hypothesis; and such conceptions as "mortal soul," and "soul of subjective multiplicity," and "soul as social structure of the instincts and passions," want henceforth to have legitimate rights in science. In that the NEW psychologist is about to put an end to the superstitions which have hitherto flourished with almost tropical luxuriance around the idea of the soul, he is really, as it were, thrusting himself into a new desert and a new distrust—it is possible that the older psychologists had a merrier and more comfortable time of it; eventually, however, he finds that precisely thereby he is also condemned to INVENT—and, who knows? perhaps to DISCOVER the new.

13. Psychologists should bethink themselves before putting down the instinct of self-preservation as the cardinal instinct of an organic being. A living thing seeks above all to DISCHARGE its strength—life itself is WILL TO POWER; self-preservation is only one of the indirect and most frequent RESULTS thereof. In short, here, as everywhere else, let us beware of SUPERFLUOUS teleological principles!—one of which is the instinct of self-preservation (we owe it to Spinoza's inconsistency). It is thus, in effect, that method ordains, which must be essentially economy of principles.

14. It is perhaps just dawning on five or six minds that natural philosophy is only a world-exposition and world-arrangement (according to us, if I may say so!) and NOT a world-explanation; but in so far as it is based on belief in the senses, it is regarded as more, and for a long time to come must be regarded as more—namely, as an explanation. It has eyes and fingers of its own, it has ocular evidence and palpableness of its own: this operates fascinatingly, persuasively, and CONVINCINGLY upon an age with fundamentally plebeian tastes—in fact, it follows instinctively the canon of truth of eternal popular sensualism. What is clear, what is "explained"? Only that which can be seen and felt—one must pursue every problem thus far. Obversely, however, the charm of the Platonic mode of thought, which was an ARISTOCRATIC mode, consisted precisely in RESISTANCE to obvious sense-evidence—perhaps among men who enjoyed even stronger and more fastidious senses than our contemporaries, but who knew how to find a higher triumph in remaining masters of them: and this by means of pale, cold, grey conceptional networks which they threw over the motley whirl of the senses—the mob of the senses, as Plato said. In this overcoming of the world, and interpreting of the world in the manner of Plato, there was an ENJOYMENT different from that which the physicists of today offer us—and likewise the Darwinists and anti-teleologists among the physiological workers, with their principle of the "smallest possible effort," and the greatest possible blunder. "Where there is nothing more to see or to grasp, there is also nothing more for men to do"—that is certainly an imperative different from the Platonic one, but it may notwithstanding be the right imperative for a hardy, laborious race of machinists and bridge-builders of the future, who have nothing but ROUGH work to perform.

15. To study physiology with a clear conscience, one must insist on the fact that the sense-organs are not phenomena in the sense of the idealistic philosophy; as such they certainly could not be causes! Sensualism, therefore, at least as regulative hypothesis, if not as heuristic principle. What? And others say even that the external world is the work of our organs? But then our body, as a part of this external world, would be the work of our organs! But then our organs themselves would be the work of our organs! It seems to me that this is a complete REDUCTIO AD ABSURDUM, if the conception CAUSA SUI is something fundamentally absurd. Consequently, the external world is NOT the work of our organs—?

16. There are still harmless self-observers who believe that there are "immediate certainties"; for instance, "I think," or as the superstition of Schopenhauer puts it, "I will"; as though cognition here got hold of its object purely and simply as "the thing in itself," without any falsification taking place either on the part of the subject or the object. I would repeat it, however, a hundred times, that "immediate certainty," as well as "absolute knowledge" and the "thing in itself," involve a CONTRADICTIO IN ADJECTO; we really ought to free ourselves from the misleading significance of words! The people on their part may think that cognition is knowing all about things, but the philosopher must say to himself: "When I analyze the process that is expressed in the sentence, 'I think,' I find a whole series of daring assertions, the argumentative proof of which would be difficult, perhaps impossible: for instance, that it is I who think, that there must necessarily be something that thinks, that thinking is an activity and operation on the part of a being who is thought of as a cause, that there is an 'ego,' and finally, that it is already determined what is to be designated by thinking— that I KNOW what thinking is. For if I had not already decided within myself what it is, by what standard could I determine whether that which is just happening is not perhaps 'willing' or 'feeling'? In short, the assertion 'I think,' assumes that I COMPARE my state at the present moment with other states of myself which I know, in order to determine what it is; on account of this retrospective connection with further 'knowledge,' it has, at any rate, no immediate certainty for me."—In place of the "immediate certainty" in which the people may believe in the special case, the philosopher thus finds a series of metaphysical questions presented to him, veritable conscience questions of the intellect, to wit: "Whence did I get the notion of 'thinking'? Why do I believe in cause and effect? What gives me the right to speak of an 'ego,' and even of an 'ego' as cause, and finally of an 'ego' as cause of thought?" He who ventures to answer these metaphysical questions at once by an appeal to a sort of INTUITIVE perception, like the person who says, "I think, and know that this, at least, is true, actual, and certain"—will encounter a smile and two notes of interrogation in a philosopher nowadays. "Sir," the philosopher will perhaps give him to understand, "it is improbable that you are not mistaken, but why should it be the truth?"

17. With regard to the superstitions of logicians, I shall never tire of emphasizing a small, terse fact, which is unwillingly recognized by these credulous minds—namely, that a thought comes when "it" wishes, and not when "I" wish; so that it is a PERVERSION of the facts of the case to say that the subject "I" is the condition of the predicate "think." ONE thinks; but that this "one" is precisely the famous old "ego," is, to put it mildly, only a supposition, an assertion, and assuredly not an "immediate certainty." After all, one has even gone too far with this "one thinks"—even the "one" contains an INTERPRETATION of the process, and does not belong to the process itself. One infers here according to the usual grammatical formula—"To think is an activity; every activity requires an agency that is active; consequently"... It was pretty much on the same lines that the older atomism sought, besides the operating "power," the material particle wherein it resides and out of which it operates—the atom. More rigorous minds, however, learnt at last to get along without this "earth-residuum," and perhaps some day we shall accustom ourselves, even from the logician's point of view, to get along without the little "one" (to which the worthy old "ego" has refined itself).

18. It is certainly not the least charm of a theory that it is refutable; it is precisely thereby that it attracts the more subtle minds. It seems that the hundred-times-refuted theory of the "free will" owes its persistence to this charm alone; some one is always appearing who feels himself strong enough to refute it.

19. Philosophers are accustomed to speak of the will as though it were the best-known thing in the world; indeed, Schopenhauer has given us to understand that the will alone is really known to us, absolutely and completely known, without deduction or addition. But it again and again seems to me that in this case Schopenhauer also only did what philosophers are in the habit of doing—he seems to have adopted a POPULAR PREJUDICE and exaggerated it. Willing seems to me to be above all something COMPLICATED, something that is a unity only in name—and it is precisely in a name that popular prejudice lurks, which has got the mastery over the inadequate precautions of philosophers in all ages. So let us for once be more cautious, let us be "unphilosophical": let us say that in all willing there is firstly a plurality of sensations, namely, the sensation of the condition "AWAY FROM WHICH we go," the sensation of the condition "TOWARDS WHICH we go," the sensation of this "FROM" and "TOWARDS" itself, and then besides, an accompanying muscular sensation, which, even without our putting in motion "arms and legs," commences its action by force of habit, directly we "will" anything. Therefore, just as sensations (and indeed many kinds of sensations) are to be recognized as ingredients of the will, so, in the second place, thinking is also to be recognized; in every act of the will there is a ruling thought;—and let us not imagine it possible to sever this thought from the "willing," as if the will would then remain over! In the third place, the will is not only a complex of sensation and thinking, but it is above all an EMOTION, and in fact the emotion of the command. That which is termed "freedom of the will" is essentially the emotion of supremacy in respect to him who must obey: "I am free, 'he' must obey"—this consciousness is inherent in every will; and equally so the straining of the attention, the straight look which fixes itself exclusively on one thing, the unconditional judgment that "this and nothing else is necessary now," the inward certainty that obedience will be rendered—and whatever else pertains to the position of the commander. A man who WILLS commands something within himself which renders obedience, or which he believes renders obedience. But now let us notice what is the strangest thing about the will,—this affair so extremely complex, for which the people have only one name. Inasmuch as in the given circumstances we are at the same time the commanding AND the obeying parties, and as the obeying party we know the sensations of constraint, impulsion, pressure, resistance, and motion, which usually commence immediately after the act of will; inasmuch as, on the other hand, we are accustomed to disregard this duality, and to deceive ourselves about it by means of the synthetic term "I": a whole series of erroneous conclusions, and consequently of false judgments about the will itself, has become attached to the act of willing—to such a degree that he who wills believes firmly that willing SUFFICES for action. Since in the majority of cases there has only been exercise of will when the effect of the command—consequently obedience, and therefore action—was to be EXPECTED, the APPEARANCE has translated itself into the sentiment, as if there were a NECESSITY OF EFFECT; in a word, he who wills believes with a fair amount of certainty that will and action are somehow one; he ascribes the success, the carrying out of the willing, to the will itself, and thereby enjoys an increase of the sensation of power which accompanies all success. "Freedom of Will"—that is the expression for the complex state of delight of the person exercising volition, who commands and at the same time identifies himself with the executor of the order—who, as such, enjoys also the triumph over obstacles, but thinks within himself that it was really his own will that overcame them. In this way the person exercising volition adds the feelings of delight of his successful executive instruments, the useful "underwills" or under-souls—indeed, our body is but a social structure composed of many souls—to his feelings of delight as commander. L'EFFET C'EST MOI. what happens here is what happens in every well-constructed and happy commonwealth, namely, that the governing class identifies itself with the successes of the commonwealth. In all willing it is absolutely a question of commanding and obeying, on the basis, as already said, of a social structure composed of many "souls", on which account a philosopher should claim the right to include willing-as-such within the sphere of morals—regarded as the doctrine of the relations of supremacy under which the phenomenon of "life" manifests itself.

20. That the separate philosophical ideas are not anything optional or autonomously evolving, but grow up in connection and relationship with each other, that, however suddenly and arbitrarily they seem to appear in the history of thought, they nevertheless belong just as much to a system as the collective members of the fauna of a Continent—is betrayed in the end by the circumstance: how unfailingly the most diverse philosophers always fill in again a definite fundamental scheme of POSSIBLE philosophies. Under an invisible spell, they always revolve once more in the same orbit, however independent of each other they may feel themselves with their critical or systematic wills, something within them leads them, something impels them in definite order the one after the other—to wit, the innate methodology and relationship of their ideas. Their thinking is, in fact, far less a discovery than a re-recognizing, a remembering, a return and a home-coming to a far-off, ancient common-household of the soul, out of which those ideas formerly grew: philosophizing is so far a kind of atavism of the highest order. The wonderful family resemblance of all Indian, Greek, and German philosophizing is easily enough explained. In fact, where there is affinity of language, owing to the common philosophy of grammar—I mean owing to the unconscious domination and guidance of similar grammatical functions—it cannot but be that everything is prepared at the outset for a similar development and succession of philosophical systems, just as the way seems barred against certain other possibilities of world-interpretation. It is highly probable that philosophers within the domain of the Ural-Altaïc languages (where the conception of the subject is least developed) look otherwise "into the world," and will be found on paths of thought different from those of the Indo-Germans and Mussulmans, the spell of certain grammatical functions is ultimately also the spell of PHYSIOLOGICAL valuations and racial conditions.—So much by way of rejecting Locke's superficiality with regard to the origin of ideas.

21. The CAUSA SUI is the best self-contradiction that has yet been conceived, it is a sort of logical violation and unnaturalness; but the extravagant pride of man has managed to entangle itself profoundly and frightfully with this very folly. The desire for "freedom of will" in the superlative, metaphysical sense, such as still holds sway, unfortunately, in the minds of the half-educated, the desire to bear the entire and ultimate responsibility for one's actions oneself, and to absolve God, the world, ancestors, chance, and society therefrom, involves nothing less than to be precisely this CAUSA SUI, and, with more than Munchausen daring, to pull oneself up into existence by the hair, out of the slough of nothingness. If any one should find out in this manner the crass stupidity of the celebrated conception of "free will" and put it out of his head altogether, I beg of him to carry his "enlightenment" a step further, and also put out of his head the contrary of this monstrous conception of "free will": I mean "non-free will," which is tantamount to a misuse of cause and effect. One should not wrongly MATERIALISE "cause" and "effect," as the natural philosophers do (and whoever like them naturalize in thinking at present), according to the prevailing mechanical doltishness which makes the cause press and push until it "effects" its end; one should use "cause" and "effect" only as pure CONCEPTIONS, that is to say, as conventional fictions for the purpose of designation and mutual understanding,— NOT for explanation. In "being-in-itself" there is nothing of "casual-connection," of "necessity," or of "psychological non-freedom"; there the effect does NOT follow the cause, there "law" does not obtain. It is WE alone who have devised cause, sequence, reciprocity, relativity, constraint, number, law, freedom, motive, and purpose; and when we interpret and intermix this symbol-world, as "being-in-itself," with things, we act once more as we have always acted—MYTHOLOGICALLY. The "non-free will" is mythology; in real life it is only a question of STRONG and WEAK wills.—It is almost always a symptom of what is lacking in himself, when a thinker, in every "causal-connection" and "psychological necessity," manifests something of compulsion, indigence, obsequiousness, oppression, and non-freedom; it is suspicious to have such feelings—the person betrays himself. And in general, if I have observed correctly, the "non-freedom of the will" is regarded as a problem from two entirely opposite standpoints, but always in a profoundly PERSONAL manner: some will not give up their "responsibility," their belief in THEMSELVES, the personal right to THEIR merits, at any price (the vain races belong to this class); others on the contrary, do not wish to be answerable for anything, or blamed for anything, and owing to an inward self-contempt, seek to GET OUT OF THE BUSINESS, no matter how. The latter, when they write books, are in the habit at present of taking the side of criminals;

a sort of socialistic sympathy is their favourite disguise. And as a matter of fact, the fatalism of the weak-willed embellishes itself surprisingly when it can pose as "la religion de la souffrance humaine"; that is ITS "good taste."

22. Let me be pardoned, as an old philologist who cannot desist from the mischief of putting his finger on bad modes of interpretation, but "Nature's conformity to law," of which you physicists talk so proudly, as though—why, it exists only owing to your interpretation and bad "philology." It is no matter of fact, no "text," but rather just a naively humanitarian adjustment and perversion of meaning, with which you make abundant concessions to the democratic instincts of the modern soul! "Everywhere equality before the law—Nature is not different in that respect, nor better than we": a fine instance of secret motive, in which the vulgar antagonism to everything privileged and autocratic—likewise a second and more refined atheism—is once more disguised. "Ni dieu, ni maitre"—that, also, is what you want; and therefore "Cheers for natural law!"—is it not so? But, as has been said, that is interpretation, not text; and somebody might come along, who, with opposite intentions and modes of interpretation, could read out of the same "Nature," and with regard to the same phenomena, just the tyrannically inconsiderate and relentless enforcement of the claims of power—an interpreter who should so place the unexceptionalness and unconditionalness of all "Will to Power" before your eyes, that almost every word, and the word "tyranny" itself, would eventually seem unsuitable, or like a weakening and softening metaphor— as being too human; and who should, nevertheless, end by asserting the same about this world as you do, namely, that it has a "necessary" and "calculable" course, NOT, however, because laws obtain in it, but because they are absolutely LACKING, and every power effects its ultimate consequences every moment. Granted that this also is only interpretation—and you will be eager enough to make this objection?—well, so much the better.

23. All psychology hitherto has run aground on moral prejudices and timidities, it has not dared to launch out into the depths. In so far as it is allowable to recognize in that which has hitherto been written, evidence of that which has hitherto been kept silent, it seems as if nobody had yet harboured the notion of psychology as the Morphology and DEVELOPMENT-DOCTRINE OF THE WILL TO POWER, as I conceive of it. The power of moral prejudices has penetrated deeply into the most intellectual world, the world apparently most indifferent and unprejudiced, and has obviously operated in an injurious, obstructive, blinding, and distorting manner. A proper physio-psychology has to contend with unconscious antagonism in the heart of the investigator, it has "the heart" against it even a doctrine of the reciprocal conditionalness of the "good" and the "bad" impulses, causes (as refined immorality) distress and aversion in a still strong and manly conscience—still more so, a doctrine of the derivation of all good impulses from bad ones. If, however, a person should regard even the emotions of hatred, envy, covetousness, and imperiousness as life-conditioning emotions, as factors which must be present, fundamentally and essentially, in the general economy of life (which must, therefore, be further developed if life is to be further developed), he will suffer from such a view of things as from sea-sickness. And yet this hypothesis is far from being the strangest and most painful in this immense and almost new domain of dangerous knowledge, and there are in fact a hundred good reasons why every one should keep away from it who CAN do so! On the other hand, if one has once drifted hither with one's bark, well! very good! now let us set our teeth firmly! let us open our eyes and keep our hand fast on the helm! We sail away right OVER morality, we crush out, we destroy perhaps the remains of our own morality by daring to make our voyage thither—but what do WE matter. Never yet did a PROFOUNDER world of insight reveal itself to daring travelers and adventurers, and the psychologist who thus "makes a sacrifice"—it is not the sacrifizio dell' intelletto, on the contrary!—will at least be entitled to demand in return that psychology shall once more be recognized as the queen of the sciences, for whose service and equipment the other sciences exist. For psychology is once more the path to the fundamental problems.

Part III: Cultural Critique And *Decay*.

The Problem of Socrates

1

Concerning life, the wisest men of all ages have judged alike: it is no good. Always and everywhere one has heard the same sound from their mouths -- a sound full of doubt, full of melancholy, full of weariness of life, full of resistance to life. Even Socrates said, as he died: "To live -- that means to be sick a long time: I owe Asclepius the Savior a rooster." Even Socrates was tired of it. What does that evidence? What does it evince? Formerly one would have said (-- oh, it has been said, and loud enough, and especially by our pessimists): "At least something of all this must be true! The consensus of the sages evidences the truth." Shall we still talk like that today? May we? "At least something must be sick here," we retort. These wisest men of all ages -- they should first be scrutinized closely. Were they all perhaps shaky on their legs? late? tottery? decadents? Could it be that wisdom appears on earth as a raven, inspired by a little whiff of carrion?

2

This irreverent thought that the great sages are types of decline first occurred to me precisely in a case where it is most strongly opposed by both scholarly and unscholarly prejudice: I recognized Socrates and Plato to be symptoms of degeneration, tools of the Greek dissolution, pseudo-Greek, anti-Greek (Birth of Tragedy, **1872**). The consensus of the sages -- I comprehended this ever more clearly -- proves least of all that they were right in what they agreed on: it shows rather that they themselves, these wisest men, agreed in some physiological respect, and hence adopted the same negative attitude to life -- had to adopt it. Judgments, judgments of value, concerning life, for it or against it, can, in the end, never be true: they have value only as symptoms, they are worthy of consideration only as symptoms; in themselves such judgments are stupidities. One must by all means stretch out one's fingers and make the attempt to grasp this amazing finesse, that the value of life cannot be estimated. Not by the living, for they are an interested party, even a bone of contention, and not judges; not by the dead, for a different reason. For a philosopher to see a problem in the value of life is thus an objection to him, a question mark concerning his wisdom, an un-wisdom. Indeed? All these great wise men -- they were not only decadents but not wise at all? But I return to the problem of Socrates.

3

In origin, Socrates belonged to the lowest class: Socrates was plebs. We know, we can still see for ourselves, how ugly he was. But ugliness, in itself an objection, is among the Greeks almost a refutation. Was Socrates a Greek at all? Ugliness is often enough the expression of a development that has been crossed, thwarted by crossing. Or it appears as declining development. The anthropologists among the criminologists tell us that the typical criminal is ugly: monstrum in fronte, monstrum in animo. ["monster in face, monster in soul"] But the criminal is a decadent. Was Socrates a typical criminal? At least that would not be contradicted by the famous judgment of the physiognomist which sounded so offensive to the friends of Socrates. A foreigner who knew about faces once passed through Athens and told Socrates to his face that he was a monstrum -- that he harbored in himself all the bad vices and appetites. And Socrates merely answered: "You know me, sir!"

4

Socrates' decadence is suggested not only by the admitted wantonness and anarchy of his instincts, but also by the hypertrophy of the logical faculty and that barbed malice which distinguishes him. Nor should we forget those auditory hallucinations which, as "the daimonion of Socrates," have been interpreted religiously. Everything in him is exaggerated, buffo, a caricature; everything is at the same time concealed, ulterior, subterranean. I seek to comprehend what idiosyncrasy begot that Socratic equation of reason, virtue, and happiness: that most bizarre of all equations which, moreover, is opposed to all the instincts of the earlier Greeks.

5

With Socrates, Greek taste changes in favor of dialectics. What really happened there? Above all, a noble taste is thus vanquished; with dialectics the plebs come to the top. Before Socrates, dialectic manners were repudiated in good society: they were considered bad manners, they were compromising. The young were warned against them. Furthermore, all such presentations of one's reasons were distrusted. Honest things, like honest men, do not carry their reasons in their hands like that. It is indecent to show all five fingers. What must first be proved is worth little. Wherever authority still forms part of good bearing, where one does not give reasons but commands, the dialectician is a kind of buffoon: one laughs at him, one does not take him seriously. Socrates was the buffoon who got himself taken seriously: what really happened there?

6

One chooses dialectic only when one has no other means. One knows that one arouses mistrust with it, that it is not very persuasive. Nothing is easier to erase than a dialectical effect: the experience of every meeting at which there are speeches proves this. It can only be self-defense for those who no longer have other weapons. One must have to enforce one's right: until one reaches that point, one makes no use of it. The Jews were dialecticians for that reason; Reynard the Fox was one -- and Socrates too?

7

Is the irony of Socrates an expression of revolt? Of plebeian ressentiment? Does he, as one oppressed, enjoy his own ferocity in the knife-thrusts of his syllogisms? Does he avenge himself on the noble people whom he fascinates? As a dialectician, one holds a merciless tool in one's hand; one can become a tyrant by means of it; one compromises those one conquers. The dialectician leaves it to his opponent to prove that he is no idiot: he makes one furious and helpless at the same time. The dialectician renders the intellect of his opponent powerless. Indeed? Is dialectic only a form of revenge in Socrates?

8

I have given to understand how it was that Socrates could repel: it is therefore all the more necessary to explain his fascination. That he discovered a new kind of agon ["contest"], that he became its first fencing master for the noble circles of Athens, is one point. He fascinated by appealing to the agonistic impulse of the Greeks -- he introduced a variation into the wrestling match between young men and youths. Socrates was also a great erotic.

9

But Socrates guessed even more. He saw through his noble Athenians; he comprehended that his own case, his idiosyncrasy, was no longer exceptional. The same kind of degeneration was quietly developing everywhere: old Athens was coming to an end. And Socrates understood that all the world needed him -- his means, his cure, his personal artifice of self-preservation. Everywhere the instincts were in anarchy everywhere one was within five paces of excess: monstrum in animo was the general danger. "The impulses want to play the tyrant; one must invent a counter-tyrant who is stronger. When the physiognomist had revealed to Socrates who he was -- a cave of bad appetites -- the great master of irony let slip another word which is the key to his character. "This is true," he said, "but I mastered them all." How did Socrates become master over himself? His case was, at bottom, merely the extreme case, only the most striking instance of what was then beginning to be a universal distress: no one was any longer master over himself, the instincts turned against each other. He fascinated, being this extreme case; his awe-inspiring ugliness proclaimed him as such to all who could see: he fascinated, of course, even more as an answer, a solution, an apparent cure of this case.

10

When one finds it necessary to turn reason into a tyrant, as Socrates did, the danger cannot be slight that something else will play the tyrant. Rationality was then hit upon as the savior; neither Socrates nor his "patients" had any choice about being rational: it was de rigeur, it was their last resort. The fanaticism with which all Greek reflection throws itself upon rationality betrays a desperate situation; there was danger, there was but one choice: either to perish or -- to be absurdly rational. The moralism of the Greek philosophers from Plato on is pathologically conditioned; so is their esteem of dialectics. Reason = virtue = happiness, that means merely that one must imitate Socrates and counter the dark appetites with a permanent daylight -- the daylight of reason. One must be clever, clear, bright at any price: any concession to the instincts, to the unconscious, leads downward.

11

I have given to understand how it was that Socrates fascinated: he seemed to be a physician, a savior. Is it necessary to go on to demonstrate the error in his faith in "rationality at any price"? It is a self-deception on the part of philosophers and moralists if they believe that they are extricating themselves from decadence when they merely wage war against it. Extrication lies beyond their strength: what they choose as a means, as salvation, is itself but another expression of decadence;

they change its expression, but they do not get rid of decadence itself. Socrates was a misunderstanding; the whole improvement-morality, including the Christian, was a misunderstanding. The most blinding daylight; rationality at any price; life, bright, cold, cautious, conscious, without instinct, in opposition to the instincts -- all this too was a mere disease, another disease, and by no means a return to "virtue," to "health," to happiness. To have to fight the instincts -- that is the formula of decadence: as long as life is ascending, happiness equals instinct.

12

Did he himself still comprehend this, this most brilliant of all self-outwitters? Was this what he said to himself in the end, in the wisdom of his courage to die? Socrates wanted to die: not Athens, but he himself chose the hemlock; he forced Athens to sentence him. "Socrates is no physician," he said softly to himself, "here death alone is the physician. Socrates himself has merely been sick a long time."

Morality as anti-nature.

1.

All passions have a time when they are merely disastrous, when they pull down with the severity of the stupidity of their victims - and a later, much later, where they marry with the mind to "spiritualize". Formerly it was because of the stupidity in the passion, the passion of the war itself: they conspired for their destruction - all the old moral monsters are unanimous about it, "il faut les tuer passions." [one must kill the passions]. The most famous formula that is what the New Testament, in that Sermon on the Mount, where, incidentally, things are not quite seen from a height. It is there, for example with practical application to the said sex "if thine eye offend thee, pluck it out": fortunately no Christian acts in accordance with this provision. The passions and desires destroy, merely to prevent their stupidity and the unpleasant consequences of their stupidity, now seems itself merely as an acute form of stupidity. We do not admire more, which tear the teeth so they do not hurt anymore... going with some equity on the other hand admitted that on the ground, has grown from Christianity, the term "spiritualization of passion" could not be conceives by the dentists. The first church was fighting, as you know, against the "intelligent" in favor of the "poor in spirit" as one might expect from it an intelligent war against passion? - The church fights passion with excision in every sense: its practice, its "cure" is the castratism. It never asks: "how spiritualized, beautified, deify a craving you?" - It has laid the emphasis at all times of discipline on extirpation (of sensuality, of pride, lust, avarice, of vengefulness). - Means to attack, but the passions at the root of the attack at the root of life: the practice of the church is hostile to life...

2.

The same agent, intersection, extermination, is instinctively chosen in the struggle with a desire by those who are too weak-willed, too degenerate, to replace the one measure in it can, from those natures, the La Trappe have need of, spoken in parable (and without a parable -), any hostility final statement, a gap between itself and a passion. Radical means are indispensable only the degenerates, and the weakness of will, some talk, the inability not to react to a stimulus, is itself merely another form of degeneration. The radical hostility, the deadly hostility against sensuality is a thoughtful symptom: it is therefore entitled to make conjectures about produce the total state of such excessive. - Those hostility, this hatred is only incidentally to its tip, even when such natures for radical cure, the cancellation of their "devil" no longer have enough strength. One of watching the whole story of the priest and philosopher, the artist added taken: the poisonous against the senses is not said of the impotent, nor by ascetics, but by the impossible ascetics, by those who would have been necessary, ascetics to be...

3.

The spiritualization of sensuality is called love (Die Vergeistigung der Sinnlichkeit heisst Liebe): it is a great triumph over Christianity. Another man triumph is our spiritualization of hostility (Feindschaft). It is that we deeply understand the value that it has to have enemies: in short, that one does, and vice versa as they formerly did, and closes shut. The church was at all times, the destruction of their enemies: we, and we immoralists and antichrist, see our advantage is that the church is... In politics, the hostility now becomes more spiritual - much wiser, more thoughtful, more gentle. Almost every party understands their self-interest of conservation is that the other party does not come by force, as does that of the great policy. Especially as a new creation, as the new Reich [kingdom], needful enemies than friends: in opposition until it feels necessary, in contrast, it is only necessary... no different we act against the "enemy within": even as we have spiritualized hostility, also because we have understood its value. It is only fruitful to be rich at the cost of opposites, it only remains young, under the condition that the soul cannot be enforced, not desire for peace... There is nothing we become stranger than that desirability of yore, by the "peace of soul," the Christian desirability, nothing makes us envy less than the moral and the joys of fat cow good conscience. One has to great life dispensed with if one renounces war... In many cases, of course, the "peace of mind" is merely a misunderstanding - about another that not only knows how to nominate honest. Without further ado or prejudice of a few cases. "Peace of mind", for example, the gentle radiance of a rich animality into the moral (or religious) being. Or the beginning of the fatigue, the first shadow cast by the evening, any evening. Or a sign that the air is humid, that south winds are approaching. Or contradict the gratitude for a happy digestive knowledge ("human love" is sometimes called). Or the silence of the genes are ends, the taste of all things new and waiting... Or the state, following a strong satisfaction of our ruling passion, the feeling of a rare good satiety. Or infirmity of our will, our cravings, our vices. Or laziness, persuaded by vanity to morally frills (aufzuputzen). Or the occurrence of a certainty, even dreadful certainty, after a long tension and torment by the uncertainty. Or the expression of maturity and mastery in the middle of doing (Thun), creativity, knitting, wool, calm breathing, attained the "freedom of the will"...

Twilight of the Idols: who knows? perhaps even a kind of "peace of the soul" ... (Götzen-Dämmerung: wer weiss? vielleicht auch nur eine Art „Frieden der Seele "...)

4.

I bring a principle in the formula. Every naturalism in morality, that is all healthy morality, is dominated by an instinct of life, - any one commandment of life is "not set" with a particular canon of "shall" and met some resistance and hostility in the way of life is made so that one side. Their moral was unnatural, that is, almost every morality which previously taught, preached and venerated, is aimed precisely reversed against the instincts of life, - it is a secret soon, soon loud and bold this condemnation (Verurtheilungdieser) instincts. By saying, "God sees the heart," God says No to the lowest and highest desires of life and God takes enemy (Feind) of life... He is Holy, in whom God is well pleased, the ideal castrato... Life is too late, where the "kingdom of God" begins...

5.

Suppose that one has understood the wicked such a revolt against life as it is in Christian morality become almost sacrosanct, so you have it, fortunately, also somewhat Andres understood: the useless, apparent, absurd, mendacious such a rebellion. A condemnation of life on the part of the last survivors is only a symptom of a certain kind of life: the question of whether law, whether with injustice, is not even raised it. You'd have a position outside of life have, and know the other, it as good as one, as many as all who have lived to touch the problem of the value of life in at all: reasons enough to realize that the problem for us an unapproachable problem (unzugängliches Problem). When we speak of values, we speak under the inspiration, under the perspective of life: life itself forces us to value to be set, life itself posits values by us, if we estimate values ... It follows that even those contradictory nature of morality, which God counter-concept and condemnation of life holds only one value-judgment of life - what life? What kind of life? - But I gave the answer: of declining, the weak, the tired, the condemned life. Morality, as has been previously understood - even as it was last formulated by Schopenhauer as "negation of the will to live" - is the décadence instinct itself, which makes itself out of an imperative: "go to bottom" it says - it is the judgment convicts... (sie ist das Urtheil Verurtheilter...)

6.

Let us finally consider what it is naivety at all to say "so and so should the man be!" Reality shows us an enchanting wealth of types, the opulence of a lavish play and change of form: and any poor loafer of a moralist comments: "No! Man ought to be different"? He even knows how it should be, these eaters and hypocrites, he paints himself against the wall and says, "Ecce homo!"... [Translator. 'Behold the man'. From John **19:5**, New Testament, title from Nietzsche's autobiography that he was soon to write in the next month, October **1888**]. But even when the moralist addresses himself only to the individual and says to him: "so and so should you be!" He listens not to make fools of themselves. The individual is a piece of fate - is from the front and rear, one law more, one necessity more for everything that is and will be. Say to him, "you change" means demand that everything changes, even backwards yet... And really, it was consistently moralists, they wanted people differently, namely, virtuous, they wanted him in their own image, namely as a bigot: this they denied the world!

No small madness! No modest kind of immodesty!... The moral, insofar as it condemns, in itself, not of respects, considerations, plans of life, is a specific error, which you should have no sympathy, one degenerates, idiosyncrasy, which has caused untold amount of damage!... We others, we have immoralists, conversely made our hearts for all kind of understand, approve of understand. Not easily denied us, we seek our honor to be answered in the affirmative. More and more we are risen, the eye for that economy (Ökonomie), which all need the still and take advantage of white, which rejects the sacred madness of the priest, the diseased reason in the priesthood for those economics in the law of life, even from the obnoxious species of the muckers, the priest, takes advantage of their virtuous,-what advantage? - But we ourselves, we are here immoralists the answer... (Aber wir selbst, wir Immoralisten sind hier die Antwort...)

Skirmishes of an Untimely Man

1.

My impossible. - Seneca, or the toreador of virtue. - Rousseau, or the return to nature in impuris naturalibus [impurities in the physical world]. Schiller: or the moral trumpeter of Säckingen. - Dante, or the hyena, which poetry in graves. - Kant: or can't as an intelligible character. - Victor Hugo, or Pharos, the sea of nonsense. - Liszt: or the School of Velocity - for women. - George Sand: or lactea ubertas [milky fertility], in German: the dairy cow with "nice" style. - Michelet: or the excitement that takes off the skirt... Carlyle: or pessimism as the poorly digested lunch. - John Stuart Mill: or insulting clarity. - Les Frères de Goncourt: Ajax or the two in the fight with Homer. Music by Offenbach. - Zola: or "the joy of stink." -

2.

Renan. - Theology, or the corruption of reason by the "original sin" (Christianity). Testimony of Renan: whom, once he even a yes or no, scores general nature, engages with embarrassing wrong regularity. He would like to join as la science and la noblesse in one: but la science belongs to democracy, but the grabs with both hands. He wants to present with no small ambition, an aristocracy of the mind: but while he is in front of the counter-doctrine, the Evangel of humbles to the knees, not just on your knees... What helps all free-thinking, modernity, mockery and turning neck suppleness, if Christ is with his bowels, and even Catholic priests has remained! Renan has his ingenuity, much like a Jesuit priest and confessor, in the seduction, his spirituality does not lacks the wide- priests smile (Geschmunzel) - he is, like all priests, dangerous only when he loves. No one does it like to worship in a dangerous way to live... This spirit of Renan, a spirit which is enervated, one more calamity for the poor, sick, ill-willed France. -

3.

Sainte-Beuve. - Nothing of man, full of a little wrath against every man spirits. Wanders around, fine, bored, curious, listening (aushorcherisch) - a wenches basically, with a wife-revenge and female sensuality. As a psychologist, a genius of slander, inexhaustibly rich in means this: no one knows better how to mix poison with praise. Plebeian of the lowest instincts, and with the resentment of Rousseau used: hence romantics - because romanticism and is hungry all the grunts in Rousseau's instinct for revenge. Revolutionary, but the fear still kept reasonably in check. Without freedom from everything which has power (public opinion, Academy, Court, even Port Royal). Embittered against everything great in person and thing, against all that believes in itself. Poet and half-female (Halbweib) enough to still feel like a big power; resistant curved, like that famous worm because he feels kicked-resistant. As a critic, is without the standard, grip and backbone, with the tongue of the cosmopolitan libertine for many things, but without the courage even to the confession of libertinage. As a historian, without philosophy, without the power of philosophical gaze, - therefore reject the task of judging in all essential things, the "objectivity" as a mask suspensions. It behaves differently to all things, where a fine, uses up taste is the highest authority: because he really has the courage to be who want to be, - because he is a master. - After a few pages a precursor of Baudelaire's. -

4.

The imitation of Christ is one of the books that I do not think without a physiological resistance in their hands: they breathed a fragrance out of the eternal feminine, to the Frenchman must have been one - or Wagnerian... This saint has a kind of love for talk that even the Parisian women are curious. - I am told that those wisest Jesuit, Auguste Comte, who wanted to lead his French by way of science to Rome, had inspired this book. I believe it: "the religion of the heart"...

5.

G. Eliot. - You are going to the Christian God and believe now hold the more the need for Christian morality: this is an English consistency, we want to blame not the moral little woman à la Eliot. In England, one for every little emancipation from theology in a fearsome way to bring back morality-fanatics in its honor. This is where the penance, which you pay for. - For us it is different from others. If one gives up the Christian faith, pulls you away to the right to Christian morality under their feet. This is understood not a bad thing saying: you have to this point, the English flat heads in defiance, always ask to light. Christianity is a system, together and thought the whole view of things. If you break one of its main idea, a belief in God out, so you break even so the whole thing: it is not necessary anymore between the fingers. Christianity presupposes that man does not know, could not know what is good for him, what evil: he believes in God, who alone knows. Christian morality is a command, its origin is transcendent; it is beyond all criticism, all right to criticism it has truth only if God is the truth - it stands or falls with faith in God. - When the English actually believe that they knew of himself, "intuitively" what is good and evil when they imagine; therefore, Christianity as a guarantee of morality is no longer necessary to have, it is itself merely the consequence of the rule of Christian value judgments and an expression of dominion (Herrschaft) strength (Stärke) and depth of this rule: so that the origin of English morality has been forgotten, so that is not felt for very- conditional (Sehr-Bedingte) their right to existence. For the English morality is not a problem...

6.

George Sand. - I read the first Lettres d'un voyageur [**1869**]: like everything that comes from Rousseau, false, made bellows exaggerated. I consider this colorful wallpaper-style is not, any more than the mob's ambition to generous feelings. The worst of course, remains with the female coquetry (Weibskoketterie) with masculinities, naughty boys with manners. - How cold she must have been at it all, this insufferable artist! She pulled up like a clock - and wrote... cold, like Hugo, like Balzac, like all romantics, if they wrote! And how smug (selbstgefällig) they may have laid here, this fruitful writing-cow, which had something German in the bad sense in itself, like Rousseau himself, her master, and in any case only in the decline of French taste was possible! - But Renan admired...

7.

Ethics for psychologists. - No backstairs psychology drive! Never watch to watch! That gives a false appearance, a squint, something forced and exaggerated. Experience as experience wanting - not the device. You may not experience himself gazing after, every look is because the "evil eye". A born psychologist guards against his instincts, to see, to see, as does that of the born painter. He never works "from nature", - he leaves it to his instincts, his camera obscura, the sifting and expressions of "if", the "nature" of the "experienced"... The general comes before him to consciousness, the end, the result: he knows not that arbitrary abstract from the individual case. - What will happen if you make it differently? For example, the type of Parisian novelists, big and small drives backstairs psychology? Lurking speak to the reality that brings every evening a handful of curiosities with home... But you only see what comes last - a heap of splotches, a mosaic at best, in any case something co-added together, restless, colors screaming. The worst thing to reach the Goncourt: they do not put together three sentences, not the eye, the psychologists simply eye-ache. - Nature, estimated artistically, is not a model. It exaggerates, it distorts, and it leaves gaps. Nature is the accident (Zufall). The study "from nature" seems to me a bad sign: it betrays submission, weakness, fatalism - this is in-dust before petits faits [little things] -- lying is unworthy of a complete artist. See is what - that belongs to another class of spirits, the anti-artistic, the actual facts. You have to know who you are... (Man muss wissen, wer man ist...)

8.

On the psychology of the artist. - So there is art, so it gives some doing and an aesthetic look, this is a physiological precondition is indispensable: the noise. The noise has only the excitability of the whole machine have increased: rather, there is no art. All so different types of intoxication are related to the force: above all, the rush of sexual excitement, this oldest and most primitive form of intoxication. Similarly, the noise, in the wake of all the great passions, all strong emotions come, and the noise of the feast of the competition, the bravura piece (Bravourstücks) of victory, all extreme movement; the intoxication of cruelty, the noise in the destruction, of intoxication under certain meteorological influences, such as the spring rush, or under the influence of narcotics, and at last the noise of the will, the ecstasy of a cluttered and swollen will. - The essence of noise on the sense of power and wealth increase. From this feeling gives off about the things they are forced to take from us, they violate (vergewaltigt) - this process is called idealizing. Let us here from a prejudice going on: there is the idealizing not, as commonly believed, in a drawing from (Abziehn) or billing of the little ones of the irrelevant. A tremendous challenge and bustle of the main features is rather decisive, so that the others disappear over it.

9.

It enriches everything in this state from his own wealth: what you see, what you want, you can see it swollen, urged strongly, overloaded with power. The man of this state transforms things until they mirror his power - until they are reflections of his perfection. This must-turn into the more perfect is - art. Everything himself, what he is not, is it still a delight in itself, is very popular in art, the human being as perfection. – It would be allowed to devise an opposite state, a specific anti-artistic (Antikünstlerthum) of instinct – a way of being (sein), all things (Dinge), which impoverished, diluted, and was consumptive. And in fact, the story is rich in such anti-artists, in such starved of life: what to take with the necessity of things yet, they wasting, they need to make leaner. This is the case for example of true Christians, Pascal's, for example: a Christian who would also artist, does not happen... One is not childish, and turn me [into] Raphael, or any homeopathic (homöopathische) Christian of the nineteenth century: Raphael said, Yes, Raphael did Yes, Raphael was therefore not a Christian...

10.

I understood what the Apollonian aesthetic introduced into the contrast- concept (Gegensatz-Begriff) and the Dionysian, as both types of intoxication? -- The Apollonian frenzy (Rausch) stops at all the eye is energized so that it gets the power of vision. The painter, the sculptor, the epic poet are visionaries par excellence. In the Dionysian state, however, is the whole affective system is excited and enhanced: so that it discharges all its means of expression at once and the power of presentation, replication, trans figuring that turn, all kind of facial expressions and acting out while driving. The essence remains the ease of metamorphosis (Metamorphose), the inability not to react (- similar to some hysterical, which also occur on every hint towards in each role). It is impossible for the Dionysian man, any suggestion is not to understand, he sees no sign of emotion, and he has the highest degree of understanding and divining instinct, as it has the highest degree of mid-healing art. He goes into every skin, into any affect: he constantly turns. - Music as we understand it today, is also a total area- excitation and -discharge (Gesammt-Erregung und -Entladung) of the emotions, but only a remnant of a much fuller expression of the emotion-world, a mere residuum of the Dionysian histrionicism (dionysischen Histrionismus). One has to allow the music as a special art, a number of senses made, still with all the muscle sense (relatively at least's talking to a certain extent even all the rhythm of our own to muscles) so that the person is no longer all that he feels immediate bodily imitates and represents. Nevertheless, the Dionysian is actually the normal state (Normalzustand), in any case the original state

(Urzustand), the music is slowly reaching the same specification at the expense of the most nearest related (die Musik ist die langsam erreichte Spezifikation desselben auf Unkosten der nächstverwandten Vermögen).

11.

The actor, the mime, the dancer, the musician, the poet are fundamentally related to their instincts and to be separated one, but gradually specialized and each other - even up to the opposition. The poet remained the longest united with the musician, the actor with the dancers. - The architect represents is neither a Dionysian nor an Apollonian condition: there is the great act of will, the will that moves mountains, the intoxication of great will to the demands of art. The most powerful people have always inspired the architects; the architect was always under the power of suggestion. The building becomes visible itself is the pride of victory over gravity, the will to power (der Wille zur Macht); architecture is a kind of eloquence in the forms of power, sometimes persuasively, even flattering, sometimes merely commanding. The highest feeling of power and clarity to the expression, which has great style. The power that has no more need of proof, which disdains to please, and the answers difficult, which feels no witnesses around; lives without the awareness that there is opposition to them, which rests in itself, fatalistically, a law under laws: the talk of itself as great style (Das redet als grosser Stil von sich). —

12.

I read Thomas Carlyle's life, without knowing or desiring this farce, this heroic and moral interpretation of dyspeptic states. - Carlyle, a man of strong words and attitudes, rhetoric from necessity, the resistant and lurid (agaçirt) by the desire for a strong faith and a sense of inability to do so (- is a typical romantic). The desire for a strong faith is not evidence of a strong faith, rather the contrary.

Has been made, we may indulge in the beautiful luxury of skepticism: it is safe enough, strong enough bound, enough for them. Carlyle somewhat stunned by the fortissimo of his reverence for people of strong faith and his rage against the less simple-minded: he requires noise. A constant passionate dishonesty against him - that is his proprium [property], so he is and remains interesting. - Of course, in England he is admired for just his honesty... Well, that is English, and given that the English are the people of perfect cant, even cheap, and not only understandable... Basically, Carlyle is an English atheist who seeks his glory in it, but it not to be.

13.

Emerson. - Much more enlightened, more roving, much simpler, refined as Carlyle, above all, happier... Such a man, who instinctively nourishes only by ambrosia, who leaves behind the indigestible in things. Carlyle held against a man of taste. - Carlyle, who loved him very much said, but of him: "He gives us enough not to bite": whatever may be said with truth, but not to the detriment of Emerson's. --Emerson has that gracious and clever cheerfulness which discourages all seriousness, he knows absolutely no idea how old he already is, and how young he will be still, - he could say in one word Lope de Vega's "yo me sucedo a mi mismo" [am my own successor]. His spirit will always find reasons to be happy and even grateful, and sometimes he wanders the serene transcendence of that good fellow (Biederman), return from amorous rendezvous, tamquam re bene gesta [as good successful]. "Ut desint vires, he said gratefully, tamen est laudanda voluptas." — [That it may lack the strength, he said gratefully, yet it is pleasure to receive your praise].

14.

Anti-Darwin. - What the famous "struggle for life" is concerned; it appears to me meanwhile claimed more than proven. It happens, but as an exception, the totality aspect of life is not the desperate situation, the hunger situation, instead of wealth, the richness, even the absurd waste - is being fought where, you are fighting for power... One should not confuse Malthus for nature. - Supposing, however, there is this fight - and in fact, it happens - so it runs unfortunately, vice versa when the school Darwin's wishes, as you might with them should wish (wünschendürfte): namely, to the detriment of the strong, the privileged, the fortunate exceptions. The species do not grow in perfection: the weak are always on the strong masters (Herr), - that is, they are the big numbers, they are also more intelligent... Darwin forgot the spirit (- that is English!), the weak have more Spirit... You have to have spirit necessary to get spirit - you will lose it, if it was no longer finds it necessary. Who has the strength of spirit to suggest (entschlägt) ("let's go there! we think in Germany today - the must we remain rich but"...). I understand by spirit, as you can see, the caution, patience, cunning, dissimulation, the great self-control, and everything that is mimicry (the latter belongs to a large part of the so-called virtue).

15.

Psychologists' casuistry. - This is a good judge: what he actually studied the human? He wants to snatch small advantages over them, or even great - he's a politician!... That is because even a good judge: and you say, who wanted nothing for himself so it was a large "impersonal." To look sharper! Allowed to feel superior to people, look down on them, no longer confused with them, maybe he even wants a worse advantage. This "impersonal" is a man-despisers: and that the former is the more humane species, which may also say the evidence. He is at least equal, he is into it...

16.

The psychological measure of the Germans seems to me by a whole series of cases called into question, to present the directory prevents me my modesty. In one case it will not fail me at a big occasion to justify my thesis: I carry (trage) it to the Germans, about Kant and his "philosophy of the back doors (Hinterthüren)," as I call them, to have sold out - that was not the type of intellectual honesty. - The other things, what might not want to hear, is a notorious "and" the Germans say "Goethe and Schiller," - I'm afraid, they say, "Schiller and Goethe" If one knows... yet this Schiller? - There are worse "and" and I heard with my own ears, but only among university professors, "Schopenhauer and Hartmann" ...

17.

The most spiritual people, provided that they are the most courageous experience, by far the most painful tragedies: but just so they honor life, because they opposed his greatest opposition.

18.

The "intellectual conscience". - Nothing seems to me now rarer than the real hypocrisy. My suspicion is great that this fruit of the gentle air of our culture is not conducive. The hypocrisy is in the era of strong faith, where they carry themselves not constrained (necessitation, Nöthigung) to another faith on display, let go of the belief that you had. Today you can release it, or, more commonly, it still puts a second to think - honestly one remains in each case. Without doubt, today is a much larger number of possible beliefs as formerly possible that is allowed, i.e. harmless. This tolerance is created against himself. — The tolerance permitted multiple convictions against itself: this live together even tolerated - they care not how the world today, to compromise himself. Compromised, which is today? If you have consistency. When you walk in a straight line. If you are less than five conflicting (fünfdeutig). If you're really... My fear is great that modern man is just too comfortable for some vices: so that they almost become extinct. Everything evil that is the strong will of reasons - and perhaps there is no evil without strength of will - degenerates, in our balmy air of virtue... The few hypocrites (Heuchler), who got to know that I, made by the hypocrisy: they were, as today nearly every tenth person, an actor. – (Die wenigen Heuchler, die ich kennen lernte, machten die Heuchelei nach: sie waren, wie heutzutage fast jeder zehnte Mensch, Schauspieler.—)

19.

Beautiful and ugly. - Nothing is related; we say limited, as our sense of beauty. Who is divorced from the desire of the people think the people would immediately lose ground under the feet. The "pretty in itself" (Schöne an sich) is only one word, not even a concept. In the beautiful man sets himself up as a measure of perfection, in selected cases he worships himself in it. A genus cannot help but say to yourself alone in such a way yes. Their lowest instinct of self- preservation and self-aggrandizement radiates even in such sublime. The man believes the world itself overwhelmed with beauty - he forgets himself as their cause. He alone has endowed them with beauty, oh! only with a very human, all too human beauty... Basically, the man is reflected in the things he keeps everything nice for what it throws back his image: the sentence "beautiful" for its generic vanity... namely the skeptic may whisper a little suspicion, the question in his ear, so that the world really is embellished, just that it takes for a person beautiful? He has anthropomorphized: that is all. But nothing, absolutely nothing guarantees us that the just man from there (abgäbe) the model of beauty. Who knows how it would look into the eyes of a higher taste judge? Perhaps risky? perhaps even amusing? perhaps a little arbitrary?... "O Dionysus, divine one, why are you dragging me by the ears?" Ariadne once asked at one of those famous dialogues on Naxos, her philosophical lover. "I feel a kind of humor in your ears, Ariadne: why are not any longer?"

20.

Nothing is beautiful, only man is beautiful: on this naiveté rests all aesthetics, it is the first truth. Let us immediately add its second still, nothing is more ugly than the degenerating man - this is the realm of aesthetic judgment bounded. - Recalculated physiologically, everything ugly weakens and afflicted people. It reminds him of decay, danger, helplessness, and he actually loses this one force. One can measure the effect of the ugly with a dynamometer. Where a person is depressed at all, because he senses the proximity of something "ugly". His feeling of power, his will to power (Wille zur Macht), his courage, his pride - that coincides with the ugly, which increases with the beautiful... In the one case as in others we make a conclusion: the premises to be heaped in immense abundance in instinct. The ugly is understood as a sign and symptom of degeneration: what reminds remotely to degeneration (Degenerescenz) that works in us the sentence "ugly". Any signs of exhaustion, of heaviness, of age, fatigue, any kind of bondage, as a spasm, as paralysis, above all, the smell, the color, the shape of the resolution, the decay, and it is also the symbol of the last dilution - all this evokes the same reaction, the value-judgment (Werthurtheil) "ugly". A hatred springs out there: who hates when man? But there is no doubt that the decline of his type. He hates because out of the deepest instincts of the species, in which hatred is shudder, caution, depth, distant view, - it is the deepest hatred, there is. For his sake, art is profound...

21.

Schopenhauer. - Schopenhauer, the last German who is eligible (- of a European event like Goethe, like Hegel, like Heinrich Heine, and not merely a local, a "national"), is a psychologist, a case of the first rank, namely as malignant ingenious attempt in favor of a nihilistic overall depreciation (Abwerthung) of life- just the other instances, the great self-affirmations of the "will to live," the exuberance of life-forms to perform in the field. He has, in turn, the art, the heroism, the genius, the beauty, the great compassion, the knowledge, the will to truth, the tragedy as consequences of the "negation" or the negative-neediness of the "will" interpreter - the biggest psychological counterfeiting, which, Christianity settled, gives in the history. More precisely, been watching this he is merely the heir to the Christian interpretation: only that he rejected even by the Christianity, the great civilization-facts of humanity even in a Christian that is to approve nihilistic sense knew (- namely as a way to "salvation", as forerunners of "salvation", as stimulants of the need for "salvation"...)

22.

I take a particular case. Schopenhauer speaks of beauty, with a melancholy glow - last reason why? Because he sees in it abridge on which we continue to reach, or thirst, gets to go on... It is the salvation of the "will" for a few moments - it attracts to salvation for ever... In particular, he praises it as a savior from the "focal of the will," from sexuality - in the beauty he sees the witness denies driving... Whimsical saint! Somebody contradicts you, I fear it is nature. Why there is even beauty in sound, color, fragrance, rhythmic movement in nature? what is driving out the beauty? - Fortunately, it also contradicts a philosopher. No less an authority than the divine Plato (- as Schopenhauer himself calls him) maintains a different proposition: that all the beauty of incentives for procreation - that those are precisely the proprium [property] their effect, from the sensible way up into the most spiritual...

Plato goes on. He says with an innocence to the one Greek must not "Christian," that there would be no Platonic philosophy, if there were not so beautiful youths in Athens: the sight of one was just what the soul of the philosopher one erotic frenzy moving and let them have no rest until they've lowered down the seeds of all things high in such a beautiful earth. Also a strange saint! - You cannot believe his ears, even supposing that you trust Plato. At the very least one guesses that philosophizes in Athens was different, first of all publicly. Nothing is less than the Greek notion of a recluse spider weaving, amor dei intellectualis [intellectual love of God] on the nature of Spinoza. Philosophy on the nature of Plato would define it more as an erotic competition as a training and internalization of the ancient agonistic gymnastics and their prerequisites... What finally grew out of this philosophical Plato's erotic? A new art form of the Greek agon [Greek: solemn contest], the dialectic. - I still remember, against Schopenhauer and Plato's honor, remember that the whole higher culture and literature of classical France on the ground of sexual interest is raised. One must look at all their gallantry, the senses, the sexual competition, the "woman" - we will never search in vain...

24

L'art pour l'art [art for art's sake]. - The fight against purpose in art is always the battle against the moralizing tendency in art, against its subordination to morality. L'art pour l'art [art for art's sake]. is called "the devil take morality!" - But even this hostility still betrays the overwhelming power of prejudice. If you have ruled out the purpose of improving human and moral preaching (predigens) of the art, it does not follow for a long time that the art at all pointless, aimless, senseless, short l'art pour l'art [art for art's sake]. - a worm that spreads its tail bites is. "Dear no use as a moral purpose" - thus speaks the mere passion. A psychologist asks the other hand, what does all art? does not praise them? does not glorify them? They choose not? They pulls out not? By all this strengthens or weakens certain valuations... Is this just the one way? a coincidence? Something where the instinct of the artist would not be implicated? Or else it is not a prerequisite to the fact that the artist can...? Is the lowest instincts of the art or not, rather on the meaning of art, the life? desirability of a life? - Art is the great stimulant to life: how could we understand it as purposeless, as aimless, as l'art pour l'art ? [art for art's sake]. - A question remains: art also brings many ugly, hard, dubious of life to manifestation - seems not to be suffering (entleiden) from life? - And in fact, there were philosophers who attribute (Liehn) this sense, "get away from the will" Schopenhauer taught as a body of art-intent, "vote for resignation," he venerated as the great utility of the tragedy. - But this - I already gave it to understand - pessimists look and "evil eye" is: - you must appeal to the artists themselves. What divides the tragic artist of himself? Is it not just the state without fear of the terrible and questionable, it is pointing? - This state is itself a high desirability, and whoever knows him, honors him with the highest honors. He informs him, he has to communicate, provided that he is an artist, a genius of communication. The bravery and freedom of feeling before a powerful enemy, before a sublime calamity, before a problem that arouses dread - this triumphant state is chosen by the tragic artist, he exalted. Before the tragedy of the warlike (Kriegerische) in our soul celebrates its Saturnalia; who is accustomed to suffering, whoever seeks out suffering, the heroic man extols the tragedy of his existence, - served him alone the tragedian the trunk of sweetest cruelty (süssesten Grausamkeit.). -

25.

To put up (Fürlieb) with people taking to keep his heart an open house, which is liberal, but that is merely liberal. You can see the heart, the noble (dervornehmen) hospitality is capable of the many curtained windows and closed shutters: their best to keep them empty spaces. But why? - Because they expect guests with whom you cannot "put up"...

26.

We do not appreciate enough more, if we communicate to us. Our actual experiences are not at all talkative. They could not communicate themselves if they wanted. That is because they lack the word. What we have words about it, we are already out. In all the talk is a grain of contempt. The language, it seems, is only invented for average, median, communicative. Vulgarization (Vulgarisirtsich) with the language is already the speaker. - From a morality for deaf-mutes and other philosophers (Aus einer Moral für Taubstumme und andere Philosophen).

27.

"This portrait is enchantingly beautiful!"... The literature-woman (Litteratur- Weib), unsatisfied, agitated, desolate heart and guts, with painful curiosity any time listening (hinhorchend) on the imperative which whispers from the depths of it organization "aut liberi aut libri": the literature-woman, educated enough, the voice of to understand nature, even if she speaks Latin and the other vain and goose enough to secretly even to speak French with them, "je me verrai, je me lirai, je m'extasierai et je dirai: Possible, que j'aie eu tant d'esprit?"... [I see, I do, I apologize and I say: maybe, I had so much spirit?"]

28.

The "impersonal" to speak. - "Nothing about us is easier than wise to be patient, superior. We drip with the oil of forbearance and compassion, we are just an absurd way, and we forgive everything. For that very reason we should keep something more severe; why we should give ourselves, from time to time, a little affection, a little vice of affect to breed. It may not concern us mad, and we may laugh at us about the aspect that we give them. But what do you want! We have no other way was left of self-control: this is our asceticism, our penance (Büsserthum)"... Personally be —the virtue of "impersonal"... (Persönlich werden — die Tugend des „Unpersönlichen"…)

29.

From a doctoral promotion. - "What is the mission of all higher education?"

From the people to make a machine. - "What is the remedy to this?" - He must learn to be bored. - "How do you achieve that?" - The term of duty. - "Who is his role model for that?" - The philologist: teaches ooze (ochsen). - "Who is the perfect man?" - The heads of state officials. - "What is the philosophy gives the formula for the highest state officials?" - Kant's: the state officials as a thing in itself the judge of the state-officials as a phenomenon (Erscheinung). -

30.

The right to stupidity. - The tired and slow breathes worker who looks good- natured, lets go of things as they go: this typical figure, the one now in the era of labor (and the "empire" -!) Met in all classes of society, will now straight art (Kunst) claim for themselves, included the book, above all, the journal - how much more the beautiful scenery, Italy... The man of the evening, with "the departed wild instincts," speaking of which Faust is subject to summer, the seaside resort, the glaciers, Bayreuth's has... In those ages the art of a right to pure folly - as a kind of holiday spirit, wit and soul. Wagner understood. The pure folly restores...

31.

Another problem of the diet. - The means by which Julius Caesar defended himself against sickness, and headaches: tremendous marches, simple lifestyle, uninterrupted stay outdoors, resistant strains - that is, into the great expected, the universal rules conservation and protection at all against the extreme vulnerability of those subtle and means under extreme pressure working machine that which is called genius. -

32.

The immoralist speaks. - A philosopher is nothing more repugnant to my taste than the man, if he wants... he sees man only in his actions, he looks lost this bravest, most cunning, even in labyrinthine hardiest animals desperate situation, as it appears admirable man! He still speaks to him... But the philosopher despises the desiring people, even the "desirable" people - and indeed all desirables, all ideals of man. When a philosopher could be a nihilist, he would be there, because he finds the nothingness behind all ideals of man. Or not even the nothing just the unworthy, the absurd, the sick, the fig, the tired, all kind of dregs (Hefen) in the finished drinking cup of his life... The man who is a reality so venerable, how is it that he deserves no respect, if he wishes? He must atone for it so hard to be a reality? Does he have his doing (Thun), the head and tension will all balance out in doing, with a folding route in the imaginary and the absurd? - The desirability of its history has been the partie honteuse [shameful part] of people: one should take care not to long to read it. What justifies man is his reality - they will justify him eternally. How much more valuable is the real man, compared with some merely desired, dreamed, people pack of lies? with some ideal man?... And the ideal man is the only philosophers against my taste (Und nur der ideale Mensch geht dem Philosophen wider den Geschmack).

33.

Natural value of egoism. - Selfishness is worth as much as the physiologically is worthy of it: it may be worth very much; they may be unworthy and contemptible. Each individual may be considered suggests that it contains is the ascending or the descending line of life. With a decision on it has also a canon of what is worthy of his selfishness. If they ascent of the line is so, in fact, its value is extraordinary - and in order of the whole-life's sake, does that with it one step further, concern for conservation, to establish its optimum of conditions even be extreme. The individual, the "individual", as he understood people, and the philosopher so far is indeed a mistake: he has nothing for himself, not an atom, not a "ring of the chain," not merely of inherited formerly, - it is all one line man up to him there myself yet... He provides the descending development, decay, chronic degeneration, disease represents (- diseases, into the Great reckoned, already consequences of the decline, not its causes), comes to him with little value, and the first equity wants him to take away as little as possible from those turn out well. He is still only the parasite (Parasit)...

34.

Christian and anarchist. - If the anarchist, as the mouthpiece of the declining strata of society, with a fine indignation "right", "justice", "equal rights" demands, it is so only under the pressure of his lack of culture that can not be comprehended know why he actually suffers - what he is poor, to life... A cause-instinct is strong in him: someone must be to blame, that he is... too bad he does the "fine indignation" itself already well, it's a pleasure for all poor wretch, to curse, - there is a small rush of power. Even the action, the notion of mourning, can give life a charm for which power can stand it: a subtle dose revenge (Rache) in any action, throwing his poor condition, possibly even his wickedness those who are different, as an injustice, forbidden (einunerlaubtes) privilege as before. "Am I a canaille, you ought to be there": this logic to make one revolution. - The self-mourning is good in any case something: it comes from weakness. Whether it is bad to others or being attaches itself - does the former socialist, the latter as a Christian - it makes no real difference. What is common to say that we also unworthy of it is that someone should be guilty because you're suffering - in short, that the sufferer is prescribed to be suffering the vengeance of the honey. The objects in this revenge-need as a pleasure-need are occasional causes: the sufferer finds everywhere causes, to cool his little revenge - he is a Christian, I repeat, he finds it in himself... The Christian and the anarchist - Both are decadents. - But if the Christian "world" condemned, slandered, sullied, he does it out of the same instincts, from which condemned the workers' socialist society (socialistische Arbeiter die Gesellschaft), defamed, defiled: the "Last Judgment" itself is still the sweet consolation of revenge - the revolution, as it expects the socialist worker, thought just a little further... This "beyond" themselves - why a beyond, if it were not a means to foul this world?... (Das „Jenseits" selbst — wozu ein Jenseits, wenn es nicht ein Mittel wäre, das Diesseits zu beschmutzen?...) [translator note: beschmutzen could be translated as "besmirch"]

35.

Critique of the moral decadence. - An "altruistic" morality, a morality in which stunted selfishness - remains under all circumstances, a bad sign. This is true of individuals; this is especially true of nations. It is missing the best when it begins to lack of selfishness. Instinctively choose the self-harmful, be-curly (Gelockt-werden) by "disinterested" motives from almost gives the formula for decadence. "Do not search a benefit" - that is merely the moral fig leaf for an entirely different, namely actual physiological: "I know my value is not found"... Disgregation the instincts! - It's over with him if the man is altruistic. - Instead of naively say, "I agree nothing more valuable," says the moral lie in the mouth of the decadent, "Nothing is worth anything - life is worth nothing"... Such a verdict will last a great danger, it is contagious, - on the whole morbid soil of society it soon proliferates up to the concept of tropical vegetation, as soon as a religion (Christianity), sometimes as a philosophy (Schopenhauerian). Under such circumstances, poisons from decomposition of vegetation growing poison-tree, with its reek widely for thousands of years to your life... (Unter Umständen vergiftet eine solche aus Fäulniss gewachsene Giftbaum-Vegetation mit ihrem Dunste weithin, auf Jahrtausende hin das Leben...)

36.

Morality for physicians. - The patient is a parasite on society. In a certain state it is indecent to live longer. The puny vegetating (Fortvegetiren) in cowardly dependence on physicians and practices, given the meaning of life should have the right to life has been lost; the society is to draw a deep contempt. The doctors in turn would have to be the mediators of this contempt - not prescriptions, but every day a new dose create disgust at their patient... A new responsibility as the doctor, just in case, where the highest interest of life, of ascending life, the most ruthless and low-pressure-aside of degenerating life demands - for example, for the right to procreation, for the right to be born, for the right to live... On a proud way to die, if it is not possible to a proud way of life. The death, voluntarily chosen, death at the right time, with light and joy, accomplished amid children and witnesses: so that a real farewell is still possible, where they are still there, of goodbye similarly, a true estimate of the reached and willed, a summation of life - all in contrast to the miserable and ghastly comedy, which has driven Christianity with the hour of death. One should never forget it for Christianity, that it is the weakness of the dying man to rape conscience that it has abused the nature of death itself to value-judgments about people and the past! - Here it is, make all acts of cowardice in spite of prejudice, and above all the right, i.e. physiological assessment of the so-called natural death: the last, only one "unnatural" is a suicide. One never goes through any one else to reason but by itself is it is the only death among the most contemptible conditions, an unfree death, death at the wrong time, a coward-death. One should, for the love of life - free of the death wish otherwise, consciously, without accident, without decadents attack... Finally, a council for the master and other pessimists. We have not given birth to in their hand, to prevent, to be: but we can make this mistake - because sometimes it is a mistake - to make amends. If you look at abolishes it does the most estimable thing there: one earns nearly so, to live... The society, what I say! life itself has more advantage of it, than by any which "life" in renunciation, anemia, and other virtues it has freed the rest of their sight, it has freed the life of an objection... Pessimism, pur, vert [pure green] proves precisely, they need Schopenhauer deny first... Pessimism, here are - you have one step further to go in his logic, not merely a negative answer to "Will and Representation," as Schopenhauer did, that life is only through the self-refutation of Mr. pessimists so contagious it is still not increasing the morbidity of a time, one race as a whole: it is their expression. He was forfeited, as one falls of cholera: one must be created morbid enough to do already. Pessimism itself does not make one more decadent, I remember the result of the statistics that the years in which the cholera rages, there is no difference in the whole-number of deaths from other year groups.

Whether we have become moral. - Against my concept of "beyond good and evil (jenseits von Gut und Böse)" has stood as one might expect, the dumbing down of whole moral ferocity (Ferocität) which is known in Germany as the morality itself - thrown into the stuff: I would like to tell stories about it. Above all, they gave me the "undeniable superiority" of our time in the moral judgments to rethink our really done here advanced: a Cesare Borgia was, in comparison with us, certainly not as a "higher man" as a kind of human being, as I do, to set up.... A Swiss editor of the "Bund", went so far, not without expressing his respect for the courage for such ventures, "understand" the meaning of my work then that I applied the same for the abolition of all decent feelings. Much obliged! - Allow me, in response, raising the question whether we have become truly moral. That all the world believes is already an objection to it... We modern people, very delicate, very fragile and a hundred considerations giving and taking, we are one, in fact, these gentle humanity that we represent, this unanimity reached in the conservation, in helpfulness (Hülfsbereitschaft), mutual trust is a positive step forward, that we may be far beyond the people of the renaissance. But just think every time they think it must. It is certain that we will not likely put into it in the renaissance-states, not even try to understand: our nerves were not from the reality, not to speak of our muscles. With this failure, but no progress has been proven, but only one other, a condition subsequent, weaker, more tender, more vulnerable, from which necessarily generates a morality rich in consideration. Think away our tenderness and late awareness, our physiological aging, it would also lose our morale of the "humanization" immediately its value - in itself has no moral value -: it would make us self-contempt. Other hand, we doubt not that we moderns, with our thick wadded humanity that wants to come up against quite a stone to his contemporaries, Cesare Borgia's a comedy would make the dead laugh. In fact, we are beyond measure involuntary jokingly, with our modern "virtues"... The decrease in hostility and distrust that awakens instincts - and that would be our "progress" - only represents one of the consequences in the general decrease in vitality: it costs a hundred times more effort to be more careful to enforce such a conditional, so late life. As you help each other because each is to some extent ill and every nurse. This means then that "virtue" -: among people who knew the life or otherwise, full, lavish, overflowing, we would have it otherwise known as "cowardice" perhaps, "wretchedness", "Indian morality"... Our softening of manners - the is my sentence, that is, if you will, my renewal - is a consequence of the decline, the hardness and terribleness of morals can conversely be a consequence of the excess of life: namely may also risked much, much challenged to be much wasted too. What spice of life formerly was, for us it would be poison to be indifferent... - this is a form of strength - this we are also too old, too late: our compassion, morality, as I warned before the first, What one might call l'Impressionism morale is more an expression of physiological hyper-excitability that all that is decadent, is suitable. That movement, which has tried with Schopenhauer's morality of pity, to demonstrate scientifically - a very unfortunate attempt! - Is the actual movement of decadence in morality, as such it is deeply related with Christian morality. The strong making (vornehmen) times, cultures see the compassion in the "charity", the lack of self-contempt and self-esteem thing. -The times are measured by their positive forces - and there results those so wasteful and disastrous busy time of the renaissance as the last great time, and we, we moderns, with our anxious self-care and charity, with our virtues of work, simplicity, the honesty, the scientific method - collecting, economically, machinery - as a weak time... Our virtues are conditional, are challenged by our weakness... The "equality", a certain amount of actual assimilation, which in the theory of "equal rights" only expresses belongs essentially to the decline: the chasm between man and man, stand and stand, the multiplicity of types, the will to be oneself, to stand out, that what I call the pathos of distance, each strong time our own. The clamping force, the span between the extremes is now getting smaller, - blur the extremes themselves finally to the similarity... All our political theories and state constitutions, the "German Reich" not entirely excluded, are consequences, consequential necessities of decline and the unconscious effect of decadence is up to the ideals of individual studies into become master. My objection to the whole sociology in England and France remains that they only knows the structure of decay of the society from experience and completely innocent of taking one's own instincts of decay as the norm of sociological value appeal. The declining life, the acceptance of organizing, i.e. separating, divides clefts, sub and organizing power formulated in the sociology of today to the ideal... Our socialists are decadents, but even Mr. Herbert Spencer is a decadent, - he sees in victory of altruism, something more desirable!...

38.

My conception of freedom. - The value of a thing sometimes lies not in what you achieved with it, but in what you pay for them - what they cost us. I'll give an example. The liberal institutions immediately cease to be liberal as soon as they are reached: there is no worse later and more thorough injuring the freedom than liberal institutions. We know, indeed, what they bring to ways: they undermine (unterminiren) the will to power, they are raised on moral leveling of hills and valleys, they make small, cowardly and pleasure, - triumphs with them every time the herd. Liberalism: in German bring herd's animalization (Heerden- Verthierung)... These same institutions as long as they are still fought for, produce very different effects, then in fact they promote freedom in a powerful way. Specifically looked on, it is war that produces these effects, the war for liberal institutions, which can take more than the war illiberal instincts. And war educates for freedom. For what is freedom! That one has the will to self-responsibility. That the distance that separates us notes. That is to toil, hardship, privation, even to the lives of indifferent. That one is willing to sacrifice its cause not the people charged. Freedom means that the male, the war and the victorious happy instincts have dominion over other instincts, for example of the "happiness". The things that has become (Derfreigewordne) man, how much more the spirit freed (freigewordne) occurs with feet on the contemptible type of well-being of the grocer, dream Christians, cows, women, Englishmen and other democrats. The free man is warrior.- What is the measure of freedom, to individuals, as nations? After the resistance that must be overcome by the effort it cost to stay on top. The highest type of free men had to be sought where the highest resistance is constantly overcome: five steps from tyranny, close to the threshold of the danger of servitude. This is psychologically true, if you here among the "tyrants" relentless and terrible instincts understand that challenge the maximum of authority and discipline against themselves - the most beautiful type of Julius Caesar - and this is politically true, they only do its course through history. The nations that were worth something, were worth, this was never under liberal institutions: great danger made something out of them, deserve the respect, the danger that we know our expedients, our virtues, our military and weapons, our spirit only teaches - which forces us to be strong... First principle: it must necessary have to be strong: it's never been otherwise. - Those large hothouses for the strong, the strongest type of person who has been given, the aristocratic community in the way of Rome and Venice freedom accurately understood in the sense that I understand the word freedom as something that you have and lacks, that you want, this one conquers...

39.

Critique of modernity. - Our institutions are good for nothing more: it is about one accord. But that is not fault in them, but rather ours. Once we have lost all the instincts of which institutions grow, we are missing at all institutions, because we are not more to them are good. Democracy, every time the decline form the organizing force: I've characterized in "Human, All Too Human," I, **318** modern democracy, together with their half-truths, like "German Reich", as degenerate form of government. So there are institutions, there must be a kind of will, instinct, imperative, anti-liberal to malice: the will to tradition, to authority, to responsibility for centuries to come, the chains of gender solidarity back and forth ad infinitum. This will is there, based somewhat like the imperium Rome: or like Russia, the only power that now has duration in the body that can wait for the promise of something still can - Russia opposed the concept of the abject European particularism and nervousness that has occurred with the founding of the German Empire in a critical condition... The entire West has grown those instincts not more, out of which institutions from which the future grows: their "modern spirit" is perhaps nothing so much against the grain. We live for today, one lives very fast one lives very irresponsibly: precisely this is called "freedom." What institutions from institutions making, is despised, hated rejected: it is believed in the danger of a new slavery (Sklaverei), where the word "authority" is just loud. So far the decadence comes in the value-instincts (Werth-Instinkte) of our politicians, our political parties: they instinctively draw from what dissolves, thus accelerating the end... the testimony of modern marriage. For the modern marriage is seen come all reason lost: but that gives no objection against the marriage, but against modernity. The reason of the marriage - it was the sole legal responsibility of the man: so had the marriage heavyweight, while limping on both legs today. The reason of the marriage - it was in their insolubility principal (principiellen): so they got an accent, which, compared to the chance of feeling, passion and the moment the hearing did create. Similarly, it was the responsibility of families for the choice of husband. It has virtually eliminated with the increasing indulgence in favor of love marriage the foundation of marriage, that which only makes an institution. One establishes an institution never more to an idiosyncrasy, one establishes the marriage, as I said, to "love" - one based it on the sex drive, on the property drive (Eigenthumstrieb) (wife and child as property), to the domination instinct who constantly needs the smallest structures of domination, the family organized, the children and heirs to an accomplished measure of power, influence, wealth and physiologically hold up long tasks to prepare instinctive solidarity between centuries. Marriage as an institution already understands the affirmation of the largest, the most enduring form of organization in itself: also if the society itself cannot vouch for as a whole up to the most distant generations, the marriage has absolutely no sense. - The modern marriage lost its meaning - consequently one abolishes it. – (Die moderne Ehe verlor ihren Sinn, — folglich schafft man sie ab. —)

40.

The Workers' question (Arbeiter-Frage). - The stupidity, basically the degeneration of instinct, which today is the cause of all stupidities, is that there is a workers question (Arbeiter-Frage). About certain things the question is not: first imperative of instinct. After having first made an issue out of it, I cannot see from what you will do with the European workers. He is much too good not to ask more step by step, to ask immodest. He has most recently the large number of its

own. The hope is completely over, that there is a modest and self-sufficient type of man, a type of emerging Chinese image to the registry (Stande): and this would have had reason, this really would have been a necessity. What has it done? - All to the requirement [presupposition, Voraussetzung] to destroy it in the bud, - you have the instincts, a worker whose virtue as possible as to itself will be destroyed by the most irresponsible thoughtlessness into the ground. It has made the military-capable workers, one he has the right-coalitions, given the political right to vote, what wonder if the worker's existence (Existenz) today as a state of emergency (Nothstand) (expressed as morally wrong -) feels? But what you want? asked again. Will you have a purpose, you just want the means: will be slaves, you are a fool if one educates them to the masters (Herrn). -

41.

"The freedom that I do not mean…" - be left in such times, as now, their instincts, is a calamity more. Contradict those instincts interfere, to destroy each other, and I already denned as the modern physiological self-contradiction. The reason of education would want to print an iron at least one of these would be paralyzed instinct systems, to allow one another, to gain strength to be strong, to be master. Today would require the individual to make it all possible by the same cuts (dasselbebeschneidet): possible, that is quite... The opposite happens: the claim to independence, to free development, is to laisser aller [letting things go] just by those made at the most heated, for which no reins would be too strict - this is true in political affairs, this applies to art. But that is a symptom of decadence (decadence) our modern concept of "freedom" is an evidence of degeneration is more instinctive. -

42.

Where faith needful. - Nothing is rarer among moralists and saints than honesty, maybe they say the opposite, and perhaps they believe it themselves. Indeed, when a belief useful, effective, convincing, as is the deliberate hypocrisy, then, by instinct, the hypocrisy soon to innocence: first principle of understanding the great saint. Even among philosophers, a different kind of saint, it brings the whole trade with them, that they allow only certain truths: namely those on the back has their craft public sanction - talked Kantian truths of practical reason. They know what they have to prove, the fact they are handy - they recognize each other because they have 'the truth' match. - "Thou shalt not lie" - in German (auf Deutsch): beware, my master (Herr) philosopher, to say the truth... ("Du sollst nicht lügen" — auf deutsch: hüten Sie sich, mein Herr Philosoph, die Wahrheit zu sagen…)

43.

The conservatives whispered in the ear. - What you formerly did not know what we know today could know - a regression, a reversal in some sense and degree is not even possible. We physiologists know this at least. But all the priests and moralists have believed - they wanted to bring back the humanity scale,

back to an earlier measure of virtue. Morale was always a Procrustean bed. Even the politicians have to imitate the preachers of virtue: there are still parties to the target than the crabs (Krebsgangaller) imagined. But no one is free to be crab. It does not help: you must forward, to say step-by-step in the decadence (- this is my definition of modern "progress"...). You can inhibit this development and, by inhibiting the degradation jam yourself, pick up, make sudden and vehement: more one cannot do. – (Man kann diese Entwicklung hemmen und, durch Hemmung, die Entartung selber stauen, aufsammeln, vehementer und plötzlicher machen: mehr kann man nicht. —)

44.

My notion [concept, Begriff] of genius. - Great men are such great times explosive substances in which an immense force is accumulated, has been its precondition (Voraussetzung) is always historically and physiologically, that long for them to collect, heaped, saved and preserved - that long held no explosion. If the tension into the crowd too large, it is suffices to most casual charm, the "genius", the "deed" to call the great destiny (Schicksal) in the world. What is then to environment, at the age where "Zeitgeist" to "public opinion"! - Take the case of Napoleon. The France of the Revolution, and still more the pre-revolution would have brought off the opposite type, when Napoleon happens: it also produced him. And because Napoleon was different, heir to a stronger, longer, older civilization than that which went into pieces and steam in France, he was the master here; he alone was master here. The great men are necessary; the period in which they appear is accidental, that they are almost always the same is master (Lord), only that they are stronger, that they are older, that has been collected on them longer out. Between a genius and his time there is a relation as between strong and weak, even as between old and young: the time is still relatively much younger, thinner, immature, insecure, childish. - That one about it in France today is very different thinking (in Germany (Deutschland) too: but it is nothing), that there the theory of the milieu, has become a true neurotic theory, sacrosanct and almost scientific, and to find among the physiologists believe that "does not smell good," which makes one sad thought. - It also knows no different in England, but that will grieve no human being. The English are open only two ways to deal with the genius and the "big man" come to terms, either democratically in the Buckle's style or religious in the manner of Carlyle. --The danger lies in people and great times is extraordinary, and the exhaustion of every kind, sterility follows them on foot. The great man is an end, the big time, the Renaissance, for example, is an end. The genius - in work, in fact - is necessarily a spendthrift that it expends itself, is its size... The instinct of self-preservation as it is posted, about the enormous pressure of the outflowing forces forbids him any such care and caution. It's called "sacrifice"; extol his "heroism" in it, his indifference to personal welfare, his devotion to an idea, a great cause, a fatherland: all misunderstandings... He flows, he flows over, he consumes itself, he spares himself no - with fatality, fatal, involuntary, like a river breaking its banks involuntarily. But because such an explosive owes much, you have given them too much, however, is such a kind of higher morality... yes, the nature of human gratitude: it misunderstands (missverstehtihre) benefactor. -

45

The criminal and what is related to him. - The criminal type is the type of the strong man under unfavorable conditions, ill-made one strong person. He lacks the wilderness, some freer and more dangerous nature and form of existence in which everything is a weapon in defense and instinct of the strong man, it is justified.

His virtues are done by the society in thrall, and his most vivid shoots, which he brought back, once fused with the depressing emotions, with the suspicion, the fear of dishonor. But this is almost a recipe for physiological degeneration. Who, what he does best, best would do, do secretly have that much tension, caution, cunning, is anemic, and because he harvests only danger, persecution, calamity of his instincts since reversed himself and his feelings towards these instincts - he feels fatalistic (fatalistisch). The society is our tame, mediocre, blended society in which a quasi-natural person who comes from the mountains or from the adventures of the sea, necessarily degenerates into a criminal. Or, almost necessarily, for there are cases where such a person proves to be stronger than the society: the Corsican Napoleon is the most famous case. For the problem considered here is the testimony Dostoyevsky's relevant - Dostoyevsky's, the only psychologist, incidentally, which I had to learn something: he is among the most fortunate circumstances of my life, more even than the discovery of Stendhal's. This deeply human, the ten time was right to estimate the superficial low Germans, has the Siberian convicts, among whom he lived a long, loud hardened criminals, for whom there was no way back to the society at all, very different feel than he himself expected - about as the best, hardest and most valuable carved wood, which grows on Russian soil at all. We generalize the case of the criminal: let us imagine natures, which is missing for some reason, the public consent, who know that they are not as beneficial, as are felt useful - that Chandala feeling that one is not regarded as equal but as expelled, unworthy, contaminating. All such natures are the color of the underground to freedom of thought and action; any paler than them is wanting those, whose existence rests on the daylight. But almost all forms of existence (Existenzformen), which we characterize today have formerly lived under this half grave air: the scientific nature, the artist, the genius, the free spirit, the actor, the merchant, the great explorers... as long as the priest as was the highest type, every valuable kind of man was devalued (entwerthet)... The time is coming - I promise - where he is regarded as the lowest, as our Chandala, as the most mendacious (verlogenste), as the most indecent kind of person... I direct attention to it, as now, under the Regiment of the mildest manners that has ever existed on earth, to say the least in Europe, any aloofness, every long, too long below, any unusual, obscure form of being that type brings close to finished the criminals. All innovators have the mind for some time the pale and fatalistic character of the Chandala on the forehead: not because they felt this way, but because they themselves feel the awful gulf that separates them from conventional one and all in honor of standing. Almost every genius knows as one of its developments, "Catilinarian existence (catilinarische Existenz)", a -hate, -revenge and -rebellion against all sense of what already is, what is not... Catiline — the form of pre-existence (Präexistenz-Form) of every Caesar. —

46.

Here the view (Aussich) is free. - It may be the soul level, if a philosopher is silent, it may be love, if he contradicts himself, it is a courtesy of the knower is possible, which is lying. You did not say without subtlety: il est de coeur des grands indigne répandre le trouble, qu'il ressentent [it is unworthy of great hearts to pour out the confusion they feel]: only need to add that before the unworthy to fear also can not be the size of the soul. A woman who loves, sacrifices her honor, a knower, who "loves" sacrifices, perhaps, her humanity, a God who loved, was Jew...(Ein Weib, das liebt, opfert seine Ehre; ein Erkennender, welcher „liebt", opfert vielleicht seine Menschlichkeit; ein Gott, welcher liebte, ward Jude...)

47.

The beauty of a coincidence. - The beauty of a race or family, their grace and kindness in all gestures will be worked out: it is equal to the genius, the final result of accumulated work of generations. You have the good taste great sacrifices have brought, you have done for his sake much, much have left - is the seventeenth-century France admirably in both -, you must have had in it a principle of choice for establishment, location, clothing, sexual satisfaction have preferred to have the advantage of beauty, the habit of mind, of inertia. Primary consideration: they must also own the right to not "let go". - The good things are costly beyond measure: and still the law holds that anyone who has them, some one else's, than he who acquires it. Everything good is inheritance: what is inherited is imperfect, is the beginning... In Athens were at the time of Cicero, who also expressed their surprise, the men and young men far superior to the women of beauty: but how much work and effort in the service of beauty there the male sex had asked for centuries by itself! - One should not lay hands on the methodology that is here: a mere breeding of feelings and thoughts is almost zero (- here lies the great misunderstanding of the German education system that is completely illusory): you must first talk about the body. The strict maintenance of significant and selected gestures, a liability, to live only with people who are "let go" is not itself, is quite enough to be chosen and significant: in two or three generations is already everything internalized. It is critical about the fate of people and humanity, that you start the culture in the right place - not the "soul" (as it was the fateful superstition of the priests and half-priests): the right place is the body which gesture, the diet, physiology, and the rest follows... The Greeks therefore remain the first culture-event history - they knew they were doing, what misery that; Christianity, the body was despised [disdained, verachtete] yet the greatest misfortune of humanity. – (das grösste Unglück der Menschheit)

48.

Progress in my sense. - Also, I'm talking about a "return to nature," although it is not really one to go back (Zurückgehn), a coming back (Hinaufkommen), but rather - up into the high, open, even terrible nature and naturalness, one that plays with great tasks, play may... To put it in parable to say that Napoleon was a piece of "return to nature", as I understand it (for example in marked (rebus) tactics, still more, how do the military, the strategic). - But Rousseau - while actually wanted back? Rousseau, the first modern man, idealist and scoundrel (canaille) in one person, the moral of "dignity" was necessary to sustain his own aspect; sick with unbridled vanity and unbridled self-contempt. Also this monstrosity, which has been stored on the threshold of the new era, wanted to "return to nature" - where, once again wanted to ask Rousseau back? - I still hate Rousseau in the Revolution: it is the world-historical expression of this duality of idealist and scoundrel (canaille). The bloody farce, with the revolution going on this does not concern me much, their "immorality", what I hate is their morality, Rousseau - the so-called "truths" of the Revolution, with which it works and everything is still flat and mediocre to talked with him. The doctrine of equality!... But there is no more poisonous poison: for it seems preached by justice itself, while it is the end of justice... "The same, the same, the unequal unequals" - That would be the true question of justice: and what follows, unequal never be the same make – "modern idea" par excellence [by excellence], a kind of glory and glow that it comes to the doctrine of the equality around so gruesome and bloody events (zugieng), this has given, then the revolution seduced as a drama, the noblest minds. The last is no reason to respect them more. - I see only one man that felt like they must be viewed with disgust (mit Ekel) -- Goethe...

<h3 style="text-align:center">49.</h3>

Goethe - not a German event, but a European: a great effort to overcome the eighteenth century by a return to nature, to come up with a naturalness of the Renaissance, a kind of self-denial on the part of this century. - He wore his strongest instincts within himself: the sense of efficacy (Gefühlsamkeit), nature- idolatry, the anti-historical (das Antihistorische), the idealistic, the unreal and revolutionary (- the latter is only one form of the unreal). He took the history, natural science, antiquity, Spinoza, similarly, to help, above all, practical action, he surrounded himself closed with a loud horizons, he broke away not from life, he stationed himself, and he was not discouraged and took as much as possible upon himself, about himself, into himself. What he wanted was totality, he fought against the separation of reason, sensuality, feeling, volition (- with frighteningly scholasticism by Kant preached the antipode of Goethe), he disciplined himself to wholeness, he created himself... Goethe was unreal amidst a minded age, a staunch realist: he said yes to everything that was related to him in this, - he had realism greater experience than that ens [existents], called Napoleon. Goethe conceives a strong, highly educated, in all bodily skillful, having himself, respect for himself as someone who dares to treat oneself to the whole range and wealth of naturalness that is strong enough for this freedom, the people of tolerance, not from weakness, but rather from strength, because that which the average nature would perish, nor need to know in his favor, the people, for there is nothing more forbidden, unless the weakness that it names now vice or virtue... Such become free (freigewordner) spirit is with a joyous and trusting fatalism (Fatalismus) in the middle of all, in belief (im Glauben) that only the individual is reprehensible that the whole, everything is redeemed and affirmed - he denies any more... But such a belief is the highest of all possible beliefs: I have him baptized in the name of Dionysus. – (Aber ein solcher Glaube ist der höchste aller möglichen Glauben: ich habe ihn auf den Namen des Dionysos getauft. —)

50.

One could say that in a certain sense the nineteenth century, all this also strives what Goethe sought as a person: a universality understands, in approve an in-itself-come approach--let from any, a daring realism, an especially reverence actual facts. How is it that in the total-result is no Goethe, but a chaos, a nihilistic sigh, a non-know-where-have-one-out (bewilderment, ein Nicht-wissen-wo-aus- noch-ein,) an instinct of fatigue that keeps on driving in practice to the eighteenth century to use? (- Such as emotional romanticism, as altruism and hyper- sentimentalism (Hyper-Sentimentalität), as feminism in taste, as socialism in politics.). Is not the nineteenth century, especially in its issue, only an

increased brutalized eighteenth century that is one century of decadence? So that Goethe not only for Germany, but rather (sondern) for Europe only one incident, would have been a pretty vain? - But one misunderstands great human beings, when looked at from the perspective of a poor public benefit. That we draw no benefit from them to know, which belongs perhaps to the greatness...

51.

Goethe was the last German for whom I have respect (Ehrfurcht): he would have felt three things that I feel - well, we see ourselves on the "cross"... I am asked often what I actually wrote in German: nowhere would I be worse read than as in the fatherland (Vaterlande). But who knows least, if I only want to be read today? - Trying to create things in vain on which time their teeth; in form, the substance to be tried by a little immortality - I've never been humble enough to demand less of me. The aphorism, the sentence in which I am the first master among Germans, are the forms of "eternity", and my ambition is to say in ten sentences what everyone else says in a book - what everyone else in a book does not say... (Der Aphorismus, die Sentenz, in denen ich als der Erste unter Deutschen Meister bin, sind die Formen der „Ewigkeit"; mein Ehrgeiz ist, in zehn Sätzen zu sagen, was jeder Andre in einem Buche sagt, — was jeder Andre in einem Buche nicht sagt…).

I have given mankind the deepest book it possesses, my Zarathustra: I give them shortly about the most independent. – (Ich habe der Menschheit das tiefste Buch gegeben, das sie besitzt, meinen Zarathustra: ich gebe ihr über kurzem das unabhängigste. —).

Part IV: Christianity And The Will To *Nothingness*

THE ANTICHRIST

1.

—Let us look each other in the face. We are Hyperboreans—we know well enough how remote our place is. "Neither by land nor by water will you find the road to the Hyperboreans": even Pindar,[1] in his day, knew that much about us. Beyond the North, beyond the ice, beyond death—our life, our happiness.... We have discovered that happiness; we know the way; we got our knowledge of it from thousands of years in the labyrinth. Who else has found it?—The man of today?—"I don't know either the way out or the way in; I am whatever doesn't know either the way out or the way in"—so sighs the man of today.... This is the sort of modernity that made us ill,—we sickened on lazy peace, cowardly compro mise, the whole virtuous dirtiness of the modern Yea and Nay. This tolerance and largeur of the heart that "forgives" everything because it "understands" everything is a sirocco to us. Rather live amid the ice than among modern virtues and other such south-winds!... We were brave enough; we spared neither ourselves nor others; but we were a long time finding out where to direct our courage. We grew dismal; they called us fatalists. Our fate—it was the fulness, the tension, the storing up of powers. We thirsted for the lightnings and great deeds; we kept as far as possible from the happiness of the weakling, from "resignation"... There was thunder in our air; nature, as we embodied it, became overcast—for we had not yet found the way. The formula of our happiness: a Yea, a Nay, a straight line, a goal....

[1]Cf. the tenth Pythian ode. See also the fourth book of Herodotus. The Hyperboreans were a mythical people beyond the Rhipaean mountains, in the far North. They enjoyed unbroken happiness and perpetual youth.

2.

What is good?—Whatever augments the feeling of power, the will to power, power itself, in man.

What is evil?—Whatever springs from weakness.

What is happiness?—The feeling that power increases—that resistance is overcome.

Not contentment, but more power; not peace at any price, but war; not virtue, but efficiency (virtue in the Renaissance sense, virtu, virtue free of moral acid).

The weak and the botched shall perish: first principle of our charity. And one should help them to it.

What is more harmful than any vice?—Practical sympathy for the botched and the weak—Christianity....

3.

The problem that I set here is not what shall replace mankind in the order of living creatures (—man is an end—): but what type of man must be bred, must be willed, as being the most valuable, the most worthy of life, the most secure guarantee of the future.

This more valuable type has appeared often enough in the past: but always as a happy accident, as an exception, never as deliberately willed. Very often it has been precisely the most feared; hitherto it has been almost the terror of terrors;—and out of that terror the contrary type has been willed, cultivated and attained: the domestic animal, the herd animal, the sick brute-man—the Christian....

4.

Mankind surely does not represent an evolution toward a better or stronger or higher level, as progress is now understood. This "progress" is merely a modern idea, which is to say, a false idea. The European of today, in his essential worth, falls far below the European of the Renaissance; the process of evolution does not necessarily mean elevation, enhancement, strengthening.

True enough, it succeeds in isolated and individual cases in various parts of the earth and under the most widely different cultures, and in these cases a higher type certainly manifests itself; something which, compared to mankind in the mass, appears as a sort of superman. Such happy strokes of high success have always been possible, and will remain possible, perhaps, for all time to come. Even whole races, tribes and nations may occasionally represent such lucky accidents.

5.

We should not deck out and embellish Christianity: it has waged a war to the death against this higher type of man, it has put all the deepest instincts of this type under its ban, it has developed its concept of evil, of the Evil One himself, out of these instincts— the strong man as the typical reprobate, the "outcast among men." Christianity has taken the part of all the weak, the low, the botched; it has made an ideal out of antagonism to all the self-preservative instincts of sound life; it has corrupted even the faculties of those natures that are intellectually most vigorous, by representing the highest intellectual values as sinful, as misleading, as full of temptation. The most lamentable example: the corruption of Pascal, who believed that his intellect had been destroyed by original sin, whereas it was actually destroyed by Christianity!—

6.

It is a painful and tragic spectacle that rises before me: I have drawn back the curtain from the rottenness of man. This word, in my mouth, is at least free from one suspicion: that it involves a moral accusation against humanity. It is used—and I wish to emphasize the fact again—without any moral significance: and this is so far true that the rottenness I speak of is most apparent to me precisely in those quarters where there has been most aspiration, hitherto, toward "virtue" and "godliness." As you probably surmise, I understand rottenness in the sense of décadence: my argument is that all the values on which mankind now fixes its highest aspirations are décadence-values.

I call an animal, a species, an individual corrupt, when it loses its instincts, when it chooses, when it prefers, what is injurious to it. A history of the "higher feelings," the "ideals of humanity"—and it is possible that I'll have to write it—would almost explain why man is so degenerate. Life itself appears to me as an instinct for growth, for survival, for the accumulation of forces, for power: whenever the will to power fails there is disaster. My contention is that all the highest values of humanity have been emptied of this will—that the values of décadence, of nihilism, now prevail under the holiest names.

7.

Christianity is called the religion of pity.—Pity stands in opposition to all the tonic passions that augment the energy of the feeling of aliveness: it is a depressant. A man loses power when he pities. Through pity that drain upon strength which suffering works is multiplied a thousandfold. Suffering is made contagious by pity; under certain circumstances it may lead to a total sacrifice of life and living energy—a loss out of all proportion to the magnitude of the cause (—the case of the death of the Nazarene). This is the first view of it; there is, however, a still more important one. If one measures the effects of pity by the gravity of the reactions it sets up, its character as a menace to life appears in a much clearer light. Pity thwarts the whole law of evolution, which is the law of natural selection. It preserves whatever is ripe for destruction; it fights on the side of those disinherited and condemned by life; by maintaining life in so many of the botched of all kinds, it gives life itself a gloomy and dubious aspect. Mankind has ventured to call pity a virtue (—in every superior moral system it appears as a weakness—); going still further, it has been called the virtue, the source and foundation of all other virtues—but let us always bear in mind that this was from the standpoint of a philosophy that was nihilistic, and upon whose shield the denial of life was inscribed. Schopenhauer was right in this: that by means of pity life is denied, and made worthy of denial—pity is the technic of nihilism. Let me repeat: this depressing and contagious instinct stands against all those instincts which work for the preservation and enhancement of life: in the rôle of protector of the miserable, it is a prime agent in the promotion of décadence—pity persuades to extinction.... Of course, one doesn't say "extinction": one says "the other world," or "God," or "the true life," or Nirvana, salvation, blessedness.... This innocent rhetoric, from the realm of religious-ethical balderdash, appears a good deal less innocent when one reflects upon the tendency that it conceals beneath sublime words: the tendency to destroy life. Schopenhauer was hostile to life: that is why pity appeared to him as a virtue.... Aristotle, as every one knows, saw in pity a sickly and dangerous state of mind, the remedy for which was an occasional purgative: he regarded tragedy as that purgative. The instinct of life should prompt us to seek some means of puncturing any such pathological and dangerous accumulation of pity as that appearing in Schopenhauer's case (and also, alack, in that of our whole literary décadence, from St. Petersburg to Paris, from Tolstoi to Wagner), that it may burst and be discharged.... Nothing is more unhealthy, amid all our unhealthy modernism, than Christian pity. To be the doctors here, to be unmerciful here, to wield the knife here—all this is our business, all this is our sort of humanity, by this sign we are philosophers, we Hyperboreans!—

8.

It is necessary to say just whom we regard as our antagonists: theologians and all who have any theological blood in their veins—this is our whole philosophy.... One must have faced that menace at close hand, better still, one must have had experience of it directly and almost succumbed to it, to realize that it is not to be taken lightly (—the alleged free-thinking of our naturalists and physiologists seems to me to be a joke—

they have no passion about such things; they have not suffered—). This poisoning goes a great deal further than most people think: I find the arrogant habit of the theologian among all who regard themselves as "idealists"—among all who, by virtue of a higher point of departure, claim a right to rise above reality, and to look upon it with suspicion.... The idealist, like the ecclesiastic, carries all sorts of lofty concepts in his hand (—and not only in his hand!); he launches them with benevolent contempt against "understanding," "the senses," "honor," "good living," "science"; he sees such things as beneath him, as pernicious and seductive forces, on which "the soul" soars as a pure thing-in-itself—as if humility, chastity, poverty, in a word, holiness, had not already done much more damage to life than all imaginable horrors and vices.... The pure soul is a pure lie.... So long as the priest, that professional denier, calumniator and poisoner of life, is accepted as a higher variety of man, there can be no answer to the question, What is truth? Truth has already been stood on its head when the obvious attorney of mere emptiness is mistaken for its representative....

9.

Upon this theological instinct I make war: I find the tracks of it everywhere. Whoever has theological blood in his veins is shifty and dishonourable in all things. The pathetic thing that grows out of this condition is called faith: in other words, closing one's eyes upon one's self once for all, to avoid suffering the sight of incurable falsehood. People erect a concept of morality, of virtue, of holiness upon this false view of all things; they ground good conscience upon faulty vision; they argue that no other sort of vision has value any more, once they have made theirs sacrosanct with the names of "God," "salvation" and "eternity." I unearth this theological instinct in all directions: it is the most widespread and the most subterranean form of falsehood to be found on earth. Whatever a theologian regards as true must be false: there you have almost a criterion of truth. His profound instinct of self-preservation stands against truth ever coming into honour in any way, or even getting stated. Wherever the in fluence of theologians is felt there is a transvaluation of values, and the concepts "true" and "false" are forced to change places: whatever is most damaging to life is there called "true," and whatever exalts it, intensifies it, approves it, justifies it and makes it triumphant is there called "false."... When theologians, working through the "consciences" of princes (or of peoples—), stretch out their hands for power, there is never any doubt as to the fundamental issue: the will to make an end, the nihilistic will exerts that power....

10.

Among Germans I am immediately understood when I say that theological blood is the ruin of philosophy. The Protestant pastor is the grandfather of German philosophy; Protestantism itself is its peccatum originale. Definition of Protestantism: hemiplegic paralysis of Christianity—and of reason.... One need only utter the words "Tübingen School" to get an understanding of what German philosophy is at bottom—a very artful form of theology.... The Suabians are the best liars in Germany; they lie innocently.... Why all the rejoicing over the appearance of Kant that went through the learned world of Germany, three-fourths of which is made up of the sons of preachers and teachers— why the German conviction still echoing, that with Kant came a change for the better? The theological instinct of German scholars made them see clearly just what had become possible again.... A backstairs leading to the old ideal stood open; the concept of the "true world," the concept of morality as the essence of the world (—the two most vicious errors that ever existed!), were once more, thanks to a subtle and wily scepticism, if not actually demonstrable, then at least no longer refutable.... Reason, the prerogative of reason, does not go so far.... Out of reality there had been made "appearance"; an absolutely false world, that of being, had been turned into reality.... The success of Kant is merely a theological success; he was, like Luther and Leibnitz, but one more impediment to German integrity, already far from steady.—

11.

A word now against Kant as a moralist. A virtue must be our invention; it must spring out of our personal need and defence. In every other case it is a source of danger. That which does not belong to our life menaces it; a virtue which has its roots in mere respect for the concept of "virtue," as Kant would have it, is pernicious. "Virtue," "duty," "good for its own sake," goodness grounded upon impersonality or a notion of universal validity—these are all chimeras, and in them one finds only an expression of the decay, the last collapse of life, the Chinese spirit of Königsberg. Quite the contrary is demanded by the most profound laws of self-preservation and of growth: to wit, that every man find his own virtue, his own categorical imperative. A nation goes to pieces when it confounds its duty with the general concept of duty. Nothing works a more complete and penetrating disaster than every "impersonal" duty, every sacrifice before the Moloch of abstraction.—To think that no one has thought of Kant's categorical imperative as dangerous to life!... The theological instinct alone took it under protection!—An action prompted by the life-instinct proves that it is a right action by the amount of pleasure that goes with it: and yet that Nihilist, with his bowels of Christian dogmatism, regarded pleasure as an objection.... What destroys a man more quickly than to work, think and feel without inner necessity, without any deep personal desire, without pleasure—as a mere automaton of duty? That is the recipe for décadence, and no less for idiocy.... Kant became an idiot.—And such a man was the contemporary of Goethe! This calamitous spinner of cobwebs passed for the German philosopher—still passes today!... I forbid myself to say what I think of the Germans.... Didn't Kant see in the French Revolution the transformation of the state from the inorganic form to the organic? Didn't he ask himself if there was a single event that could be explained save on the assumption of a moral faculty in man, so that on the basis of it, "the tendency of mankind toward the good" could be explained, once and for all time? Kant's answer: "That is revolution." Instinct at fault in everything and anything, instinct as a revolt against nature, German décadence as a philosophy—that is Kant! —

12.

I put aside a few sceptics, the types of decency in the history of philosophy: the rest haven't the slightest conception of intellectual integrity. They behave like women, all these great enthusiasts and prodigies—they regard "beautiful feelings" as arguments, the "heaving breast" as the bellows of divine inspiration, conviction as the criterion of truth. In the end, with "German" innocence, Kant tried to give a scientific flavour to this form of corruption, this dearth of intellectual conscience, by calling it "practical reason." He deliberately invented a variety of reasons for use on occasions when it was desirable not to trouble with reason—that is, when morality, when the sublime command "thou shalt," was heard. When one recalls the fact that, among all peoples, the philosopher is no more than a development from the old type of priest, this inheritance from the priest, this fraud upon self, ceases to be remarkable. When a man feels that he has a divine mission, say to lift up, to save or to liberate mankind—when a man feels the divine spark in his heart and believes that he is the mouthpiece of super natural imperatives—when such a mission inflames him, it is only natural that he should stand beyond all merely reasonable standards of judgment. He feels that he is himself sanctified by this mission, that he is himself a type of a higher order!... What has a priest to do with philosophy! He stands far above it!—And hitherto the priest has ruled!—He has determined the meaning of "true" and "not true"!...

13.

Let us not underestimate this fact: that we ourselves, we free spirits, are already a "transvaluation of all values," a visualized declaration of war and victory against all the old concepts of "true" and "not true." The most valuable intuitions are the last to be attained; the most valuable of all are those which determine methods. All the methods, all the principles of the scientific spirit of today, were the targets for thousands of years of the most profound contempt; if a man inclined to them he was excluded from the society of "decent" people—he passed as "an enemy of God," as a scoffer at the truth, as one "possessed." As a man of science, he belonged to the Chandala[2].... We have had the whole pathetic stupidity of mankind against us—their every notion of what the truth ought to be, of what the service of the truth ought to be—their every "thou shalt" was launched against us.... Our objectives, our methods, our quiet, cautious, distrustful manner—all appeared to them as absolutely discreditable and contemptible.—Looking back, one may almost ask one's self with reason if it was not actually an aesthetic sense that kept men blind so long: what they demanded of the truth was picturesque effectiveness, and of the learned a strong appeal to their senses. It was our modesty that stood out longest against their taste.... How well they guessed that, these turkey-cocks of God!

[2]The lowest of the Hindu castes.

14.

We have unlearned something. We have become more modest in every way. We no longer derive man from the "spirit," from the "godhead"; we have dropped him back among the beasts. We regard him as the strongest of the beasts because he is the craftiest; one of the re sults thereof is his intellectuality. On the other hand, we guard ourselves against a conceit which would assert itself even here: that man is the great second thought in the process of organic evolution. He is, in truth, anything but the crown of creation: beside him stand many other animals, all at similar stages of development.... And even when we say that we say a bit too much, for man, relatively speaking, is the most botched of all the animals and the sickliest, and he has wandered the most dangerously from his instincts—though for all that, to be sure, he remains the most interesting!—As regards the lower animals, it was Descartes who first had the really admirable daring to describe them as machina; the whole of our physiology is directed toward proving the truth of this doctrine. Moreover, it is illogical to set man apart, as Descartes did: what we know of man today is limited precisely by the extent to which we have regarded him, too, as a machine. Formerly we accorded to man, as his inheritance from some higher order of beings, what was called "free will"; now we have taken even this will from him, for the term no longer describes anything that we can understand. The old word "will" now connotes only a sort of result, an individual reaction, that follows inevitably upon a series of partly discordant and partly harmonious stimuli—the will no longer "acts," or "moves."... Formerly it was thought that man's consciousness, his "spirit," offered evidence of his high origin, his divinity. That he might be perfected, he was advised, tortoise-like, to draw his senses in, to have no traffic with earthly things, to shuffle off his mortal coil—then only the important part of him, the "pure spirit," would remain. Here again we have thought out the thing better: to us consciousness, or "the spirit," appears as a symptom of a relative imperfection of the organism, as an experiment, a groping, a misunderstanding, as an affliction which uses up nervous force unnecessarily—we deny that anything can be done perfectly so long as it is done consciously. The "pure spirit" is a piece of pure stupidity: take away the nervous system and the senses, the so-called "mortal shell," and the rest is miscalculation—that is all!...

15.

Under Christianity neither morality nor religion has any point of contact with actuality. It offers purely imaginary causes ("God," "soul," "ego," "spirit," "free will"—or even "unfree"), and purely imaginary effects ("sin," "salvation," "grace," "punishment," "forgiveness of sins"). Intercourse between imaginary beings ("God," "spirits," "souls"); an imaginary natural history (anthropocentric; a total denial of the concept of natural causes); an imaginary psychology (misunderstandings of self, misinterpretations of agreeable or disagreeable general feelings—for example, of the states of the nervus sympathicus with the help of the sign-language of religio-ethical balderdash—, "repentance," "pangs of conscience," "temptation by the devil," "the presence of God"); an imaginary teleology (the "kingdom of God," "the last judgment," "eternal life").—This purely fictitious world, greatly to its disadvantage, is to be differentiated from the world of dreams; the latter at least reflects reality, whereas the former falsifies it, cheapens it and denies it. Once the concept of "nature" had been opposed to the concept of "God," the word "natural" necessarily took on the meaning of "abominable"—the whole of that fictitious world has its sources in hatred of the natural (—the real!—), and is no more than evidence of a profound uneasiness in the presence of reality.... This explains everything. Who alone has any reason for living his way out of reality? The man who suffers under it. But to suffer from reality one must be a botched reality.... The preponderance of pains over pleasures is the cause of this fictitious morality and religion: but such a preponderance also supplies the formula for décadence....

16.

A criticism of the Christian concept of God leads inevitably to the same conclusion.—A nation that still believes in itself holds fast to its own god. In him it does honour to the conditions which enable it to survive, to its virtues—it projects its joy in itself, its feeling of power, into a being to whom one may offer thanks. He who is rich will give of his riches; a proud people need a god to whom they can make sacrifices.... Religion, within these limits, is a form of gratitude. A man is grateful for his own existence: to that end he needs a god.——Such a god must be able to work both benefits and injuries; he must be able to play either friend or foe——he is wondered at for the good he does as well as for the evil he does. But the castration, against all nature, of such a god, making him a god of goodness alone, would be contrary to human inclination. Mankind has just as much need for an evil god as for a good god; it doesn't have to thank mere tolerance and humanitarianism for its own existence.... What would be the value of a god who knew nothing of anger, revenge, envy, scorn, cunning, violence? who had perhaps never experienced the rapturous ardeurs of victory and of destruction? No one would understand such a god: why should any one want him?——True enough, when a nation is on the downward path, when it feels its belief in its own future, its hope of freedom slipping from it, when it begins to see submission as a first necessity and the virtues of submission as measures of self-preservation, then it must overhaul its god. He then becomes a hypocrite, timorous and demure; he counsels "peace of soul," hate-no-more, leniency, "love" of friend and foe. He moralizes endlessly; he creeps into every private virtue; he becomes the god of every man; he becomes a private citizen, a cosmopolitan.... Formerly he represented a people, the strength of a people, everything aggressive and thirsty for power in the soul of a people; now he is simply the good god.... The truth is that there is no other alternative for gods: either they are the will to power——in which case they are national gods——or incapacity for power——in which case they have to be good....

17.

Wherever the will to power begins to decline, in whatever form, there is always an accompanying decline physiologically, a décadence. The divinity of this décadence, shorn of its masculine virtues and passions, is converted perforce into a god of the physiologically degraded, of the weak. Of course, they do not call themselves the weak; they call themselves "the good."... No hint is needed to indicate the moments in history at which the dualistic fiction of a good and an evil god first became possible. The same instinct which prompts the inferior to reduce their own god to "goodness-in-itself" also prompts them to eliminate all good qualities from the god of their superiors; they make revenge on their masters by making a devil of the latter's god.—— The good god, and the devil like him——both are abortions of décadence.——How can we be so tolerant of the naïveté of Christian theologians as to join in their doctrine that the evolution of the concept of god from "the god of Israel," the god of a people, to the Christian god, the essence of all goodness, is to be described as progress?——But even Renan does this. As if Renan had a right to be naïve! The contrary actually stares one in the face. When everything necessary to ascending life; when all that is strong, courageous, masterful and proud has been eliminated from the concept of a god; when he has sunk step by step to the level of a staff for the weary, a sheet-anchor for the drowning; when he becomes the poor man's god, the sinner's god, the invalid's god par excellence, and the attribute of "saviour" or "redeemer" remains as the one essential attribute of divinity——just what is the significance of such a metamorphosis? what does such a reduction of the godhead imply?——To be sure, the "kingdom of God" has thus grown larger. Formerly he had only his own people, his "chosen" people. But since then he has gone wandering, like his people themselves, into foreign parts; he has given up settling down quietly anywhere; finally he has come to feel at home everywhere, and is the great cosmopolitan——until now he has the "great majority" on his side, and half the earth. But this god of the "great majority," this democrat among gods, has not become a proud heathen god: on the contrary, he remains a Jew, he remains a god in a corner, a god of all the dark nooks and crevices, of all the noisesome quarters of the world!... His earthly kingdom, now as always, is a kingdom of the underworld, a souterrain kingdom, a ghetto kingdom.... And he himself is so pale, so weak, so décadent.... Even the palest of the pale are able to master him—messieurs the metaphysicians, those albinos of the intellect. They spun their webs around him for so long that finally he was hypnotized, and began to spin himself, and became another metaphysician. Thereafter he resumed once more his old busi ness of spinning the world out of his inmost being sub specie Spinozae; thereafter he became ever thinner and paler—became the "ideal," became "pure spirit," became "the absolute," became "the thing-in-itself."... The collapse of a god: he became a "thing-in-itself."

18.

The Christian concept of a god—the god as the patron of the sick, the god as a spinner of cobwebs, the god as a spirit—is one of the most corrupt concepts that has ever been set up in the world: it probably touches low-water mark in the ebbing evolution of the god-type. God degenerated into the contradiction of life. Instead of being its transfiguration and eternal Yea! In him war is declared on life, on nature, on the will to live! God becomes the formula for every slander upon the "here and now," and for every lie about the "beyond"! In him nothingness is deified, and the will to nothingness is made holy!...

19.

The fact that the strong races of northern Europe did not repudiate this Christian god does little credit to their gift for religion—and not much more to their taste. They ought to have been able to make an end of such a moribund and worn-out product of the décadence. A curse lies upon them because they were not equal to it; they made illness, decrepitude and contradiction a part of their instincts—and since then they have not managed to create any more gods. Two thousand years have come and gone—and not a single new god! Instead, there still exists, and as if by some intrinsic right,—as if he were the ultimatum and maximum of the power to create gods, of the creator spiritus in mankind—this pitiful god of Christian monotono-theism! This hybrid image of decay, conjured up out of emptiness, contradiction and vain imagining, in which all the instincts of décadence, all the cowardices and wearinesses of the soul find their sanction!—

20.

In my condemnation of Christianity I surely hope I do no injustice to a related religion with an even larger number of believers: I allude to Buddhism. Both are to be reckoned among the nihilistic religions—they are both décadence religions—but they are separated from each other in a very remarkable way. For the fact that he is able to compare them at all the critic of Christianity is indebted to the scholars of India.—Buddhism is a hundred times as realistic as Christianity—it is part of its living heritage that it is able to face problems objectively and coolly; it is the product of long centuries of philosophical speculation. The concept, "god," was already disposed of before it appeared. Buddhism is the only genuinely positive religion to be encountered in history, and this applies even to its epistemology (which is a strict phenomenalism). It does not speak of a "struggle with sin," but, yielding to reality, of the "struggle with suffering." Sharply differentiating itself from Christianity, it puts the self-deception that lies in moral concepts behind it; it is, in my phrase, beyond good and evil.— The two physiological facts upon which it grounds itself and upon which it bestows its chief attention are: first, an excessive sensitiveness to sensation, which manifests itself as a refined susceptibility to pain, and secondly, an extraordinary spirituality, a too protracted concern with concepts and logical procedures, under the influence of which the instinct of personality has yielded to a notion of the "impersonal." (—Both of these states will be familiar to a few of my readers, the objectivists, by experience, as they are to me). These physiological states produced a depression, and Buddha tried to combat it by hygienic measures. Against it he prescribed a life in the open, a life of travel; moderation in eating and a careful selection of foods; caution in the use of intoxicants; the same caution in arousing any of the passions that foster a bilious habit and heat the blood; finally, no worry, either on one's own account or on account of others. He encourages ideas that make for either quiet contentment or good cheer—he finds means to combat ideas of other sorts. He understands good, the state of goodness, as something which promotes health. Prayer is not included, and neither is asceticism. There is no categorical imperative nor any disciplines, even within the walls of a monastery (—it is always possible to leave—). These things would have been simply means of increasing the excessive sensitiveness above mentioned. For the same reason he does not advocate any conflict with unbelievers; his teaching is antagonistic to nothing so much as to revenge, aversion, ressentiment (—"enmity never brings an end to enmity": the moving refrain of all Buddhism....) And in all this he was right, for it is precisely these passions which, in view of his main regiminal purpose, are unhealthful. The mental fatigue that he observes, already plainly displayed in too much "objectivity" (that is, in the individual's loss of interest in himself, in loss of balance and of "egoism"), he combats by strong efforts to lead even the spiritual interests back to the ego. In Buddha's teaching egoism is a duty. The "one thing needful," the question "how can you be delivered from suffering," regulates and determines the whole spiritual diet. (—Perhaps one will here recall that Athenian who also declared war upon pure "scientificality," to wit, Socrates, who also elevated egoism to the estate of a morality).

21.

The things necessary to Buddhism are a very mild climate, customs of great gentleness and liberality, and no militarism; moreover, it must get its start among the higher and better edu cated classes. Cheerfulness, quiet and the absence of desire are the chief desiderata, and they are attained. Buddhism is not a religion in which perfection is merely an object of aspiration: perfection is actually normal.—

Under Christianity the instincts of the subjugated and the oppressed come to the fore: it is only those who are at the bottom who seek their salvation in it. Here the prevailing pastime, the favourite remedy for boredom is the discussion of sin, self-criticism, the inquisition of conscience; here the emotion produced by power (called "God") is pumped up (by prayer); here the highest good is regarded as unattainable, as a gift, as "grace." Here, too, open dealing is lacking; concealment and the darkened room are

Christian. Here body is despised and hygiene is denounced as sensual; the church even ranges itself against cleanliness (—the first Christian order after the banishment of the Moors closed the public baths, of which there were **270** in Cordova alone). Christian, too, is a certain cruelty toward one's self and toward others; hatred of unbelievers; the will to persecute. Sombre and disquieting ideas are in the foreground; the most esteemed states of mind, bearing the most respectable names, are epileptoid; the diet is so regulated as to engender morbid symptoms and over-stimulate the nerves. Christian, again, is all deadly enmity to the rulers of the earth, to the "aristocratic"— along with a sort of secret rivalry with them (—one resigns one's "body" to them; one wants only one's "soul"...). And Christian is all hatred of the intellect, of pride, of courage, of freedom, of intellectual libertinage; Christian is all hatred of the senses, of joy in the senses, of joy in general....

22.

When Christianity departed from its native soil, that of the lowest orders, the underworld of the ancient world, and began seeking power among barbarian peoples, it no longer had to deal with exhausted men, but with men still inwardly savage and capable of self-torture—in brief, strong men, but bungled men. Here, unlike in the case of the Buddhists, the cause of discontent with self, suffering through self, is not merely a general sensitiveness and susceptibility to pain, but, on the contrary, an inordinate thirst for inflicting pain on others, a tendency to obtain subjective satisfaction in hostile deeds and ideas. Christianity had to embrace barbaric concepts and valuations in order to obtain mastery over barbarians: of such sort, for example, are the sacrifices of the first-born, the drinking of blood as a sacrament, the disdain of the intellect and of culture; torture in all its forms, whether bodily or not; the whole pomp of the cult. Buddhism is a religion for peoples in a further state of development, for races that have become kind, gentle and over-spiritualized (—Europe is not yet ripe for it—): it is a summons that takes them back to peace and cheerfulness, to a careful rationing of the spirit, to a certain hardening of the body. Christianity aims at mastering beasts of prey; its modus operandi is to make them ill—to make feeble is the Christian recipe for taming, for "civilizing." Buddhism is a religion for the closing, over-wearied stages of civilization. Christianity appears before civilization has so much as begun—under certain circumstances it lays the very foundations thereof.

23.

Buddhism, I repeat, is a hundred times more austere, more honest, more objective. It no longer has to justify its pains, its susceptibility to suffering, by interpreting these things in terms of sin—it simply says, as it simply thinks, "I suffer." To the barbarian, however, suffering in itself is scarcely understandable: what he needs, first of all, is an explanation as to why he suffers. (His mere instinct prompts him to deny his suffering altogether, or to endure it in silence.) Here the word "devil" was a blessing: man had to have an omnipotent and terrible enemy—there was no need to be ashamed of suffering at the hands of such an enemy.—

At the bottom of Christianity there are several subtleties that belong to the Orient. In the first place, it knows that it is of very little consequence whether a thing be true or not, so long as it is believed to be true. Truth and faith: here we have two wholly distinct worlds of ideas, almost two diametrically opposite worlds—the road to the one and the road to the other lie miles apart. To understand that fact thoroughly—this is almost enough, in the Orient, to make one a sage. The Brahmins knew it, Plato knew it, every student of the esoteric knows it. When, for example, a man gets any pleasure out of the notion that he has been saved from sin, it is not necessary for him to be actually sinful, but merely to feel sinful. But when faith is thus exalted above everything else, it necessarily follows that reason, knowledge and patient inquiry have to be discredited: the road to the truth becomes a forbidden road.—Hope, in its stronger forms, is a great deal more powerful stimulans to life than any sort of realized joy can ever be. Man must be sustained in suffering by a hope so high that no conflict with actuality can dash it—so high, indeed, that no fulfilment can satisfy it: a hope reaching out beyond this world. (Precisely because of this power that hope has of making the suffering hold out, the Greeks regarded it as the evil of evils, as the most malign of evils; it remained behind at the source of all evil.)[3]—In order that love may be possible, God must become a person; in order that the lower instincts may take a hand in the matter God must be young. To satisfy the ardor of the woman a beautiful saint must appear on the scene, and to satisfy that of the men there must be a virgin. These things are necessary if Christianity is to assume lordship over a soil on which some aphrodisiacal or Adonis cult has already established a notion as to what a cult ought to be. To insist upon chastity greatly strengthens the vehemence and subjectivity of the religious instinct—it makes the cult warmer, more enthusiastic, more soulful.—Love is the state in which man sees things most decidedly as they are not. The force of illusion reaches its highest here, and so does the capacity for sweetening, for transfiguring. When a man is in love he endures more than at any other time; he submits to anything. The problem was to devise a religion which would allow one to love: by this means the worst that life has to offer is overcome—it is scarcely even noticed.—So much for the three Christian virtues: faith, hope and charity: I call them the three Christian ingenuities.—Buddhism is in too late a stage of development, too full of positivism, to be shrewd in any such way.—

[3]That is, in Pandora's box.

24.

Here I barely touch upon the problem of the origin of Christianity. The first thing necessary to its solution is this: that Christianity is to be understood only by examining the soil from which it sprung—it is not a reaction against Jewish instincts; it is their inevitable product; it is simply one more step in the awe-inspiring logic of the Jews. In the words of the Saviour, "salvation is of the Jews."[4]—The second thing to remember is this: that the psychological type of the Galilean is still to be recognized, but it was only in its most degenerate form (which is at once maimed and overladen with foreign features) that it could serve in the manner in which it has been used: as a type of the Saviour of mankind.—

[4]John iv, 22.

The Jews are the most remarkable people in the history of the world, for when they were confronted with the question, to be or not to be, they chose, with perfectly unearthly deliberation, to be at any price: this price involved a radical falsification of all nature, of all naturalness, of all reality, of the whole inner world, as well as of the outer. They put themselves against all those conditions under which, hitherto, a people had been able to live, or had even been permitted to live; out of themselves they evolved an idea which stood in direct opposition to natural conditions—one by one they distorted religion, civilization, morality, history and psychology until each became a contradiction of its natural significance. We meet with the same phenomenon later on, in an incalculably exaggerated form, but only as a copy: the Christian church, put beside the "people of God," shows a complete lack of any claim to originality. Precisely for this reason the Jews are the most fateful people in the history of the world: their influence has so falsified the reasoning of mankind in this matter that today the Christian can cherish anti-Semitism without realizing that it is no more than the final consequence of Judaism.

In my "Genealogy of Morals" I give the first psychological explanation of the concepts underlying those two antithetical things, a noble morality and a ressentiment morality, the second of which is a mere product of the denial of the former. The Judaeo-Christian moral system belongs to the second division, and in every detail. In order to be able to say Nay to everything representing an ascending evolution of life—that is, to well-being, to power, to beauty, to self-approval—the instincts of ressentiment, here become downright genius, had to invent an other world in which the acceptance of life appeared as the most evil and abominable thing imaginable. Psychologically, the Jews are a people gifted with the very strongest vitality, so much so that when they found themselves facing impossible conditions of life they chose voluntarily, and with a profound talent for self-preservation, the side of all those instincts which make for décadence—not as if mastered by them, but as if detecting in them a power by which "the world" could be defied. The Jews are the very opposite of décadents: they have simply been forced into appearing in that guise, and with a degree of skill approaching the non plus ultra of histrionic genius they have managed to put themselves at the head of all décadent movements (—for example, the Christianity of Paul—), and so make of them something stronger than any party frankly saying Yes to life. To the sort of men who reach out for power under Judaism and Christianity,—that is to say, to the priestly class—décadence is no more than a means to an end. Men of this sort have a vital interest in making mankind sick, and in confusing the values of "good" and "bad," "true" and "false" in a manner that is not only dangerous to life, but also slanders it.

25.

The history of Israel is invaluable as a typical history of an attempt to denaturize all natural values: I point to five facts which bear this out. Originally, and above all in the time of the monarchy, Israel maintained the right attitude of things, which is to say, the natural attitude. Its Jahveh was an expression of its consciousness of power, its joy in itself, its hopes for itself: to him the Jews looked for victory and salvation and through him they expected nature to give them whatever was necessary to their existence— above all, rain. Jahveh is the god of Israel, and consequently the god of justice: this is the logic of every race that has power in its hands and a good conscience in the use of it. In the religious ceremonial of the Jews both aspects of this self-approval stand revealed. The nation is grateful for the high destiny that has enabled it to obtain dominion; it is grateful for the benign procession of the seasons, and for the good fortune attending its herds and its crops.—This view of things remained an ideal for a long while, even after it had been robbed of validity by tragic blows: anarchy within and the Assyrian without. But the people still retained, as a projection of their highest yearnings, that vision of a king who was at once a gallant warrior and an upright judge—a vision best visualized in the typical prophet (i. e., critic and satirist of the moment), Isaiah.—But every hope remained unfulfilled. The old god no longer could do what he used to do. He ought to have been abandoned. But what actually happened? Simply this: the conception of him was changed—the conception of him was denaturized; this was the price that had to be paid for keeping him.—Jahveh, the god of "justice"—he is in accord with Israel no more, he no longer vizualizes the national egoism; he is now a god only conditionally.... The public notion of this god now becomes merely a weapon in the hands of clerical agitators, who interpret all happiness as a reward and all unhappiness as a punishment for obedience or disobedience to him, for "sin": that most fraudulent of all imaginable interpretations, whereby a "moral order of the world" is set up, and the fundamental concepts, "cause" and "effect," are stood on their heads. Once natural causation has been swept out of the world by doctrines of reward and punishment some sort of un-natural causation becomes necessary: and all other varieties of the denial of nature follow it. A god who demands—in place of a god who helps, who gives counsel, who is at bottom merely a name for every happy inspiration of courage and self-reliance.... Morality is no longer a reflection of the conditions which make for the sound life and development of the people; it is no longer the primary life-instinct; instead it has become abstract and in opposition to life—a fundamental perversion of the fancy, an "evil eye" on all things. What is Jewish, what is Christian morality? Chance robbed of its innocence; unhappiness polluted with the idea of "sin"; well-being represented as a danger, as a "temptation"; a physiological disorder produced by the canker worm of conscience....

26.

The concept of god falsified; the concept of morality falsified;—but even here Jewish priest-craft did not stop. The whole history of Israel ceased to be of any value: out with it!—These priests accomplished that miracle of falsification of which a great part of the Bible is the documentary evidence; with a degree of contempt unparalleled, and in the face of all tradition and all historical reality, they translated the past of their people into religious terms, which is to say, they converted it into an idiotic mechanism of salvation, whereby all offences against Jahveh were punished and all devotion to him was rewarded. We would regard this act of historical falsification as something far more shameful if familiarity with the ecclesiastical interpretation of history for thousands of years had not blunted our inclinations for uprightness in historicis. And the philosophers support the church: the lie about a "moral order of the world" runs through the whole of philosophy, even the newest. What is the meaning of a "moral order of the world"? That there is a thing called the will of God which, once and for all time, determines what man ought to do and what he ought not to do; that the worth of a people, or of an individual thereof, is to be measured by the extent to which they or he obey this will of God; that the destinies of a people or of an individual are controlled by this will of God, which rewards or punishes according to the degree of obedience manifested.—In place of all that pitiable lie reality has this to say: the priest, a parasitical variety of man who can exist only at the cost of every sound view of life, takes the name of God in vain: he calls that state of human society in which he himself determines the value of all things "the kingdom of God"; he calls the means whereby that state of affairs is attained "the will of God"; with cold-blooded cynicism he estimates all peoples, all ages and all individuals by the extent of their subservience or opposition to the power of the priestly order. One observes him at work: under the hand of the Jewish priesthood the great age of Israel became an age of decline; the Exile, with its long series of misfortunes, was transformed into a punishment for that great age—during which priests had not yet come into existence. Out of the powerful and wholly free heroes of Israel's history they fashioned, according to their changing needs, either wretched bigots and hypocrites or men entirely "godless." They reduced every great event to the idiotic formula: "obedient or disobedient to God."—They went a step further: the "will of God" (in other words some means necessary for preserving the power of the priests) had to be determined—and to this end they had to have a "revelation." In plain English, a gigantic literary fraud had to be perpetrated, and "holy scriptures" had to be concocted—and so, with the utmost hierarchical pomp, and days of penance and much lamentation over the long days of "sin" now ended, they were duly published. The "will of God," it appears, had long stood like a rock; the trouble was that mankind had neglected the "holy scriptures".... But the "will of God" had already been revealed to Moses.... What happened? Simply this: the priest had formulated, once and for all time and with the strictest meticulousness, what tithes were to be paid to him, from the largest to the smallest (—not forgetting the most appetizing cuts of meat, for the priest is a great consumer of beefsteaks); in brief, he let it be known just what he wanted, what "the will of God" was.... From this time forward things were so arranged that the priest became indispensable everywhere; at all the great natural events of life, at birth, at marriage, in sickness, at death, not to say at the "sacrifice" (that is, at meal-times), the holy parasite put in his appearance, and proceeded to denaturize it—in his own phrase, to "sanctify" it.... For this should be noted: that every natural habit, every natural institution (the state, the administration of justice, marriage, the care of the sick and of the poor), everything demanded by the life-instinct, in short, everything that has any value in itself, is reduced to absolute worthlessness and even made the reverse of valuable by the parasitism of priests (or, if you chose, by the "moral order of the world"). The fact requires a sanction—a power to grant values becomes necessary, and the only way it can create such values is by denying nature.... The priest depreciates and desecrates nature: it is only at this price that he can exist at all.—Disobedience to God, which actually means to the priest, to "the law," now gets the name of "sin"; the means prescribed for "reconciliation with God" are, of course, precisely the means which bring one most effectively under the thumb of the priest; he alone can "save".... Psychologically considered, "sins" are indispensable to every society organized on an ecclesiastical basis; they are the only reliable weapons of power; the priest lives upon sins; it is necessary to him that there be "sinning".... Prime axiom: "God forgiveth him that repenteth"—in plain English, him that submitteth to the priest.

27.

Christianity sprang from a soil so corrupt that on it everything natural, every natural value, every reality was opposed by the deepest instincts of the ruling class—it grew up as a sort of war to the death upon reality, and as such it has never been surpassed. The "holy people," who had adopted priestly values and priestly names for all things, and who, with a terrible logical consistency, had rejected everything of the earth as "unholy," "worldly," "sinful"—this people put its instinct into a final for mula that was logical to the point of self-annihilation: as Christianity it actually denied even the last form of reality, the "holy people," the "chosen people," Jewish reality itself. The phenomenon is of the first order of importance: the small insurrectionary movement which took the name of Jesus of Nazareth is simply the Jewish instinct redivivus—in other words, it is the priestly instinct come to such a pass that it can no longer endure the priest as a fact; it is the discovery of a state of existence even more fantastic than any before it, of a vision of life even more unreal than that necessary to an ecclesiastical organization. Christianity actually denies the church....

I am unable to determine what was the target of the insurrection said to have been led (whether rightly or wrongly) by Jesus, if it was not the Jewish church—"church" being here used in exactly the same sense that the word has today. It was an insurrection against the "good and just," against the "prophets of Israel," against the whole hierarchy of society—not against corruption, but against caste, privilege, order, formalism. It was unbelief in "superior men," a Nay flung at everything that priests and theologians stood for. But the hierarchy that was called into question, if only for an instant, by this movement was the structure of piles which, above everything, was necessary to the safety of the Jewish people in the midst of the "waters"—it represented their last possibility of survival; it was the final residuum of their independent political existence; an attack upon it was an attack upon the most profound national instinct, the most powerful national will to live, that has ever appeared on earth. This saintly anarchist, who aroused the people of the abyss, the outcasts and "sinners," the Chandala of Judaism, to rise in revolt against the established order of things—and in language which, if the Gospels are to be credited, would get him sent to Siberia today—this man was certainly a political criminal, at least in so far as it was possible to be one in so absurdly unpolitical a community. This is what brought him to the cross: the proof thereof is to be found in the inscription that was put upon the cross. He died for his own sins—there is not the slightest ground for believing, no matter how often it is asserted, that he died for the sins of others. —

28.

As to whether he himself was conscious of this contradiction—whether, in fact, this was the only contradiction he was cognizant of—that is quite another question. Here, for the first time, I touch upon the problem of the psychology of the Saviour.—I confess, to begin with, that there are very few books which offer me harder reading than the Gospels. My difficulties are quite different from those which enabled the learned curiosity of the German mind to achieve one of its most unforgettable triumphs. It is a long while since I, like all other young scholars, enjoyed with all the sapient laboriousness of a fastidious philologist the work of the incomparable Strauss.[5] At that time I was twenty years old: now I am too serious for that sort of thing. What do I care for the contradictions of "tradition"? How can any one call pious legends "traditions"? The histories of saints present the most dubious variety of literature in existence; to examine them by the scientific method, in the entire ab sence of corroborative documents, seems to me to condemn the whole inquiry from the start—it is simply learned idling....

[5]David Friedrich Strauss (**1808-74**), author of "Das Leben Jesu" (**1835-6**), a very famous work in its day. Nietzsche here refers to it.

29.

What concerns me is the psychological type of the Saviour. This type might be depicted in the Gospels, in however mutilated a form and however much overladen with extraneous characters—that is, in spite of the Gospels; just as the figure of Francis of Assisi shows itself in his legends in spite of his legends. It is not a question of mere truthful evidence as to what he did, what he said and how he actually died; the question is, whether his type is still conceivable, whether it has been handed down to us.—All the attempts that I know of to read the history of a "soul" in the Gospels seem to me to reveal only a lamentable psychological levity. M. Renan, that mountebank in psychologicus, has contributed the two most unseemly notions to this business of explaining the type of Jesus: the notion of the genius and that of the hero ("héros"). But if there is anything essentially unevangelical, it is surely the concept of the hero. What the Gospels make instinctive is precisely the reverse of all heroic struggle, of all taste for conflict: the very incapacity for resistance is here converted into something moral: ("resist not evil!"—the most profound sentence in the Gospels, perhaps the true key to them), to wit, the blessedness of peace, of gentleness, the inability to be an enemy. What is the meaning of "glad tidings"?—The true life, the life eternal has been found—it is not merely promised, it is here, it is in you; it is the life that lies in love free from all retreats and exclusions, from all keeping of distances. Every one is the child of God—Jesus claims nothing for himself alone—as the child of God each man is the equal of every other man.... Imagine making Jesus a hero!—And what a tremendous misunderstanding appears in the word "genius"! Our whole conception of the "spiritual," the whole conception of our civilization, could have had no meaning in the world that Jesus lived in. In the strict sense of the physiologist, a quite different word ought to be used here.... We all know that there is a morbid sensibility of the tactile nerves which causes those suffering from it to recoil from every touch, and from every effort to grasp a solid object. Brought to its logical conclusion, such a physiological habitus becomes an instinctive hatred of all reality, a flight into the "intangible," into the "incomprehensible"; a distaste for all formulae, for all conceptions of time and space, for everything established—customs, institutions, the church—; a feeling of being at home in a world in which no sort of reality survives, a merely "inner" world, a "true" world, an "eternal" world.... "The Kingdom of God is within you"....

30.

The instinctive hatred of reality: the consequence of an extreme susceptibility to pain and irritation—so great that merely to be "touched" becomes unendurable, for every sensation is too profound.

The instinctive exclusion of all aversion, all hostility, all bounds and distances in feeling: the consequence of an extreme susceptibility to pain and irritation—so great that it senses all resistance, all compulsion to resistance, as unbearable anguish (—that is to say, as harmful, as prohibited by the instinct of self-preservation), and regards blessedness (joy) as possible only when it is no longer necessary to offer resistance to anybody or anything, however evil or dangerous—love, as the only, as the ultimate possibility of life....

These are the two physiological realities upon and out of which the doctrine of salvation has sprung. I call them a sublime super-development of hedonism upon a thoroughly unsalubrious soil. What stands most closely related to them, though with a large admixture of Greek vitality and nerve-force, is epicureanism, the theory of salvation of paganism. Epicurus was a typical décadent: I was the first to recognize him.—The fear of pain, even of infinitely slight pain—the end of this can be nothing save a religion of love....

31.

I have already given my answer to the problem. The prerequisite to it is the assumption that the type of the Saviour has reached us only in a greatly distorted form. This distortion is very probable: there are many reasons why a type of that sort should not be handed down in a pure form, complete and free of additions. The milieu in which this strange figure moved must have left marks upon him, and more must have been imprinted by the history, the destiny, of the early Christian communities; the latter indeed, must have embellished the type retrospectively with characters which can be understood only as serving the purposes of war and of propaganda. That strange and sickly world into which the Gospels lead us—a world apparently out of a Russian novel, in which the scum of society, nervous maladies and "childish" idiocy keep a tryst— must, in any case, have coarsened the type: the first disciples, in particular, must have been forced to translate an existence visible only in symbols and incomprehensibilities into their own crudity, in order to understand it at all—in their sight the type could take on reality only after it had been recast in a familiar mould.... The prophet, the messiah, the future judge, the teacher of morals, the worker of wonders, John the Baptist—all these merely presented chances to misunderstand it.... Finally, let us not underrate the proprium of all great, and especially all sectarian veneration: it tends to erase from the venerated objects all its original traits and idiosyncrasies, often so painfully strange—it does not even see them. It is greatly to be regretted that no Dostoyevsky lived in the neighbourhood of this most interesting décadent—I mean some one who would have felt the poignant charm of such a compound of the sublime, the morbid and the childish. In the last analysis, the type, as a type of the décadence, may actually have been peculiarly complex and contradictory: such a possibility is not to be lost sight of. Nevertheless, the probabilities seem to be against it, for in that case tradition would have been particularly accurate and objective, whereas we have reasons for assuming the contrary. Meanwhile, there is a contradiction between the peaceful preacher of the mount, the sea-shore and the fields, who appears like a new Buddha on a soil very unlike India's, and the aggressive fanatic, the mortal enemy of theologians and ecclesiastics, who stands glorified by Renan's malice as "le grand maître en ironie." I myself haven't any doubt that the greater part of this venom (and no less of esprit) got itself into the concept of the Master only as a result of the excited nature of Christian propaganda: we all know the unscrupulousness of sectarians when they set out to turn their leader into an apologia for themselves. When the early Christians had need of an adroit, contentious, pugnacious and maliciously subtle theologian to tackle other theologians, they created a "god" that met that need, just as they put into his mouth without hesitation certain ideas that were necessary to them but that were utterly at odds with the Gospels—"the second coming," "the last judgment," all sorts of expectations and promises, current at the time.—

32.

I can only repeat that I set myself against all efforts to intrude the fanatic into the figure of the Saviour: the very word impérieux, used by Renan, is alone enough to annul the type. What the "glad tidings" tell us is simply that there are no more contradictions; the kingdom of heaven belongs to children; the faith that is voiced here is no more an embattled faith—it is at hand, it has been from the beginning, it is a sort of recrudescent childishness of the spirit. The physiologists, at all events, are familiar with such a delayed and incomplete puberty in the living organism, the result of degeneration. A faith of this sort is not furious, it does not de nounce, it does not defend itself: it does not come with "the sword"—it does not realize how it will one day set man against man. It does not manifest itself either by miracles, or by rewards and promises, or by "scriptures": it is itself, first and last, its own miracle, its own reward, its own promise, its own "kingdom of God." This faith does not formulate itself—it simply lives, and so guards itself against formulae. To be sure, the accident of environment, of educational background gives prominence to concepts of a certain sort: in primitive Christianity one finds only concepts of a Judaeo-Semitic character (—that of eating and drinking at the last supper belongs to this category—an idea which, like everything else Jewish, has been badly mauled by the church). But let us be careful not to see in all this anything more than symbolical language, semantics[6] an opportunity to speak in parables. It is only on the theory that no work is to be taken literally that this anti-realist is able to speak at all. Set down among Hindus he would have made use of the concepts of Sankhya,[7] and among Chinese he would have employed those of Lao-tse[8]—and in neither case would it have made any difference to him.—With a little freedom in the use of words, one might actually call Jesus a "free spirit"[9]—he cares nothing for what is established: the word killeth,[10] whatever is established killeth. The idea of "life" as an experience, as he alone conceives it, stands opposed to his mind to every sort of word, formula, law, belief and dogma. He speaks only of inner things: "life" or "truth" or "light" is his word for the innermost—in his sight everything else, the whole of reality, all nature, even language, has significance only as sign, as allegory.—Here it is of paramount importance to be led into no error by the temptations lying in Christian, or rather ecclesiastical prejudices: such a symbolism par excellence stands outside all religion, all notions of worship, all history, all natural science, all worldly experience, all knowledge, all politics, all psychology, all books, all art—his "wisdom" is precisely a pure ignorance[11] of all such things. He has never heard of culture; he doesn't have to make war on it—he doesn't even deny it.... The same thing may be said of the state, of the whole bourgeoise social order, of labour, of war—he has no ground for denying "the world," for he knows nothing of the ecclesiastical concept of "the world".... Denial is precisely the thing that is impossible to him.—In the same way he lacks argumentative capacity, and has no belief that an article of faith, a "truth," may be established by proofs (—his proofs are inner "lights," subjective sensations of happiness and self-approval, simple "proofs of power"—). Such a doctrine cannot contradict: it doesn't know that other doctrines exist, or can exist, and is wholly incapable of imagining anything opposed to it.... If anything of the sort is ever encountered, it laments the "blindness" with sincere sympathy—for it alone has "light"—but it does not offer objections....

[6]The word Semiotik is in the text, but it is probable that Semantik is what Nietzsche had in mind.

[7]One of the six great systems of Hindu philosophy.

[8]The reputed founder of Taoism.

[9]Nietzsche's name for one accepting his own philosophy.

[10]That is, the strict letter of the law—the chief target of Jesus's early preaching.

[11]A reference to the "pure ignorance" (reine Thorheit) of Parsifal.

33.

In the whole psychology of the "Gospels" the concepts of guilt and punishment are lacking, and so is that of reward. "Sin," which means anything that puts a distance between God and man, is abolished—this is precisely the "glad tidings." Eternal bliss is not merely promised, nor is it bound up with conditions: it is conceived as the only reality—what remains consists merely of signs useful in speaking of it.

The results of such a point of view project themselves into a new way of life, the special evangelical way of life. It is not a "belief" that marks off the Christian; he is distinguished by a different mode of action; he acts differently. He offers no resistance, either by word or in his heart, to those who stand against him. He draws no distinction between strangers and countrymen, Jews and Gentiles ("neighbour," of course, means fellow-believer, Jew). He is angry with no one, and he despises no one. He neither appeals to the courts of justice nor heeds their mandates ("Swear not at all").[12] He never under any circumstances divorces his wife, even when he has proofs of her infidelity.—And under all of this is one principle; all of it arises from one instinct.—

[12]Matthew v, **34**.

The life of the Saviour was simply a carrying out of this way of life—and so was his death.... He no longer needed any formula or ritual in his relations with God—not even prayer. He had rejected the whole of the Jewish doctrine of repentance and atonement; he knew that it was only by a way of life that one could feel one's self "divine," "blessed," "evangelical," a "child of God." Not by "repentance," not by "prayer and forgiveness" is the way to God: only the Gospel way leads to God—it is itself "God!"—What the Gospels abolished was the Judaism in the concepts of "sin," "forgiveness of sin," "faith," "salvation through faith"—the whole ecclesiastical dogma of the Jews was denied by the "glad tidings."

The deep instinct which prompts the Christian how to live so that he will feel that he is "in heaven" and is "immortal," despite many reasons for feeling that he is not "in heaven": this is the only psychological reality in "salvation."—A new way of life, not a new faith....

34

If I understand anything at all about this great symbolist, it is this: that he regarded only subjective realities as realities, as "truths"—that he saw everything else, everything natural, temporal, spatial and historical, merely as signs, as materials for parables. The concept of "the Son of God" does not connote a concrete person in history, an isolated and definite individual, but an "eternal" fact, a psychological symbol set free from the concept of time. The same thing is true, and in the highest sense, of the God of this typical symbolist, of the "kingdom of God," and of the "sonship of God." Nothing could be more un-Christian than the crude ecclesiastical notions of God as a person, of a "kingdom of God" that is to come, of a "kingdom of heaven" beyond, and of a "son of God" as the second person of the Trinity. All this—if I may be forgiven the phrase—is like thrusting one's fist into the eye (and what an eye!) of the Gospels: a disrespect for symbols amounting to world-historical cynicism.... But it is nevertheless obvious enough what is meant by the symbols "Father" and "Son"—not, of course, to every one—: the word "Son" expresses entrance into the feeling that there is a general transformation of all things (beatitude), and "Father" expresses that feeling itself—the sensation of eternity and of perfection.—I am ashamed to remind you of what the church has made of this symbolism: has it not set an Amphitryon story[13] at the threshold of the Christian "faith"? And a dogma of "immaculate conception" for good measure?... And thereby it has robbed conception of its immaculateness—

[13]Amphitryon was the son of Alcaeus, King of Tiryns. His wife was Alcmene. During his absence she was visited by Zeus, and bore Heracles.

The "kingdom of heaven" is a state of the heart—not something to come "beyond the world" or "after death." The whole idea of natural death is absent from the Gospels: death is not a bridge, not a passing; it is absent because it belongs to a quite different, a merely apparent world, useful only as a symbol. The "hour of death" is not a Christian idea—"hours," time, the physical life and its crises have no existence for the bearer of "glad tidings."... The "kingdom of God" is not something that men wait for: it had no yesterday and no day after tomorrow, it is not going to come at a "millennium"—it is an experience of the heart, it is everywhere and it is nowhere....

35.

This "bearer of glad tidings" died as he lived and taught—not to "save mankind," but to show mankind how to live. It was a way of life that he bequeathed to man: his demeanour before the judges, before the officers, before his accusers—his demeanour on the cross. He does not resist; he does not defend his rights; he makes no effort to ward off the most extreme penalty—more, he invites it.... And he prays, suffers and loves with those, in those, who do him evil.... Not to defend one's self, not to show anger, not to lay blames.... On the contrary, to submit even to the Evil One— to love him....

36.

—We free spirits—we are the first to have the necessary prerequisite to understanding what nineteen centuries have misunderstood—that instinct and passion for integrity which makes war upon the "holy lie" even more than upon all other lies.... Mankind was unspeakably far from our benevolent and cautious neutrality, from that discipline of the spirit which alone makes possible the solution of such strange and subtle things: what men always sought, with shameless egoism, was their own advantage therein; they created the church out of denial of the Gospels....

Whoever sought for signs of an ironical divinity's hand in the great drama of existence would find no small indication thereof in the stupendous question-mark that is called Christianity. That mankind should be on its knees before the very antithesis of what was the origin, the meaning and the law of the Gospels—that in the concept of the "church" the very things should be pronounced holy that the "bearer of glad tidings" regards as beneath him and behind him—it would be impossible to surpass this as a grand example of world-historical irony—

37.

—Our age is proud of its historical sense: how, then, could it delude itself into believing that the crude fable of the wonder-worker and Saviour constituted the beginnings of Christianity—and that everything spiritual and symbolical in it only came later? Quite to the contrary, the whole history of Christianity—from the death on the cross onward—is the history of a progressively clumsier misunderstanding of an original symbolism. With every extension of Christianity among larger and ruder masses, even less capable of grasping the principles that gave birth to it, the need arose to make it more and more vulgar and barbarous—it absorbed the teachings and rites of all the subterranean cults of the imperium Romanum, and the absurdities engendered by all sorts of sickly reasoning. It was the fate of Christianity that its faith had to become as sickly, as low and as vulgar as the needs were sickly, low and vulgar to which it had to administer. A sickly barbarism finally lifts itself to power as the church—the church, that incarnation of deadly hostility to all honesty, to all loftiness of soul, to all discipline of the spirit, to all spontaneous and kindly humanity.—Christian values— noble values: it is only we, we free spirits, who have re-established this greatest of all antitheses in values!...

38.

—I cannot, at this place, avoid a sigh. There are days when I am visited by a feeling blacker than the blackest melancholy—contempt of man. Let me leave no doubt as to what I despise, whom I despise: it is the man of today, the man with whom I am unhappily contemporaneous. The man of today—I am suffocated by his foul breath!... Toward the past, like all who understand, I am full of tolerance, which is to say, generous self-control: with gloomy caution I pass through whole millenniums of this madhouse of a world, call it "Christianity," "Christian faith" or the "Christian church," as you will—I take care not to hold mankind responsible for its lunacies. But my feeling changes and breaks out irresistibly the moment I enter modern times, our times. Our age knows better.... What was formerly merely sickly now becomes indecent—it is indecent to be a Christian today. And here my disgust begins.—I look about me: not a word survives of what was once called "truth"; we can no longer bear to hear a priest pronounce the word. Even a man who makes the most modest pretensions to integrity must know that a theologian, a priest, a pope of today not only errs when he speaks, but actually lies— and that he no longer escapes blame for his lie through "innocence" or "ignorance."

The priest knows, as every one knows, that there is no longer any "God," or any "sinner," or any "Saviour"—that "free will" and the "moral order of the world" are lies—: serious reflection, the profound self-conquest of the spirit, allow no man to pretend that he does not know it.... All the ideas of the church are now recognized for what they are—as the worst counterfeits in existence, invented to debase nature and all natural values; the priest himself is seen as he actually is—as the most dangerous form of parasite, as the venomous spider of creation.... We know, our conscience now knows—just what the real value of all those sinister inventions of priest and church has been and what ends they have served, with their debasement of humanity to a state of self-pollution, the very sight of which excites loathing,—the concepts "the other world," "the last judgment," "the immortality of the soul," the "soul" itself: they are all merely so many instruments of torture, systems of cruelty, whereby the priest becomes master and remains master.... Every one knows this, but nevertheless things remain as before. What has become of the last trace of decent feeling, of self-respect, when our statesmen, otherwise an unconventional class of men and thoroughly anti-Christian in their acts, now call themselves Christians and go to the communion-table?... A prince at the head of his armies, magnificent as the expression of the egoism and arrogance of his people—and yet acknowledging, without any shame, that he is a Christian!... Whom, then, does Christianity deny? what does it call "the world"? To be a soldier, to be a judge, to be a patriot; to defend one's self; to be careful of one's honour; to desire one's own advantage; to be proud ... every act of everyday, every instinct, every valuation that shows itself in a deed, is now anti-Christian: what a monster of falsehood the modern man must be to call himself nevertheless, and without shame, a Christian!—

39.

—I shall go back a bit, and tell you the authentic history of Christianity.—The very word "Christianity" is a misunderstanding—at bottom there was only one Christian, and he died on the cross. The "Gospels" died on the cross. What, from that moment onward, was called the "Gospels" was the very reverse of what he had lived: "bad tidings," a Dysangelium.[14] It is an error amounting to nonsensicality to see in "faith," and particularly in faith in salvation through Christ, the distinguishing mark of the Christian: only the Christian way of life, the life lived by him who died on the cross, is Christian.... To this day such a life is still possible, and for certain men even necessary: genuine, primitive Christianity will remain possible in all ages.... Not faith, but acts; above all, an avoidance of acts, a different state of being.... States of consciousness, faith of a sort, the acceptance, for example, of anything as true—as every psychologist knows, the value of these things is perfectly indifferent and fifth-rate compared to that of the instincts: strictly speaking, the whole concept of intellectual causality is false. To reduce being a Christian, the state of Christianity, to an acceptance of truth, to a mere phenomenon of consciousness, is to formulate the negation of Christianity. In fact, there are no Christians. The "Christian"—he who for two thousand years has passed as a Christian—is simply a psycho logical self-delusion. Closely examined, it appears that, despite all his "faith," he has been ruled only by his instincts—and what instincts!—In all ages—for example, in the case of Luther—"faith" has been no more than a cloak, a pretense, a curtain behind which the instincts have played their game—a shrewd blindness to the domination of certain of the instincts.... I have already called "faith" the specially Christian form of shrewdness—people always talk of their "faith" and act according to their instincts.... In the world of ideas of the Christian there is nothing that so much as touches reality: on the contrary, one recognizes an instinctive hatred of reality as the motive power, the only motive power at the bottom of Christianity. What follows therefrom? That even here, in psychologicis, there is a radical error, which is to say one conditioning fundamentals, which is to say, one in substance. Take away one idea and put a genuine reality in its place—and the whole of Christianity crumbles to nothingness!—Viewed calmly, this strangest of all phenomena, a religion not only depending on errors, but inventive and ingenious only in devising injurious errors, poisonous to life and to the heart—this remains a spectacle for the gods—for those gods who are also philosophers, and whom I have encountered, for example, in the celebrated dialogues at Naxos. At the moment when their disgust leaves them (— and us!) they will be thankful for the spectacle afforded by the Christians: perhaps because of this curious exhibition alone the wretched little planet called the earth deserves a glance from omnipotence, a show of divine interest.... Therefore, let us not underestimate the Christians: the Christian, false to the point of innocence, is far above the ape—in its application to the Christians a well-known theory of descent becomes a mere piece of politeness....

[14]So in the text. One of Nietzsche's numerous coinages, obviously suggested by Evangelium, the German for gospel.

<h2 style="text-align:center">40.</h2>

—The fate of the Gospels was decided by death—it hung on the "cross."... It was only death, that unexpected and shameful death; it was only the cross, which was usually reserved for the canaille only—it was only this appalling paradox which brought the disciples face to face with the real riddle: "Who was it? what was it?"—The feeling of dis may, of profound affront and injury; the suspicion that such a death might involve a refutation of their cause; the terrible question, "Why just in this way?"—this state of mind is only too easy to understand. Here everything must be accounted for as necessary; everything must have a meaning, a reason, the highest sort of reason; the love of a disciple excludes all chance. Only then did the chasm of doubt yawn: "Who put him to death? who was his natural enemy?"—this question flashed like a lightning-stroke. Answer: dominant Judaism, its ruling class. From that moment, one found one's self in revolt against the established order, and began to understand Jesus as in revolt against the established order. Until then this militant, this nay-saying, nay-doing element in his character had been lacking; what is more, he had appeared to present its opposite. Obviously, the little community had not understood what was precisely the most important thing of all: the example offered by this way of dying, the freedom from and superiority to every feeling of ressentiment—a plain indication of how little he was understood at all! All that Jesus could hope to accomplish by his death, in itself, was to offer the strongest possible proof, or example, of his teachings in the most public manner.... But his disciples were very far from forgiving his death— though to have done so would have accorded with the Gospels in the highest degree; and neither were they prepared to offer themselves, with gentle and serene calmness of heart, for a similar death.... On the contrary, it was precisely the most unevangelical of feelings, revenge, that now possessed them. It seemed impossible that the cause should perish with his death: "recompense" and "judgment" became necessary (—

yet what could be less evangelical than "recompense," "punishment," and "sitting in judgment"!). Once more the popular belief in the coming of a messiah appeared in the foreground; attention was rivetted upon an historical moment: the "kingdom of God" is to come, with judgment upon his enemies.... But in all this there was a wholesale misunderstanding: imagine the "kingdom of God" as a last act, as a mere promise! The Gospels had been, in fact, the incarnation, the fulfilment, the realization of this "kingdom of God." It was only now that all the familiar contempt for and bitterness against Pharisees and theologians began to appear in the character of the Master—he was thereby turned into a Pharisee and theologian himself! On the other hand, the savage veneration of these completely unbalanced souls could no longer endure the Gospel doctrine, taught by Jesus, of the equal right of all men to be children of God: their revenge took the form of elevating Jesus in an extravagant fashion, and thus separating him from themselves: just as, in earlier times, the Jews, to revenge themselves upon their enemies, separated themselves from their God, and placed him on a great height. The One God and the Only Son of God: both were products of ressentiment....

41.

—And from that time onward an absurd problem offered itself: "how could God allow it!" To which the deranged reason of the little community formulated an answer that was terrifying in its absurdity: God gave his son as a sacrifice for the forgiveness of sins. At once there was an end of the gospels! Sacrifice for sin, and in its most obnoxious and barbarous form: sacrifice of the innocent for the sins of the guilty! What appalling paganism!—Jesus him self had done away with the very concept of "guilt," he denied that there was any gulf fixed between God and man; he lived this unity between God and man, and that was precisely his "glad tidings".... And not as a mere privilege!—From this time forward the type of the Saviour was corrupted, bit by bit, by the doctrine of judgment and of the second coming, the doctrine of death as a sacrifice, the doctrine of the resurrection, by means of which the entire concept of "blessedness," the whole and only reality of the gospels, is juggled away—in favour of a state of existence after death!... St. Paul, with that rabbinical impudence which shows itself in all his doings, gave a logical quality to that conception, that indecent conception, in this way: "If Christ did not rise from the dead, then all our faith is in vain!"—And at once there sprang from the Gospels the most contemptible of all unfulfillable promises, the shameless doctrine of personal immortality.... Paul even preached it as a reward....

42.

One now begins to see just what it was that came to an end with the death on the cross: a new and thoroughly original effort to found a Buddhistic peace movement, and so establish happiness on earth—real, not merely promised. For this remains—as I have already pointed out—the essential difference between the two religions of décadence: Buddhism promises nothing, but actually fulfils; Christianity promises everything, but fulfils nothing.—Hard upon the heels of the "glad tidings" came the worst imaginable: those of Paul. In Paul is incarnated the very opposite of the "bearer of glad tidings"; he represents the genius for hatred, the vision of hatred, the relentless logic of hatred. What, indeed, has not this dysangelist sacrificed to hatred! Above all, the Saviour: he nailed him to his own cross. The life, the example, the teaching, the death of Christ, the meaning and the law of the whole gospels—nothing was left of all this after that counterfeiter in hatred had reduced it to his uses. Surely not reality; surely not historical truth!... Once more the priestly instinct of the Jew perpetrated the same old master crime against history—he simply struck out the yesterday and the day before yesterday of Christianity, and invented his own history of Christian beginnings. Going further, he treated the history of Israel to another falsification, so that it became a mere prologue to his achievement: all the prophets, it now appeared, had referred to his "Saviour."... Later on the church even falsified the history of man in order to make it a prologue to Christianity.... The figure of the Saviour, his teaching, his way of life, his death, the meaning of his death, even the consequences of his death—nothing remained untouched, nothing remained in even remote contact with reality. Paul simply shifted the centre of gravity of that whole life to a place behind this existence—in the lie of the "risen" Jesus. At bottom, he had no use for the life of the Saviour—what he needed was the death on the cross, and something more. To see anything honest in such a man as Paul, whose home was at the centre of the Stoical enlightenment, when he converts an hallucination into a proof of the resurrection of the Saviour, or even to believe his tale that he suffered from this hallucination himself—this would be a genuine niaiserie in a psychologist. Paul willed the end; therefore he also willed the means.... What he himself didn't believe was swallowed readily enough by the idiots among whom he spread his teaching.—What he wanted was power; in Paul the priest once more reached out for power—he had use only for such concepts, teachings and symbols as served the purpose of tyrannizing over the masses and organizing mobs. What was the only part of Christianity that Mohammed borrowed later on? Paul's invention, his device for establishing priestly tyranny and organizing the mob: the belief in the immortality of the soul—that is to say, the doctrine of "judgment"....

43.

When the centre of gravity of life is placed, not in life itself, but in "the beyond"—in nothingness—then one has taken away its centre of gravity altogether. The vast lie of personal immortality destroys all reason, all natural instinct—henceforth, everything in the instincts that is beneficial, that fosters life and that safeguards the future is a cause of suspicion. So to live that life no longer has any meaning: this is now the "meaning" of life.... Why be public-spirited? Why take any pride in descent and forefathers? Why labour together, trust one another, or concern one's self about the common welfare, and try to serve it?... Merely so many "temptations," so many strayings from the "straight path."—"One thing only is necessary".... That every man, because he has an "immortal soul," is as good as every other man; that in an infinite universe of things the "salvation" of every individual may lay claim to eternal importance; that insignificant bigots and the three-fourths insane may assume that the laws of nature are constantly suspended in their behalf—it is impossible to lavish too much contempt upon such a magnification of every sort of selfishness to infinity, to insolence. And yet Christianity has to thank precisely this miserable flattery of personal vanity for its triumph—it was thus that it lured all the botched, the dissatisfied, the fallen upon evil days, the whole refuse and off-scouring of humanity to its side. The "salvation of the soul"—in plain English: "the world revolves around me."... The poisonous doctrine, "equal rights for all," has been propagated as a Christian principle: out of the secret nooks and crannies of bad instinct Christianity has waged a deadly war upon all feelings of reverence and distance between man and man, which is to say, upon the first prerequisite to every step upward, to every development of civilization—out of the ressentiment of the masses it has forged its chief weapons against us, against everything noble, joyous and high-spirited on earth, against our happiness on earth.... To allow "immortality" to every Peter and Paul was the greatest, the most vicious outrage upon noble humanity ever perpetrated.—And let us not underestimate the fatal influence that Christianity has had, even upon politics! Nowadays no one has courage any more for special rights, for the right of dominion, for feelings of honourable pride in himself and his equals—for the pathos of distance.... Our politics is sick with this lack of courage!— The aristocratic attitude of mind has been undermined by the lie of the equality of souls; and if belief in the "privileges of the majority" makes and will continue to make revolutions—it is Christianity, let us not doubt, and Christian valuations, which convert every revolution into a carnival of blood and crime! Christianity is a revolt of all creatures that creep on the ground against everything that is lofty: the gospel of the "lowly" lowers....

44.

—The gospels are invaluable as evidence of the corruption that was already persistent within the primitive community. That which Paul, with the cynical logic of a rabbi, later developed to a conclusion was at bottom merely a process of decay that had begun with the death of the Saviour.—These gospels cannot be read too carefully; difficulties lurk behind every word. I confess—I hope it will not be held against me— that it is precisely for this reason that they offer first-rate joy to a psychologist—as the opposite of all merely naïve corruption, as refinement par excellence, as an artistic triumph in psychological corruption. The gospels, in fact, stand alone. The Bible as a whole is not to be compared to them. Here we are among Jews: this is the first thing to be borne in mind if we are not to lose the thread of the matter. This positive genius for conjuring up a delusion of personal "holiness" unmatched anywhere else, either in books or by men; this elevation of fraud in word and attitude to the level of an art—all this is not an accident due to the chance talents of an individual, or to any violation of nature. The thing responsible is race. The whole of Judaism appears in Christianity as the art of concocting holy lies, and there, after many centuries of earnest Jewish training and hard practice of Jewish technic, the business comes to the stage of mastery. The Christian, that ultima ratio of lying, is the Jew all over again—he is threefold the Jew.... The underlying will to make use only of such concepts, symbols and attitudes as fit into priestly practice, the instinctive repudiation of every other mode of thought, and every other method of estimating values and utilities—this is not only tradition, it is inheritance: only as an inheritance is it able to operate with the force of nature. The whole of mankind, even the best minds of the best ages (with one exception, perhaps hardly human—), have permitted themselves to be deceived. The gospels have been read as a book of innocence ... surely no small indication of the high skill with which the trick has been done.—Of course, if we could actually see these astounding bigots and bogus saints, even if only for an instant, the farce would come to an end,—and it is precisely because I cannot read a word of theirs without seeing their attitudinizing that I have made an end of them.... I simply cannot endure the way they have of rolling up their eyes.—For the majority, happily enough, books are mere literature.—Let us not be led astray: they say "judge not," and yet they condemn to hell whoever stands in their way. In letting God sit in judgment they judge themselves; in glorifying God they glorify themselves; in demanding that every one show the virtues which they themselves happen to be capable of—still more, which they must have in order to remain on top—they assume the grand air of men struggling for virtue, of men engaging in a war that virtue may prevail. "We live, we die, we sacrifice ourselves for the good" (—"the truth," "the light," "the kingdom of God"): in point of fact, they simply do what they cannot help doing. Forced, like hypocrites, to be sneaky, to hide in corners, to slink along in the shadows, they convert their necessity into a duty: it is on grounds of duty that they account for their lives of humility, and that humility becomes merely one more proof of their piety.... Ah, that humble, chaste, charitable brand of fraud! "Virtue itself shall bear witness for us."... One may read the gospels as books of moral seduction: these petty folks fasten themselves to morality—they know the uses of morality! Morality is the best of all devices for leading mankind by the nose!— The fact is that the conscious conceit of the chosen here disguises itself as modesty: it is in this way that they, the "community," the "good and just," range themselves, once and for always, on one side, the side of "the truth"—and the rest of mankind, "the world," on the other.... In that we observe the most fatal sort of megalomania that the earth has ever seen: little abortions of bigots and liars began to claim exclusive rights in the concepts of "God," "the truth," "the light," "the spirit," "love," "wisdom" and "life," as if these things were synonyms of themselves and thereby they sought to fence themselves off from the "world"; little super-Jews, ripe for some sort of madhouse, turned values upside down in order to meet their notions, just as if the Christian were the meaning, the salt, the standard and even the last judgment of all the rest.... The whole disaster was only made possible by the fact that there already existed in the world a similar megalomania, allied to this one in race, to wit, the Jewish: once a chasm began to yawn between Jews and Judaeo-Christians, the latter had no choice but to employ the self-preservative measures that the Jewish instinct had devised, even against the Jews themselves, whereas the Jews had employed them only against non-Jews. The Christian is simply a Jew of the "reformed" confession.—

45.

—I offer a few examples of the sort of thing these petty people have got into their heads—what they have put into the mouth of the Master: the unalloyed creed of "beautiful souls."—

"And whosoever shall not receive you, nor hear you, when ye depart thence, shake off the dust under your feet for a testimony against them. Verily I say unto you, it shall be more tolerable for Sodom and Gomorrha in the day of judgment, than for that city" (Mark vi, **11**)—How evangelical!...

"And whosoever shall offend one of these little ones that believe in me, it is better for him that a millstone were hanged about his neck, and he were cast into the sea" (Mark ix, **42**).—How evangelical!...

"And if thine eye offend thee, pluck it out: it is better for thee to enter into the kingdom of God with one eye, than having two eyes to be cast into hell fire; Where the worm dieth not, and the fire is not quenched." (Mark ix, **47**.[**15**])—It is not exactly the eye that is meant....

[15]To which, without mentioning it, Nietzsche adds verse **48**.

"Verily I say unto you, That there be some of them that stand here, which shall not taste of death, till they have seen the kingdom of God come with power." (Mark ix, **1**.)—Well lied, lion![16]....

[16]A paraphrase of Demetrius' "Well roar'd, Lion!" in act v, scene **1** of "A Midsummer Night's Dream." The lion, of course, is the familiar Christian symbol for Mark.

"Whosoever will come after me, let him deny himself, and take up his cross, and follow me. For..." (Note of a psychologist. Christian morality is refuted by its fors: its reasons are against it,—this makes it Christian.) Mark viii, **34**.—

"Judge not, that ye be not judged. With what measure ye mete, it shall be measured to you again." (Matthew vii, **1**.[17])—What a notion of justice, of a "just" judge!...

[17]Nietzsche also quotes part of verse **2**.

"For if ye love them which love you, what reward have ye? do not even the publicans the same? And if ye salute your brethren only, what do ye more than others? do not even the publicans so?" (Matthew v, **46**.[18])—Principle of "Christian love": it insists upon being well paid in the end....

[18]The quotation also includes verse **47**.

"But if ye forgive not men their trespasses, neither will your Father forgive your trespasses." (Matthew vi, **15**.)—Very compromising for the said "father."...

"But seek ye first the kingdom of God, and his righteousness; and all these things shall be added unto you." (Matthew vi, **33**.)—All these things: namely, food, clothing, all the necessities of life. An error, to put it mildly.... A bit before this God appears as a tailor, at least in certain cases....

"Rejoice ye in that day, and leap for joy: for, behold, your reward is great in heaven: for in the like manner did their fathers unto the prophets." (Luke vi, **23**.)—Impudent rabble! It compares itself to the prophets....

"Know ye not that ye are the temple of God, and that the spirit of God dwelleth in you? If any man defile the temple of God, him shall God destroy; for the temple of God is holy, which temple ye are." (Paul, **1** Corinthians iii, **16**.[19])—For that sort of thing one cannot have enough contempt....

[19]And **17**.

"Do ye not know that the saints shall judge the world? and if the world shall be judged by you, are ye unworthy to judge the smallest matters?" (Paul, **1** Corinthians vi, **2**.)—Unfortunately, not merely the speech of a lunatic.... This frightful impostor then proceeds: "Know ye not that we shall judge angels? how much more things that pertain to this life?"...

"Hath not God made foolish the wisdom of this world? For after that in the wisdom of God the world by wisdom knew not God, it pleased God by the foolishness of preaching to save them that believe.... Not many wise men after the flesh, not men mighty, not many noble are called: But God hath chosen the foolish things of the world to confound the wise; and God hath chosen the weak things of the world to confound the things which are mighty; And base things of the world, and things which are despised, hath God chosen, yea, and things which are not, to bring to nought things that are: That no flesh should glory in his presence." (Paul, **1** Corinthians i, **20**ff.**[20]**)—In order to understand this passage, a first-rate example of the psychology underlying every Chandala-morality, one should read the first part of my "Genealogy of Morals": there, for the first time, the antagonism between a noble morality and a morality born of ressentiment and impotent vengefulness is exhibited. Paul was the greatest of all apostles of revenge....

[20]Verses **20, 21, 26, 27, 28, 29**.

46.

—What follows, then? That one had better put on gloves before reading the New Testament. The presence of so much filth makes it very advisable. One would as little choose "early Christians" for companions as Polish Jews: not that one need seek out an objection to them.... Neither has a pleasant smell.—I have searched the New Testament in vain for a single sympathetic touch; nothing is there that is free, kindly, open-hearted or upright. In it humanity does not even make the first step upward—the instinct for cleanliness is lacking.... Only evil instincts are there, and there is not even the courage of these evil instincts. It is all coward ice; it is all a shutting of the eyes, a self-deception. Every other book becomes clean, once one has read the New Testament: for example, immediately after reading Paul I took up with delight that most charming and wanton of scoffers, Petronius, of whom one may say what Domenico Boccaccio wrote of Cæsar Borgia to the Duke of Parma: "è tutto festo"—immortally healthy, immortally cheerful and sound.... These petty bigots make a capital miscalculation. They attack, but everything they attack is thereby distinguished. Whoever is attacked by an "early Christian" is surely not befouled.... On the contrary, it is an honour to have an "early Christian" as an opponent. One cannot read the New Testament without acquired admiration for whatever it abuses—not to speak of the "wisdom of this world," which an impudent wind-bag tries to dispose of "by the foolishness of preaching."... Even the scribes and pharisees are benefitted by such opposition: they must certainly have been worth something to have been hated in such an indecent manner. Hypocrisy—as if this were a charge that the "early Christians" dared to make!—After all, they were the privileged, and that was enough: the hatred of the Chandala needed no other excuse. The "early Christian"—and also, I fear, the "last Christian," whom I may perhaps live to see—is a rebel against all privilege by profound instinct—he lives and makes war for ever for "equal rights."... Strictly speaking, he has no alternative. When a man proposes to represent, in his own person, the "chosen of God"—or to be a "temple of God," or a "judge of the angels"—then every other criterion, whether based upon honesty, upon intellect, upon manliness and pride, or upon beauty and freedom of the heart, becomes simply "worldly"—evil in itself.... Moral: every word that comes from the lips of an "early Christian" is a lie, and his every act is instinctively dishonest—all his values, all his aims are noxious, but whoever he hates, whatever he hates, has real value.... The Christian, and particularly the Christian priest, is thus a criterion of values.

—Must I add that, in the whole New Testament, there appears but a solitary figure worthy of honour? Pilate, the Roman viceroy. To regard a Jewish imbroglio seriously—that was quite beyond him. One Jew more or less—what did it matter?... The noble scorn of a Roman, before whom the word "truth" was shamelessly mishandled, enriched the New Testament with the only saying that has any value—and that is at once its criticism and its destruction: "What is truth?..."

<h2 style="text-align:center">47.</h2>

—The thing that sets us apart is not that we are unable to find God, either in history, or in nature, or behind nature—but that we regard what has been honoured as God, not as "divine," but as pitiable, as absurd, as injurious; not as a mere error, but as a crime against life.... We deny that God is God.... If any one were to show us this Christian God, we'd be still less inclined to believe in him.—In a formula: deus, qualem Paulus creavit, dei negatio.—Such a religion as Christianity, which does not touch reality at a single point and which goes to pieces the moment reality asserts its rights at any point, must be inevitably the deadly enemy of the "wisdom of this world," which is to say, of science—and it will give the name of good to whatever means serve to poison, calumniate and cry down all intellectual discipline, all lucidity and strictness in matters of intellectual conscience, and all noble coolness and freedom of the mind. "Faith," as an imperative, vetoes science—in praxi, lying at any price.... Paul well knew that lying—that "faith"—was necessary; later on the church borrowed the fact from Paul.—The God that Paul invented for himself, a God who "reduced to absurdity" "the wisdom of this world" (especially the two great enemies of superstition, philology and medicine), is in truth only an indication of Paul's resolute determination to accomplish that very thing himself: to give one's own will the name of God, thora— that is essentially Jewish. Paul wants to dispose of the "wisdom of this world": his enemies are the good philologians and physicians of the Alexandrine school—on them he makes his war. As a matter of fact no man can be a philologian or a physician without being also Antichrist. That is to say, as a philologian a man sees behind the "holy books," and as a physician he sees behind the physiological degeneration of the typical Christian. The physician says "incurable"; the philologian says "fraud."...

<h2 style="text-align:center">48.</h2>

—Has any one ever clearly understood the celebrated story at the beginning of the Bible—of God's mortal terror of science?... No one, in fact, has understood it. This priest-book par excellence opens, as is fitting, with the great inner difficulty of the priest: he faces only one great danger; ergo, "God" faces only one great danger.—

The old God, wholly "spirit," wholly the high-priest, wholly perfect, is promenading his garden: he is bored and trying to kill time. Against boredom even gods struggle in vain.[21] What does he do? He creates man—man is entertaining.... But then he notices that man is also bored. God's pity for the only form of distress that invades all paradises knows no bounds: so he forthwith creates other animals. God's first mistake: to man these other animals were not entertaining—he sought dominion over them; he did not want to be an "animal" himself.—So God created woman. In the act he brought boredom to an end—and also many other things! Woman was the second mistake of God.—"Woman, at bottom, is a serpent, Heva"—every priest knows that; "from woman comes every evil in the world"—every priest knows that, too. Ergo, she is also to blame for science.... It was through woman that man learned to taste of the tree of knowledge.—What happened? The old God was seized by mortal terror. Man himself had been his greatest blunder; he had created a rival to himself; science makes men godlike—it is all up with priests and gods when man becomes scientific!—Moral: science is the forbidden per se; it alone is forbidden. Science is the first of sins, the germ of all sins, the original sin. This is all there is of morality.—"Thou shall not know":— the rest follows from that.—God's mortal terror, however, did not hinder him from being shrewd. How is one to protect one's self against science? For a long while this was the capital problem. Answer: Out of paradise with man! Happiness, leisure, foster thought—and all thoughts are bad thoughts!—Man must not think.—And so the priest invents distress, death, the mortal dangers of childbirth, all sorts of misery, old age, decrepitude, above all, sickness—nothing but devices for making war on science! The troubles of man don't allow him to think.... Nevertheless—how terrible!—, the edifice of knowledge begins to tower aloft, invading heaven, shadowing the gods—what is to be done?—The old God invents war; he separates the peoples; he makes men destroy one another (—the priests have always had need of war....). War—among other things, a great disturber of science!—Incredible! Knowledge, deliverance from the priests, prospers in spite of war.—So the old God comes to his final resolution: "Man has become scientific—there is no help for it: he must be drowned!"...

[21]A paraphrase of Schiller's "Against stupidity even gods struggle in vain."

49.

—I have been understood. At the opening of the Bible there is the whole psychology of the priest.—The priest knows of only one great danger: that is science—the sound comprehension of cause and effect. But science flourishes, on the whole, only under favourable conditions—a man must have time, he must have an overflowing intellect, in order to "know."... "Therefore, man must be made unhappy,"—this has been, in all ages, the logic of the priest.—It is easy to see just what, by this logic, was the first thing to come into the world:—"sin."... The concept of guilt and punishment, the whole "moral order of the world," was set up against science—against the deliverance of man from priests.... Man must not look outward; he must look inward. He must not look at things shrewdly and cautiously, to learn about them; he must not look at all; he must suffer.... And he must suffer so much that he is always in need of the priest.—Away with physicians! What is needed is a Saviour.—The concept of guilt and punishment, including the doctrines of "grace," of "salvation," of "forgiveness"— lies through and through, and absolutely without psychological reality—were devised to destroy man's sense of causality: they are an attack upon the concept of cause and effect!—And not an attack with the fist, with the knife, with honesty in hate and love! On the contrary, one inspired by the most cowardly, the most crafty, the most ignoble of instincts! An attack of priests! An attack of parasites! The vampirism of pale, subterranean leeches!... When the natural consequences of an act are no longer "natural," but are regarded as produced by the ghostly creations of superstition— by "God," by "spirits," by "souls"—and reckoned as merely "moral" consequences, as rewards, as punishments, as hints, as lessons, then the whole ground-work of knowledge is destroyed—then the greatest of crimes against humanity has been perpetrated.—I repeat that sin, man's self-desecration par excellence, was invented in order to make science, culture, and every elevation and ennobling of man impossible; the priest rules through the invention of sin.—

50.

—In this place I can't permit myself to omit a psychology of "belief," of the "believer," for the special benefit of "believers." If there remain any today who do not yet know how indecent it is to be "believing"—or how much a sign of décadence, of a broken will to live—then they will know it well enough tomorrow. My voice reaches even the deaf.—It appears, unless I have been incorrectly informed, that there prevails among Christians a sort of criterion of truth that is called "proof by power." "Faith makes blessed: therefore it is true."—It might be objected right here that blessedness is not dem onstrated, it is merely promised: it hangs upon "faith" as a condition— one shall be blessed because one believes.... But what of the thing that the priest promises to the believer, the wholly transcendental "beyond"—how is that to be demonstrated?—The "proof by power," thus assumed, is actually no more at bottom than a belief that the effects which faith promises will not fail to appear. In a formula: "I believe that faith makes for blessedness—therefore, it is true."... But this is as far as we may go. This "therefore" would be absurdum itself as a criterion of truth.—But let us admit, for the sake of politeness, that blessedness by faith may be demonstrated (— not merely hoped for, and not merely promised by the suspicious lips of a priest): even so, could blessedness—in a technical term, pleasure—ever be a proof of truth? So little is this true that it is almost a proof against truth when sensations of pleasure influence the answer to the question "What is true?" or, at all events, it is enough to make that "truth" highly suspicious. The proof by "pleasure" is a proof of "pleasure"—nothing more; why in the world should it be assumed that true judgments give more pleasure than false ones, and that, in conformity to some pre-established harmony, they necessarily bring agreeable feelings in their train?—The experience of all disciplined and profound minds teaches the contrary. Man has had to fight for every atom of the truth, and has had to pay for it almost everything that the heart, that human love, that human trust cling to. Greatness of soul is needed for this business: the service of truth is the hardest of all services.—What, then, is the meaning of integrity in things intellectual? It means that a man must be severe with his own heart, that he must scorn "beautiful feelings," and that he makes every Yea and Nay a matter of conscience!— Faith makes blessed: therefore, it lies....

51.

The fact that faith, under certain circumstances, may work for blessedness, but that this blessedness produced by an idée fixe by no means makes the idea itself true, and the fact that faith actually moves no mountains, but instead raises them up where there were none before: all this is made sufficiently clear by a walk through a lunatic asylum. Not, of course, to a priest: for his instincts prompt him to the lie that sickness is not sickness and lunatic asylums not lunatic asylums. Christianity finds sickness necessary, just as the Greek spirit had need of a superabundance of health—the actual ulterior purpose of the whole system of salvation of the church is to make people ill. And the church itself— doesn't it set up a Catholic lunatic asylum as the ultimate ideal?—The whole earth as a madhouse?—The sort of religious man that the church wants is a typical décadent; the moment at which a religious crisis dominates a people is always marked by epidemics of nervous disorder; the "inner world" of the religious man is so much like the "inner world" of the overstrung and exhausted that it is difficult to distinguish between them; the "highest" states of mind, held up before mankind by Christianity as of supreme worth, are actually epileptoid in form—the church has granted the name of holy only to lunatics or to gigantic frauds in majorem dei honorem.... Once I ventured to designate the whole Christian system of training[22] in penance and salvation (now best studied in England) as a method of producing a folie circulaire upon a soil already prepared for it, which is to say, a soil thoroughly unhealthy. Not every one may be a Christian: one is not "converted" to Christianity—one must first be sick enough for it.... We others, who have the courage for health and likewise for contempt,—we may well despise a religion that teaches misunderstanding of the body! that refuses to rid itself of the superstition about the soul! that makes a "virtue" of insufficient nourishment! that combats health as a sort of enemy, devil, temptation! that persuades itself that it is possible to carry about a "perfect soul" in a cadaver of a body, and that, to this end, had to devise for itself a new concept of "perfection," a pale, sickly, idiotically ecstatic state of existence, so-called "holiness"—a holiness that is itself merely a series of symptoms of an impoverished, enervated and incurably disordered body!... The Christian movement, as a European movement, was from the start no more than a general uprising of all sorts of outcast and refuse elements (—who now, under cover of Christianity, aspire to power). It does not represent the decay of a race; it represents, on the contrary, a conglomeration of décadence products from all directions, crowding together and seeking one another out. It was not, as has been thought, the corruption of antiquity, of noble antiquity, which made Christianity possible; one cannot too sharply challenge the learned imbecility which today maintains that theory. At the time when the sick and rotten Chandala classes in the whole imperium were Christianized, the contrary type, the nobility, reached its finest and ripest development. The majority became master; democracy, with its Christian instincts, triumphed.... Christianity was not "national," it was not based on race—it appealed to all the varieties of men disinherited by life, it had its allies everywhere. Christianity has the rancour of the sick at its very core—the instinct against the healthy, against health. Everything that is well-constituted, proud, gallant and, above all, beautiful gives offence to its ears and eyes. Again I remind you of Paul's priceless saying: "And God hath chosen the weak things of the world, the foolish things of the world, the base things of the world, and things which are despised":[23] this was the formula, in hoc signo the décadence triumphed.—God on the cross—is man always to miss the frightful inner significance of this symbol?—Everything that suffers, everything that hangs on the cross, is divine.... We all hang on the cross, consequently we are divine.... We alone are divine.... Christianity was thus a victory: a nobler attitude of mind was destroyed by it—Christianity remains to this day the greatest misfortune of humanity.—

[22]The word training is in English in the text.

[23]1 Corinthians i, **27, 28.**

Christianity also stands in opposition to all intellectual well-being,—sick reasoning is the only sort that it can use as Christian reasoning; it takes the side of everything that is idiotic; it pronounces a curse upon "intellect," upon the superbia of the healthy intellect. Since sickness is inherent in Christianity, it follows that the typically Christian state of "faith" must be a form of sickness too, and that all straight, straightforward and scientific paths to knowledge must be banned by the church as forbidden ways. Doubt is thus a sin from the start.... The complete lack of psychological cleanliness in the priest—revealed by a glance at him—is a phenomenon resulting from décadence,—one may observe in hysterical women and in rachitic children how regularly the falsification of instincts, delight in lying for the mere sake of lying, and incapacity for looking straight and walking straight are symptoms of décadence. "Faith" means the will to avoid knowing what is true. The pietist, the priest of either sex, is a fraud because he is sick: his instinct demands that the truth shall never be allowed its rights on any point. "Whatever makes for illness is good; whatever issues from abundance, from superabundance, from power, is evil": so argues the believer. The impulse to lie—it is by this that I recognize every foreordained theologian.—Another characteristic of the theologian is his unfitness for philology. What I here mean by philology is, in a general sense, the art of reading with profit—the capacity for absorbing facts without interpreting them falsely, and without losing caution, patience and subtlety in the effort to understand them. Philology as ephexis[24] in interpretation: whether one be dealing with books, with newspaper reports, with the most fateful events or with weather statistics—not to mention the "salvation of the soul.".... The way in which a theologian, whether in Berlin or in Rome, is ready to explain, say, a "passage of Scripture," or an experience, or a victory by the national army, by turning upon it the high illumination of the Psalms of David, is always so daring that it is enough to make a philologian run up a wall. But what shall he do when pietists and other such cows from Suabia[25] use the "finger of God" to convert their miserably commonplace and huggermugger existence into a miracle of "grace," a "providence" and an "experience of salvation"? The most modest exercise of the intellect, not to say of decency, should certainly be enough to convince these interpreters of the perfect childishness and unworthiness of such a misuse of the divine digital dexterity. However small our piety, if we ever encountered a god who always cured us of a cold in the head at just the right time, or got us into our carriage at the very instant heavy rain began to fall, he would seem so absurd a god that he'd have to be abolished even if he existed. God as a domestic servant, as a letter carrier, as an almanac-man—at bottom, he is a mere name for the stupidest sort of chance.... "Divine Prov idence," which every third man in "educated Germany" still believes in, is so strong an argument against God that it would be impossible to think of a stronger. And in any case it is an argument against Germans!...

[24]That is, to say, scepticism. Among the Greeks scepticism was also occasionally called ephecticism.

[25]A reference to the University of Tübingen and its famous school of Biblical criticism. The leader of this school was F. C. Baur, and one of the men greatly influenced by it was Nietzsche's pet abomination, David F. Strauss, himself a Suabian. Vide § **10** and § **28**.

—It is so little true that martyrs offer any support to the truth of a cause that I am inclined to deny that any martyr has ever had anything to do with the truth at all. In the very tone in which a martyr flings what he fancies to be true at the head of the world there appears so low a grade of intellectual honesty and such insensibility to the problem of "truth," that it is never necessary to refute him. Truth is not something that one man has and another man has not: at best, only peasants, or peasant-apostles like Luther, can think of truth in any such way. One may rest assured that the greater the degree of a man's intellectual conscience the greater will be his modesty, his discretion, on this point. To know in five cases, and to refuse, with delicacy, to know anything further.... "Truth," as the word is understood by every prophet, every sectarian, every free-thinker, every Socialist and every churchman, is simply a complete proof that not even a beginning has been made in the intellectual discipline and self-control that are necessary to the unearthing of even the smallest truth.—The deaths of the martyrs, it may be said in passing, have been misfortunes of history: they have misled.... The conclusion that all idiots, women and plebeians come to, that there must be something in a cause for which any one goes to his death (or which, as under primitive Christianity, sets off epidemics of death-seeking)—this conclusion has been an unspeakable drag upon the testing of facts, upon the whole spirit of inquiry and investigation. The martyrs have damaged the truth.... Even to this day the crude fact of persecution is enough to give an honourable name to the most empty sort of sectarianism.—But why? Is the worth of a cause altered by the fact that some one had laid down his life for it?—An error that becomes honourable is simply an error that has acquired one seductive charm the more: do you suppose, Messrs. Theologians, that we shall give you the chance to be martyred for your lies?—One best disposes of a cause by respectfully putting it on ice—that is also the best way to dispose of theologians.... This was precisely the world- historical stupidity of all the persecutors: that they gave the appearance of honour to the cause they opposed—that they made it a present of the fascination of martyrdom.... Women are still on their knees before an error because they have been told that some one died on the cross for it. Is the cross, then, an argument?—But about all these things there is one, and one only, who has said what has been needed for thousands of years—Zarathustra.

They made signs in blood along the way that they went, and their folly taught them that the truth is proved by blood.

But blood is the worst of all testimonies to the truth; blood poisoneth even the purest teaching and turneth it into madness and hatred in the heart.

And when one goeth through fire for his teaching—what doth that prove? Verily, it is more when one's teaching cometh out of one's own burning![26]

[26]The quotations are from "Also sprach Zarathustra" ii, **24**: "Of Priests."

54

Do not let yourself be deceived: great intellects are sceptical. Zarathustra is a sceptic. The strength, the freedom which proceed from intellectual power, from a superabundance of intellectual power, manifest themselves as scep ticism. Men of fixed convictions do not count when it comes to determining what is fundamental in values and lack of values. Men of convictions are prisoners. They do not see far enough, they do not see what is below them: whereas a man who would talk to any purpose about value and non-value must be able to see five hundred convictions beneath him— and behind him.... A mind that aspires to great things, and that wills the means thereto, is necessarily sceptical. Freedom from any sort of conviction belongs to strength, and to an independent point of view.... That grand passion which is at once the foundation and the power of a sceptic's existence, and is both more enlightened and more despotic than he is himself, drafts the whole of his intellect into its service; it makes him unscrupulous; it gives him courage to employ unholy means; under certain circumstances it does not begrudge him even convictions. Conviction as a means: one may achieve a good deal by means of a conviction. A grand passion makes use of and uses up convictions; it does not yield to them—it knows itself to be sovereign.—On the contrary, the need of faith, of something unconditioned by yea or nay, of Carlylism, if I may be allowed the word, is a need of weakness. The man of faith, the "believer" of any sort, is necessarily a dependent man—such a man cannot posit himself as a goal, nor can he find goals within himself. The "believer" does not belong to himself; he can only be a means to an end; he must be used up; he needs some one to use him up. His instinct gives the highest honours to an ethic of self-effacement; he is prompted to embrace it by everything: his prudence, his experience, his vanity. Every sort of faith is in itself an evidence of self-effacement, of self-estrangement.... When one reflects how necessary it is to the great majority that there be regulations to restrain them from without and hold them fast, and to what extent control, or, in a higher sense, slavery, is the one and only condition which makes for the well-being of the weak-willed man, and especially woman, then one at once understands conviction and "faith." To the man with convictions they are his backbone. To avoid seeing many things, to be impartial about nothing, to be a party man through and through, to estimate all values strictly and infallibly—these are conditions necessary to the existence of such a man. But by the same token they are antagonists of the truthful man—of the truth.... The believer is not free to answer the question, "true" or "not true," according to the dictates of his own conscience: integrity on this point would work his instant downfall. The pathological limitations of his vision turn the man of convictions into a fanatic—Savonarola, Luther, Rousseau, Robespierre, Saint-Simon—these types stand in opposition to the strong, emancipated spirit. But the grandiose attitudes of these sick intellects, these intellectual epileptics, are of influence upon the great masses—fanatics are picturesque, and mankind prefers observing poses to listening to reasons....

55.

—One step further in the psychology of conviction, of "faith." It is now a good while since I first proposed for consideration the question whether convictions are not even more dangerous enemies to truth than lies. ("Human, All-Too-Human," I, aphorism **483**.)[27] This time I desire to put the question definitely: is there any actual difference between a lie and a conviction?—All the world believes that there is; but what is not believed by all the world!—Every conviction has its history, its primitive forms, its stage of tentativeness and error: it becomes a conviction only after having been, for a long time, not one, and then, for an even longer time, hardly one. What if falsehood be also one of these embryonic forms of conviction?—Sometimes all that is needed is a change in persons: what was a lie in the father becomes a conviction in the son.—I call it lying to refuse to see what one sees, or to refuse to see it as it is: whether the lie be uttered before witnesses or not before witnesses is of no consequence. The most common sort of lie is that by which a man deceives himself: the deception of others is a relatively rare offence.—Now, this will not to see what one sees, this will not to see it as it is, is almost the first requisite for all who belong to a party of whatever sort: the party man becomes inevitably a liar. For example, the German historians are convinced that Rome was synonymous with despotism and that the Germanic peoples brought the spirit of liberty into the world: what is the difference between this conviction and a lie? Is it to be wondered at that all partisans, including the German historians, instinctively roll the fine phrases of morality upon their tongues—that morality almost owes its very survival to the fact that the party man of every sort has need of it every moment?—"This is our conviction: we publish it to the whole world; we live and die for it—let us respect all who have convictions!"—I have actually heard such sentiments from the mouths of anti-Semites. On the contrary, gentlemen! An anti-Semite surely does not become more respectable because he lies on principle.... The priests, who have more finesse in such matters, and who well understand the objection that lies against the notion of a conviction, which is to say, of a falsehood that becomes a matter of principle because it serves a purpose, have borrowed from the Jews the shrewd device of sneaking in the concepts, "God," "the will of God" and "the revelation of God" at this place. Kant, too, with his categorical imperative, was on the same road: this was his practical reason.[28] There are questions regarding the truth or untruth of which it is not for man to decide; all the capital questions, all the capital problems of valuation, are beyond human reason.... To know the limits of reason—that alone is genuine philosophy.... Why did God make a revelation to man? Would God have done anything superfluous? Man could not find out for himself what was good and what was evil, so God taught him His will.... Moral: the priest does not lie—the question, "true" or "untrue," has nothing to do with such things as the priest discusses; it is impossible to lie about these things. In order to lie here it would be necessary to know what is true. But this is more than man can know; therefore, the priest is simply the mouthpiece of God.—Such a priestly syllogism is by no means merely Jewish and Christian; the right to lie and the shrewd dodge of "revelation" belong to the general priestly type—to the priest of the décadence as well as to the priest of pagan times (—Pagans are all those who say yes to life, and to whom "God" is a word signifying acquiescence in all things).—The "law," the "will of God," the "holy book," and "inspiration"—all these things are merely words for the conditions under which the priest comes to power and with which he maintains his power,—these concepts are to be found at the bottom of all priestly organizations, and of all priestly or priestly-philosophical schemes of governments. The "holy lie"—common alike to Confucius, to the Code of Manu, to Mohammed and to the Christian church—is not even wanting in Plato. "Truth is here": this means, no matter where it is heard, the priest lies....

[27]The aphorism, which is headed "The Enemies of Truth," makes the direct statement: "Convictions are more dangerous enemies of truth than lies."

[28]A reference, of course, to Kant's "Kritik der praktischen Vernunft" (Critique of Practical Reason).

56.

—In the last analysis it comes to this: what is the end of lying? The fact that, in Christianity, "holy" ends are not visible is my objection to the means it employs. Only bad ends appear: the poisoning, the calumniation, the denial of life, the despising of the body, the degradation and self-contamination of man by the concept of sin— therefore, its means are also bad.—I have a contrary feeling when I read the Code of Manu, an incomparably more intellectual and superior work, which it would be a sin against the intelligence to so much as name in the same breath with the Bible. It is easy to see why: there is a genuine philosophy behind it, in it, not merely an evil-smelling mess of Jewish rabbinism and superstition,—it gives even the most fastidious psychologist something to sink his teeth into. And, not to forget what is most important, it differs fundamentally from every kind of Bible: by means of it the nobles, the philosophers and the warriors keep the whip-hand over the majority; it is full of noble valuations, it shows a feeling of perfection, an acceptance of life, and triumphant feeling toward self and life—the sun shines upon the whole book.—All the things on which Christianity vents its fathomless vulgarity—for example, procreation, women and marriage—are here handled earnestly, with reverence and with love and confidence. How can any one really put into the hands of children and ladies a book which contains such vile things as this: "to avoid fornication, let every man have his own wife, and let every woman have her own husband; ... it is better to marry than to burn"?[29] And is it possible to be a Christian so long as the origin of man is Christianized, which is to say, befouled, by the doctrine of the immaculata conceptio?... I know of no book in which so many delicate and kindly things are said of women as in the Code of Manu; these old grey-beards and saints have a way of being gallant to women that it would be impossible, perhaps, to surpass. "The mouth of a woman," it says in one place, "the breasts of a maiden, the prayer of a child and the smoke of sacrifice are always pure." In another place: "there is nothing purer than the light of the sun, the shadow cast by a cow, air, water, fire and the breath of a maiden." Finally, in still another place—perhaps this is also a holy lie—: "all the orifices of the body above the navel are pure, and all below are impure. Only in the maiden is the whole body pure."

[29]1 Corinthians vii, **2**, **9**.

57.

One catches the unholiness of Christian means in flagranti by the simple process of putting the ends sought by Christianity beside the ends sought by the Code of Manu— by putting these enormously antithetical ends under a strong light. The critic of Christianity cannot evade the necessity of making Christianity contemptible.—A book of laws such as the Code of Manu has the same origin as every other good law-book: it epitomizes the experience, the sagacity and the ethical experimentation of long centuries; it brings things to a conclusion; it no longer creates. The prerequisite to a codification of this sort is recognition of the fact that the means which establish the authority of a slowly and painfully attained truth are fundamentally different from those which one would make use of to prove it. A law-book never recites the utility, the grounds, the casuistical antecedents of a law: for if it did so it would lose the imperative tone, the "thou shall," on which obedience is based. The problem lies exactly here.—At a certain point in the evolution of a people, the class within it of the greatest insight, which is to say, the greatest hindsight and foresight, declares that the series of experiences determining how all shall live—or can live—has come to an end. The object now is to reap as rich and as complete a harvest as possible from the days of experiment and hard experience. In consequence, the thing that is to be avoided above everything is further experimentation—the continuation of the state in which values are fluent, and are tested, chosen and criticized ad infinitum. Against this a double wall is set up: on the one hand, revelation, which is the assumption that the reasons lying behind the laws are not of human origin, that they were not sought out and found by a slow process and after many errors, but that they are of divine ancestry, and came into being complete, perfect, without a history, as a free gift, a miracle...; and on the other hand, tradition, which is the assumption that the law has stood unchanged from time immemorial, and that it is impious and a crime against one's forefathers to bring it into question. The authority of the law is thus grounded on the thesis: God gave it, and the fathers lived it.—The higher motive of such procedure lies in the design to distract consciousness, step by step, from its concern with notions of right living (that is to say, those that have been proved to be right by wide and carefully considered experience), so that instinct attains to a perfect automatism—a primary necessity to every sort of mastery, to every sort of perfection in the art of life. To draw up such a law-book as Manu's means to lay before a people the possibility of future mastery, of attainable perfection—it permits them to aspire to the highest reaches of the art of life. To that end the thing must be made unconscious: that is the aim of every holy lie.—The order of castes, the highest, the dominating law, is merely the ratification of an order of nature, of a natural law of the first rank, over which no arbitrary fiat, no "modern idea," can exert any influence. In every healthy society there are three physiological types, gravitating toward differentiation but mutually conditioning one another, and each of these has its own hygiene, its own sphere of work, its own special mastery and feeling of perfection. It is not Manu but nature that sets off in one class those who are chiefly intellectual, in another those who are marked by muscular strength and temperament, and in a third those who are distinguished in neither one way or the other, but show only mediocrity—the last-named represents the great majority, and the first two the select. The superior caste—I call it the fewest—has, as the most perfect, the privileges of the few: it stands for happiness, for beauty, for everything good upon earth. Only the most intellectual of men have any right to beauty, to the beautiful; only in them can goodness escape being weakness. Pulchrum est paucorum hominum:[30] goodness is a privilege. Nothing could be more unbecoming to them than uncouth manners or a pessimistic look, or an eye that sees ugliness—or indignation against the general aspect of things. Indigna tion is the privilege of the Chandala; so is pessimism. "The world is perfect"—so prompts the instinct of the intellectual, the instinct of the man who says yes to life. "Imperfection, whatever is inferior to us, distance, the pathos of distance, even the Chandala themselves are parts of this perfection." The most intelligent men, like the strongest, find their happiness where others would find only disaster: in the labyrinth, in being hard with themselves and with others, in effort; their delight is in self-mastery; in them asceticism becomes second nature, a necessity, an instinct. They regard a difficult task as a privilege; it is to them a recreation to play with burdens that would crush all others.... Knowledge—a form of asceticism.—They are the most honourable kind of men: but that does not prevent them being the most cheerful and most amiable. They rule, not because they want to, but because they are; they are not at liberty to play second.—

The second caste: to this belong the guardians of the law, the keepers of order and security, the more noble warriors, above all, the king as the highest form of warrior, judge and preserver of the law. The second in rank constitute the executive arm of the intellectuals, the next to them in rank, taking from them all that is rough in the business of ruling—their followers, their right hand, their most apt disciples.—In all this, I repeat, there is nothing arbitrary, nothing "made up"; whatever is to the contrary is made up—by it nature is brought to shame.... The order of castes, the order of rank, simply formulates the supreme law of life itself; the separation of the three types is necessary to the maintenance of society, and to the evolution of higher types, and the highest types—the inequality of rights is essential to the existence of any rights at all.—A right is a privilege. Every one enjoys the privileges that accord with his state of existence. Let us not underestimate the privileges of the mediocre. Life is always harder as one mounts the heights—the cold increases, responsibility increases. A high civilization is a pyramid: it can stand only on a broad base; its primary prerequisite is a strong and soundly consolidated mediocrity. The handicrafts, commerce, agriculture, science, the greater part of art, in brief, the whole range of occupational activities, are compatible only with mediocre ability and aspiration; such callings would be out of place for exceptional men; the instincts which belong to them stand as much opposed to aristocracy as to anarchism. The fact that a man is publicly useful, that he is a wheel, a function, is evidence of a natural predisposition; it is not society, but the only sort of happiness that the majority are capable of, that makes them intelligent machines. To the mediocre mediocrity is a form of happiness; they have a natural instinct for mastering one thing, for specialization. It would be altogether unworthy of a profound intellect to see anything objectionable in mediocrity in itself. It is, in fact, the first prerequisite to the appearance of the exceptional: it is a necessary condition to a high degree of civilization. When the exceptional man handles the mediocre man with more delicate fingers than he applies to himself or to his equals, this is not merely kindness of heart—it is simply his duty.... Whom do I hate most heartily among the rabbles of today? The rabble of Socialists, the apostles to the Chandala, who undermine the workingman's instincts, his pleasure, his feeling of contentment with his petty existence—who make him envious and teach him revenge.... Wrong never lies in unequal rights; it lies in the assertion of "equal" rights.... What is bad? But I have already answered: all that proceeds from weakness, from envy, from revenge.—The anarchist and the Christian have the same ancestry....

[**30**]Few men are noble.

58.

In point of fact, the end for which one lies makes a great difference: whether one preserves thereby or destroys. There is a perfect likeness between Christian and anarchist: their object, their instinct, points only toward destruction. One need only turn to history for a proof of this: there it appears with appalling distinctness. We have just studied a code of religious legislation whose object it was to convert the conditions which cause life to flourish into an "eternal" social organization,—Christianity found its mission in putting an end to such an organization, because life flourished under it. There the benefits that reason had produced during long ages of experiment and insecurity were applied to the most remote uses, and an effort was made to bring in a harvest that should be as large, as rich and as complete as possible; here, on the contrary, the harvest is blighted overnight.... That which stood there aere perennis, the imperium Romanum, the most magnificent form of organization under difficult conditions that has ever been achieved, and compared to which everything before it and after it appears as patchwork, bungling, dilletantism—those holy anarchists made it a matter of "piety" to destroy "the world," which is to say, the imperium Romanum, so that in the end not a stone stood upon another—and even Germans and other such louts were able to become its masters.... The Christian and the anarchist: both are décadents; both are incapable of any act that is not disintegrating, poisonous, degenerating, blood-sucking; both have an instinct of mortal hatred of everything that stands up, and is great, and has durability, and promises life a future.... Christianity was the vampire of the imperium Romanum,—overnight it destroyed the vast achievement of the Romans: the conquest of the soil for a great culture that could await its time. Can it be that this fact is not yet understood? The imperium Romanum that we know, and that the history of the Roman provinces teaches us to know better and better,—this most admirable of all works of art in the grand manner was merely the beginning, and the structure to follow was not to prove its worth for thousands of years. To this day, noth ing on a like scale sub specie aeterni has been brought into being, or even dreamed of!—This organization was strong enough to withstand bad emperors: the accident of personality has nothing to do with such things—the first principle of all genuinely great architecture. But it was not strong enough to stand up against the corruptest of all forms of corruption—against Christians.... These stealthy worms, which under the cover of night, mist and duplicity, crept upon every individual, sucking him dry of all earnest interest in real things, of all instinct for reality—this cowardly, effeminate and sugar-coated gang gradually alienated all "souls," step by step, from that colossal edifice, turning against it all the meritorious, manly and noble natures that had found in the cause of Rome their own cause, their own serious purpose, their own pride. The sneakishness of hypocrisy, the secrecy of the conventicle, concepts as black as hell, such as the sacrifice of the innocent, the unio mystica in the drinking of blood, above all, the slowly rekindled fire of revenge, of Chandala revenge—all that sort of thing became master of Rome: the same kind of religion which, in a pre-existent form, Epicurus had combatted. One has but to read Lucretius to know what Epicurus made war upon—not paganism, but "Christianity," which is to say, the corruption of souls by means of the concepts of guilt, punishment and immortality.—He combatted the subterranean cults, the whole of latent Christianity—to deny immortality was already a form of genuine salvation.— Epicurus had triumphed, and every respectable intellect in Rome was Epicurean— when Paul appeared ... Paul, the Chandala hatred of Rome, of "the world," in the flesh and inspired by genius—the Jew, the eternal Jew par excellence.... What he saw was how, with the aid of the small sectarian Christian movement that stood apart from Judaism, a "world conflagration" might be kindled; how, with the symbol of "God on the cross," all secret seditions, all the fruits of anarchistic intrigues in the empire, might be amalgamated into one immense power. "Salvation is of the Jews."—Christianity is the formula for exceeding and summing up the subterranean cults of all varieties, that of Osiris, that of the Great Mother, that of Mithras, for instance: in his discernment of this fact the genius of Paul showed itself. His instinct was here so sure that, with reckless violence to the truth, he put the ideas which lent fascination to every sort of Chandala religion into the mouth of the "Saviour" as his own inventions, and not only into the mouth—he made out of him something that even a priest of Mithras could understand.... This was his revelation at Damascus: he grasped the fact that he needed the belief in immortality in order to rob "the world" of its value, that the concept of "hell" would master Rome—that the notion of a "beyond" is the death of life.... Nihilist and Christian: they rhyme in German, and they do more than rhyme....

59.

The whole labour of the ancient world gone for naught: I have no word to describe the feelings that such an enormity arouses in me.—And, considering the fact that its labour was merely preparatory, that with adamantine self-consciousness it laid only the foundations for a work to go on for thousands of years, the whole meaning of antiquity disappears!... To what end the Greeks? to what end the Romans?—All the prerequisites to a learned culture, all the methods of science, were already there; man had already perfected the great and incomparable art of read ing profitably—that first necessity to the tradition of culture, the unity of the sciences; the natural sciences, in alliance with mathematics and mechanics, were on the right road,—the sense of fact, the last and more valuable of all the senses, had its schools, and its traditions were already centuries old! Is all this properly understood? Every essential to the beginning of the work was ready:—and the most essential, it cannot be said too often, are methods, and also the most difficult to develop, and the longest opposed by habit and laziness. What we have today reconquered, with unspeakable self-discipline, for ourselves—for certain bad instincts, certain Christian instincts, still lurk in our bodies—that is to say, the keen eye for reality, the cautious hand, patience and seriousness in the smallest things, the whole integrity of knowledge—all these things were already there, and had been there for two thousand years! More, there was also a refined and excellent tact and taste! Not as mere brain-drilling! Not as "German" culture, with its loutish manners! But as body, as bearing, as instinct—in short, as reality.... All gone for naught! Overnight it became merely a memory!—The Greeks! The Romans! Instinctive nobility, taste, methodical inquiry, genius for organization and administration, faith in and the will to secure the future of man, a great yes to everything entering into the imperium Romanum and palpable to all the senses, a grand style that was beyond mere art, but had become reality, truth, life....—All overwhelmed in a night, but not by a convulsion of nature! Not trampled to death by Teutons and others of heavy hoof! But brought to shame by crafty, sneaking, invisible, anæmic vampires! Not conquered,—only sucked dry!... Hidden vengefulness, petty envy, became master! Everything wretched, intrinsically ailing, and invaded by bad feelings, the whole ghetto-world of the soul, was at once on top!—One needs but read any of the Christian agitators, for example, St. Augustine, in order to realize, in order to smell, what filthy fellows came to the top. It would be an error, however, to assume that there was any lack of understanding in the leaders of the Christian movement:—ah, but they were clever, clever to the point of holiness, these fathers of the church! What they lacked was something quite different. Nature neglected—perhaps forgot—to give them even the most modest endowment of respectable, of upright, of cleanly instincts.... Between ourselves, they are not even men.... If Islam despises Christianity, it has a thousandfold right to do so: Islam at least assumes that it is dealing with men....

60.

Christianity destroyed for us the whole harvest of ancient civilization, and later it also destroyed for us the whole harvest of Mohammedan civilization. The wonderful culture of the Moors in Spain, which was fundamentally nearer to us and appealed more to our senses and tastes than that of Rome and Greece, was trampled down (—I do not say by what sort of feet—) Why? Because it had to thank noble and manly instincts for its origin—because it said yes to life, even to the rare and refined luxuriousness of Moorish life!... The crusaders later made war on something before which it would have been more fitting for them to have grovelled in the dust—a civilization beside which even that of our nineteenth century seems very poor and very "senile."—What they wanted, of course, was booty: the orient was rich.... Let us put aside our prejudices! The crusades were a higher form of piracy, nothing more! The German nobility, which is fundamentally a Viking nobility, was in its element there: the church knew only too well how the German nobility was to be won.... The German noble, always the "Swiss guard" of the church, always in the service of every bad instinct of the church—but well paid.... Consider the fact that it is precisely the aid of German swords and German blood and valour that has enabled the church to carry through its war to the death upon everything noble on earth! At this point a host of painful questions suggest themselves. The German nobility stands outside the history of the higher civilization: the reason is obvious.... Christianity, alcohol—the two great means of corruption.... Intrinsically there should be no more choice between Islam and Christianity than there is between an Arab and a Jew. The decision is already reached; nobody remains at liberty to choose here. Either a man is a Chandala or he is not.... "War to the knife with Rome! Peace and friendship with Islam!": this was the feeling, this was the act, of that great free spirit, that genius among German emperors, Frederick II. What! must a German first be a genius, a free spirit, before he can feel decently? I can't make out how a German could ever feel Christian....

61.

Here it becomes necessary to call up a memory that must be a hundred times more painful to Germans. The Germans have destroyed for Europe the last great harvest of civilization that Europe was ever to reap—the Renaissance. Is it understood at last, will it ever be understood, what the Renaissance was? The transvaluation of Christian values,—an attempt with all available means, all instincts and all the resources of genius to bring about a triumph of the opposite values, the more noble values.... This has been the one great war of the past; there has never been a more critical question than that of the Renaissance—it is my question too—; there has never been a form of attack more fundamental, more direct, or more violently delivered by a whole front upon the center of the enemy! To attack at the critical place, at the very seat of Christianity, and there enthrone the more noble values—that is to say, to insinuate them into the instincts, into the most fundamental needs and appetites of those sitting there.... I see before me the possibility of a perfectly heavenly enchantment and spectacle:—it seems to me to scintillate with all the vibrations of a fine and delicate beauty, and within it there is an art so divine, so infernally divine, that one might search in vain for thousands of years for another such possibility; I see a spectacle so rich in significance and at the same time so wonderfully full of paradox that it should arouse all the gods on Olympus to immortal laughter—Cæsar Borgia as pope!... Am I understood?... Well then, that would have been the sort of triumph that I alone am longing for today—: by it Christianity would have been swept away!—What happened? A German monk, Luther, came to Rome. This monk, with all the vengeful instincts of an unsuccessful priest in him, raised a rebellion against the Renaissance in Rome.... Instead of grasping, with profound thanksgiving, the miracle that had taken place: the conquest of Christianity at its capital—instead of this, his hatred was stimulated by the spectacle. A religious man thinks only of himself.—Luther saw only the depravity of the papacy at the very moment when the oppo site was becoming apparent: the old corruption, the peccatum originale, Christianity itself, no longer occupied the papal chair! Instead there was life! Instead there was the triumph of life! Instead there was a great yea to all lofty, beautiful and daring things!... And Luther restored the church: he attacked it.... The Renaissance—an event without meaning, a great futility!—Ah, these Germans, what they have not cost us! Futility—that has always been the work of the Germans.—The Reformation; Leibnitz; Kant and so-called German philosophy; the war of "liberation"; the empire—every time a futile substitute for something that once existed, for something irrecoverable.... These Germans, I confess, are my enemies: I despise all their uncleanliness in concept and valuation, their cowardice before every honest yea and nay. For nearly a thousand years they have tangled and confused everything their fingers have touched; they have on their conscience all the half-way measures, all the three-eighths-way measures, that Europe is sick of,—they also have on their conscience the uncleanest variety of Christianity that exists, and the most incurable and indestructible—Protestantism.... If man kind never manages to get rid of Christianity the Germans will be to blame....

62.

—With this I come to a conclusion and pronounce my judgment. I condemn Christianity; I bring against the Christian church the most terrible of all the accusations that an accuser has ever had in his mouth. It is, to me, the greatest of all imaginable corruptions; it seeks to work the ultimate corruption, the worst possible corruption. The Christian church has left nothing untouched by its depravity; it has turned every value into worthlessness, and every truth into a lie, and every integrity into baseness of soul. Let any one dare to speak to me of its "humanitarian" blessings! Its deepest necessities range it against any effort to abolish distress; it lives by distress; it creates distress to make itself immortal.... For example, the worm of sin: it was the church that first enriched mankind with this misery!—The "equality of souls before God"—this fraud, this pretext for the rancunes of all the base-minded—this explosive concept, ending in revolution, the modern idea, and the notion of overthrowing the whole social order—this is Christian dynamite.... The "humanitarian" blessings of Christianity forsooth! To breed out of humanitas a self-contradiction, an art of self-pollution, a will to lie at any price, an aversion and contempt for all good and honest instincts! All this, to me, is the "humanitarianism" of Christianity!—Parasitism as the only practice of the church; with its anæmic and "holy" ideals, sucking all the blood, all the love, all the hope out of life; the beyond as the will to deny all reality; the cross as the distinguishing mark of the most subterranean conspiracy ever heard of,—against health, beauty, well-being, intellect, kindness of soul—against life itself....

This eternal accusation against Christianity I shall write upon all walls, wherever walls are to be found—I have letters that even the blind will be able to see.... I call Christianity the one great curse, the one great intrinsic depravity, the one great instinct of revenge, for which no means are venomous enough, or secret, subterranean and small enough,—I call it the one immortal blemish upon the human race....

And mankind reckons time from the *dies nefastus* when this fatality befell—from the first day of Christianity!—Why not rather from its last?—From today?—The transvaluation of all values!...

Part V: Beyond Nihilism-The *Overcoming*

ZARATHUSTRA'S PROLOGUE

1.

When Zarathustra was thirty years old, he left his home and the lake of his home, and went into the mountains. There he enjoyed his spirit and solitude, and for ten years did not weary of it. But at last his heart changed,—and rising one morning with the rosy dawn, he went before the sun, and spake thus unto it:

Thou great star! What would be thy happiness if thou hadst not those for whom thou shinest!

For ten years hast thou climbed hither unto my cave: thou wouldst have wearied of thy light and of the journey, had it not been for me, mine eagle, and my serpent.

But we awaited thee every morning, took from thee thine overflow and blessed thee for it.

Lo! I am weary of my wisdom, like the bee that hath gathered too much honey; I need hands outstretched to take it.

I would fain bestow and distribute, until the wise have once more become joyous in their folly, and the poor happy in their riches.

Therefore must I descend into the deep: as thou doest in the evening, when thou goest behind the sea, and givest light also to the nether-world, thou exuberant star!

Like thee must I GO DOWN, as men say, to whom I shall descend.

Bless me, then, thou tranquil eye, that canst behold even the greatest happiness without envy!

Bless the cup that is about to overflow, that the water may flow golden out of it, and carry everywhere the reflection of thy bliss!

Lo! This cup is again going to empty itself, and Zarathustra is again going to be a man.

Thus began Zarathustra's down-going.

2.

Zarathustra went down the mountain alone, no one meeting him. When he entered the forest, however, there suddenly stood before him an old man, who had left his holy cot to seek roots. And thus spake the old man to Zarathustra:

"No stranger to me is this wanderer: many years ago passed he by. Zarathustra he was called; but he hath altered.

Then thou carriedst thine ashes into the mountains: wilt thou now carry thy fire into the valleys? Fearest thou not the incendiary's doom?

Yea, I recognise Zarathustra. Pure is his eye, and no loathing lurketh about his mouth. Goeth he not along like a dancer?

Altered is Zarathustra; a child hath Zarathustra become; an awakened one is Zarathustra: what wilt thou do in the land of the sleepers?

As in the sea hast thou lived in solitude, and it hath borne thee up. Alas, wilt thou now go ashore? Alas, wilt thou again drag thy body thyself?"

Zarathustra answered: "I love mankind."

"Why," said the saint, "did I go into the forest and the desert? Was it not because I loved men far too well?

Now I love God: men, I do not love. Man is a thing too imperfect for me. Love to man would be fatal to me."

Zarathustra answered: "What spake I of love! I am bringing gifts unto men."

"Give them nothing," said the saint. "Take rather part of their load, and carry it along with them—that will be most agreeable unto them: if only it be agreeable unto thee!

If, however, thou wilt give unto them, give them no more than an alms, and let them also beg for it!"

"No," replied Zarathustra, "I give no alms. I am not poor enough for that."

The saint laughed at Zarathustra, and spake thus: "Then see to it that they accept thy treasures! They are distrustful of anchorites, and do not believe that we come with gifts.

The fall of our footsteps ringeth too hollow through their streets. And just as at night, when they are in bed and hear a man abroad long before sunrise, so they ask themselves concerning us: Where goeth the thief?

Go not to men, but stay in the forest! Go rather to the animals! Why not be like me—a bear amongst bears, a bird amongst birds?"

"And what doeth the saint in the forest?" asked Zarathustra.

The saint answered: "I make hymns and sing them; and in making hymns I laugh and weep and mumble: thus do I praise God.

With singing, weeping, laughing, and mumbling do I praise the God who is my God. But what dost thou bring us as a gift?"

When Zarathustra had heard these words, he bowed to the saint and said: "What should I have to give thee! Let me rather hurry hence lest I take aught away from thee!"— And thus they parted from one another, the old man and Zarathustra, laughing like schoolboys.

When Zarathustra was alone, however, he said to his heart: "Could it be possible! This old saint in the forest hath not yet heard of it, that GOD IS DEAD!"

3.

When Zarathustra arrived at the nearest town which adjoineth the forest, he found many people assembled in the market-place; for it had been announced that a rope-dancer would give a performance. And Zarathustra spake thus unto the people:

I TEACH YOU THE SUPERMAN. Man is something that is to be surpassed. What have ye done to surpass man?

All beings hitherto have created something beyond themselves: and ye want to be the ebb of that great tide, and would rather go back to the beast than surpass man?

What is the ape to man? A laughing-stock, a thing of shame. And just the same shall man be to the Superman: a laughing-stock, a thing of shame.

Ye have made your way from the worm to man, and much within you is still worm. Once were ye apes, and even yet man is more of an ape than any of the apes.

Even the wisest among you is only a disharmony and hybrid of plant and phantom. But do I bid you become phantoms or plants?

Lo, I teach you the Superman!

The Superman is the meaning of the earth. Let your will say: The Superman SHALL BE the meaning of the earth!

I conjure you, my brethren, REMAIN TRUE TO THE EARTH, and believe not those who speak unto you of superearthly hopes! Poisoners are they, whether they know it or not.

Despisers of life are they, decaying ones and poisoned ones themselves, of whom the earth is weary: so away with them!

Once blasphemy against God was the greatest blasphemy; but God died, and therewith also those blasphemers. To blaspheme the earth is now the dreadfulest sin, and to rate the heart of the unknowable higher than the meaning of the earth!

Once the soul looked contemptuously on the body, and then that contempt was the supreme thing:—the soul wished the body meagre, ghastly, and famished. Thus it thought to escape from the body and the earth.

Oh, that soul was itself meagre, ghastly, and famished; and cruelty was the delight of that soul!

But ye, also, my brethren, tell me: What doth your body say about your soul? Is your soul not poverty and pollution and wretched self-complacency?

Verily, a polluted stream is man. One must be a sea, to receive a polluted stream without becoming impure.

Lo, I teach you the Superman: he is that sea; in him can your great contempt be submerged.

What is the greatest thing ye can experience? It is the hour of great contempt. The hour in which even your happiness becometh loathsome unto you, and so also your reason and virtue.

The hour when ye say: "What good is my happiness! It is poverty and pollution and wretched self-complacency. But my happiness should justify existence itself!"

The hour when ye say: "What good is my reason! Doth it long for knowledge as the lion for his food? It is poverty and pollution and wretched self-complacency!"

The hour when ye say: "What good is my virtue! As yet it hath not made me passionate. How weary I am of my good and my bad! It is all poverty and pollution and wretched self-complacency!"

The hour when ye say: "What good is my justice! I do not see that I am fervour and fuel. The just, however, are fervour and fuel!"

The hour when ye say: "What good is my pity! Is not pity the cross on which he is nailed who loveth man? But my pity is not a crucifixion."

Have ye ever spoken thus? Have ye ever cried thus? Ah! would that I had heard you crying thus!

It is not your sin—it is your self-satisfaction that crieth unto heaven; your very sparingness in sin crieth unto heaven!

Where is the lightning to lick you with its tongue? Where is the frenzy with which ye should be inoculated?

Lo, I teach you the Superman: he is that lightning, he is that frenzy!—

When Zarathustra had thus spoken, one of the people called out: "We have now heard enough of the rope-dancer; it is time now for us to see him!" And all the people laughed at Zarathustra. But the rope-dancer, who thought the words applied to him, began his performance.

4.

Zarathustra, however, looked at the people and wondered. Then he spake thus:

Man is a rope stretched between the animal and the Superman—a rope over an abyss.

A dangerous crossing, a dangerous wayfaring, a dangerous looking-back, a dangerous trembling and halting.

What is great in man is that he is a bridge and not a goal: what is lovable in man is that he is an OVER-GOING and a DOWN-GOING.

I love those that know not how to live except as down-goers, for they are the over-goers.

I love the great despisers, because they are the great adorers, and arrows of longing for the other shore.

I love those who do not first seek a reason beyond the stars for going down and being sacrifices, but sacrifice themselves to the earth, that the earth of the Superman may hereafter arrive.

I love him who liveth in order to know, and seeketh to know in order that the Superman may hereafter live. Thus seeketh he his own down-going.

I love him who laboureth and inventeth, that he may build the house for the Superman, and prepare for him earth, animal, and plant: for thus seeketh he his own down-going.

I love him who loveth his virtue: for virtue is the will to down-going, and an arrow of longing.

I love him who reserveth no share of spirit for himself, but wanteth to be wholly the spirit of his virtue: thus walketh he as spirit over the bridge.

I love him who maketh his virtue his inclination and destiny: thus, for the sake of his virtue, he is willing to live on, or live no more.

I love him who desireth not too many virtues. One virtue is more of a virtue than two, because it is more of a knot for one's destiny to cling to.

I love him whose soul is lavish, who wanteth no thanks and doth not give back: for he always bestoweth, and desireth not to keep for himself.

I love him who is ashamed when the dice fall in his favour, and who then asketh: "Am I a dishonest player?"—for he is willing to succumb.

I love him who scattereth golden words in advance of his deeds, and always doeth more than he promiseth: for he seeketh his own down-going.

I love him who justifieth the future ones, and redeemeth the past ones: for he is willing to succumb through the present ones.

I love him who chasteneth his God, because he loveth his God: for he must succumb through the wrath of his God.

I love him whose soul is deep even in the wounding, and may succumb through a small matter: thus goeth he willingly over the bridge.

I love him whose soul is so overfull that he forgetteth himself, and all things are in him: thus all things become his down-going.

I love him who is of a free spirit and a free heart: thus is his head only the bowels of his heart; his heart, however, causeth his down-going.

I love all who are like heavy drops falling one by one out of the dark cloud that lowereth over man: they herald the coming of the lightning, and succumb as heralds.

Lo, I am a herald of the lightning, and a heavy drop out of the cloud: the lightning, however, is the SUPERMAN.—

5.

When Zarathustra had spoken these words, he again looked at the people, and was silent. "There they stand," said he to his heart; "there they laugh: they understand me not; I am not the mouth for these ears.

Must one first batter their ears, that they may learn to hear with their eyes? Must one clatter like kettledrums and penitential preachers? Or do they only believe the stammerer?

They have something whereof they are proud. What do they call it, that which maketh them proud? Culture, they call it; it distinguisheth them from the goatherds.

They dislike, therefore, to hear of 'contempt' of themselves. So I will appeal to their pride.

I will speak unto them of the most contemptible thing: that, however, is THE LAST MAN!"

And thus spake Zarathustra unto the people:

It is time for man to fix his goal. It is time for man to plant the germ of his highest hope.

Still is his soil rich enough for it. But that soil will one day be poor and exhausted, and no lofty tree will any longer be able to grow thereon.

Alas! there cometh the time when man will no longer launch the arrow of his longing beyond man—and the string of his bow will have unlearned to whizz!

I tell you: one must still have chaos in one, to give birth to a dancing star. I tell you: ye have still chaos in you.

Alas! There cometh the time when man will no longer give birth to any star. Alas! There cometh the time of the most despicable man, who can no longer despise himself.

Lo! I show you THE LAST MAN.

"What is love? What is creation? What is longing? What is a star?"—so asketh the last man and blinketh.

The earth hath then become small, and on it there hoppeth the last man who maketh everything small. His species is ineradicable like that of the ground-flea; the last man liveth longest.

"We have discovered happiness"—say the last men, and blink thereby.

They have left the regions where it is hard to live; for they need warmth. One still loveth one's neighbour and rubbeth against him; for one needeth warmth.

Turning ill and being distrustful, they consider sinful: they walk warily. He is a fool who still stumbleth over stones or men!

A little poison now and then: that maketh pleasant dreams. And much poison at last for a pleasant death.

One still worketh, for work is a pastime. But one is careful lest the pastime should hurt one.

One no longer becometh poor or rich; both are too burdensome. Who still wanteth to rule? Who still wanteth to obey? Both are too burdensome.

No shepherd, and one herd! Every one wanteth the same; every one is equal: he who hath other sentiments goeth voluntarily into the madhouse.

"Formerly all the world was insane,"—say the subtlest of them, and blink thereby.

They are clever and know all that hath happened: so there is no end to their raillery. People still fall out, but are soon reconciled—otherwise it spoileth their stomachs.

They have their little pleasures for the day, and their little pleasures for the night, but they have a regard for health.

"We have discovered happiness,"—say the last men, and blink thereby.—

And here ended the first discourse of Zarathustra, which is also called "The Prologue": for at this point the shouting and mirth of the multitude interrupted him. "Give us this last man, O Zarathustra,"—they called out—"make us into these last men! Then will we make thee a present of the Superman!" And all the people exulted and smacked their lips. Zarathustra, however, turned sad, and said to his heart:

"They understand me not: I am not the mouth for these ears.

Too long, perhaps, have I lived in the mountains; too much have I hearkened unto the brooks and trees: now do I speak unto them as unto the goatherds.

Calm is my soul, and clear, like the mountains in the morning. But they think me cold, and a mocker with terrible jests.

And now do they look at me and laugh: and while they laugh they hate me too. There is ice in their laughter."

6.

Then, however, something happened which made every mouth mute and every eye fixed. In the meantime, of course, the rope-dancer had commenced his performance: he had come out at a little door, and was going along the rope which was stretched between two towers, so that it hung above the market-place and the people. When he was just midway across, the little door opened once more, and a gaudily-dressed fellow like a buffoon sprang out, and went rapidly after the first one. "Go on, halt-foot," cried his frightful voice, "go on, lazy-bones, interloper, sallow-face!—lest I tickle thee with my heel! What dost thou here between the towers? In the tower is the place for thee, thou shouldst be locked up; to one better than thyself thou blockest the way!"—And with every word he came nearer and nearer the first one. When, however, he was but a step behind, there happened the frightful thing which made every mouth mute and every eye fixed—he uttered a yell like a devil, and jumped over the other who was in his way. The latter, however, when he thus saw his rival triumph, lost at the same time his head and his footing on the rope; he threw his pole away, and shot downwards faster than it, like an eddy of arms and legs, into the depth. The market-place and the people were like the sea when the storm cometh on: they all flew apart and in disorder, especially where the body was about to fall.

Zarathustra, however, remained standing, and just beside him fell the body, badly injured and disfigured, but not yet dead. After a while consciousness returned to the shattered man, and he saw Zarathustra kneeling beside him. "What art thou doing there?" said he at last, "I knew long ago that the devil would trip me up. Now he draggeth me to hell: wilt thou prevent him?"

"On mine honour, my friend," answered Zarathustra, "there is nothing of all that whereof thou speakest: there is no devil and no hell. Thy soul will be dead even sooner than thy body: fear, therefore, nothing any more!"

The man looked up distrustfully. "If thou speakest the truth," said he, "I lose nothing when I lose my life. I am not much more than an animal which hath been taught to dance by blows and scanty fare."

"Not at all," said Zarathustra, "thou hast made danger thy calling; therein there is nothing contemptible. Now thou perishest by thy calling: therefore will I bury thee with mine own hands."

When Zarathustra had said this the dying one did not reply further; but he moved his hand as if he sought the hand of Zarathustra in gratitude.

7.

Meanwhile the evening came on, and the market-place veiled itself in gloom. Then the people dispersed, for even curiosity and terror become fatigued. Zarathustra, however, still sat beside the dead man on the ground, absorbed in thought: so he forgot the time. But at last it became night, and a cold wind blew upon the lonely one. Then arose Zarathustra and said to his heart:

Verily, a fine catch of fish hath Zarathustra made to-day! It is not a man he hath caught, but a corpse.

Sombre is human life, and as yet without meaning: a buffoon may be fateful to it.

I want to teach men the sense of their existence, which is the Superman, the lightning out of the dark cloud—man.

But still am I far from them, and my sense speaketh not unto their sense. To men I am still something between a fool and a corpse.

Gloomy is the night, gloomy are the ways of Zarathustra. Come, thou cold and stiff companion! I carry thee to the place where I shall bury thee with mine own hands.

8.

When Zarathustra had said this to his heart, he put the corpse upon his shoulders and set out on his way. Yet had he not gone a hundred steps, when there stole a man up to him and whispered in his ear—and lo! he that spake was the buffoon from the tower. "Leave this town, O Zarathustra," said he, "there are too many here who hate thee. The good and just hate thee, and call thee their enemy and despiser; the believers in the orthodox belief hate thee, and call thee a danger to the multitude. It was thy good fortune to be laughed at: and verily thou spakest like a buffoon. It was thy good fortune to associate with the dead dog; by so humiliating thyself thou hast saved thy life to-day. Depart, however, from this town,—or to-morrow I shall jump over thee, a living man over a dead one." And when he had said this, the buffoon vanished; Zarathustra, however, went on through the dark streets.

At the gate of the town the grave-diggers met him: they shone their torch on his face, and, recognising Zarathustra, they sorely derided him. "Zarathustra is carrying away the dead dog: a fine thing that Zarathustra hath turned a grave-digger! For our hands are too cleanly for that roast. Will Zarathustra steal the bite from the devil? Well then, good luck to the repast! If only the devil is not a better thief than Zarathustra!—he will steal them both, he will eat them both!" And they laughed among themselves, and put their heads together.

Zarathustra made no answer thereto, but went on his way. When he had gone on for two hours, past forests and swamps, he had heard too much of the hungry howling of the wolves, and he himself became a-hungry. So he halted at a lonely house in which a light was burning.

"Hunger attacketh me," said Zarathustra, "like a robber. Among forests and swamps my hunger attacketh me, and late in the night.

"Strange humours hath my hunger. Often it cometh to me only after a repast, and all day it hath failed to come: where hath it been?"

And thereupon Zarathustra knocked at the door of the house. An old man appeared, who carried a light, and asked: "Who cometh unto me and my bad sleep?"

"A living man and a dead one," said Zarathustra. "Give me something to eat and drink, I forgot it during the day. He that feedeth the hungry refresheth his own soul, saith wisdom."

The old man withdrew, but came back immediately and offered Zarathustra bread and wine. "A bad country for the hungry," said he; "that is why I live here. Animal and man come unto me, the anchorite. But bid thy companion eat and drink also, he is wearier than thou." Zarathustra answered: "My companion is dead; I shall hardly be able to persuade him to eat." "That doth not concern me," said the old man sullenly; "he that knocketh at my door must take what I offer him. Eat, and fare ye well!"—

Thereafter Zarathustra again went on for two hours, trusting to the path and the light of the stars: for he was an experienced night-walker, and liked to look into the face of all that slept. When the morning dawned, however, Zarathustra found himself in a thick forest, and no path was any longer visible. He then put the dead man in a hollow tree at his head—for he wanted to protect him from the wolves—and laid himself down on the ground and moss. And immediately he fell asleep, tired in body, but with a tranquil soul.

9.

Long slept Zarathustra; and not only the rosy dawn passed over his head, but also the morning. At last, however, his eyes opened, and amazedly he gazed into the forest and the stillness, amazedly he gazed into himself. Then he arose quickly, like a seafarer who all at once seeth the land; and he shouted for joy: for he saw a new truth. And he spake thus to his heart:

A light hath dawned upon me: I need companions—living ones; not dead companions and corpses, which I carry with me where I will.

But I need living companions, who will follow me because they want to follow themselves—and to the place where I will.

A light hath dawned upon me. Not to the people is Zarathustra to speak, but to companions! Zarathustra shall not be the herd's herdsman and hound!

To allure many from the herd—for that purpose have I come. The people and the herd must be angry with me: a robber shall Zarathustra be called by the herdsmen.

Herdsmen, I say, but they call themselves the good and just. Herdsmen, I say, but they call themselves the believers in the orthodox belief.

Behold the good and just! Whom do they hate most? Him who breaketh up their tables of values, the breaker, the law-breaker:—he, however, is the creator.

Behold the believers of all beliefs! Whom do they hate most? Him who breaketh up their tables of values, the breaker, the law-breaker—he, however, is the creator.

Companions, the creator seeketh, not corpses—and not herds or believers either. Fellow-creators the creator seeketh—those who grave new values on new tables.

Companions, the creator seeketh, and fellow-reapers: for everything is ripe for the harvest with him. But he lacketh the hundred sickles: so he plucketh the ears of corn and is vexed.

Companions, the creator seeketh, and such as know how to whet their sickles. Destroyers, will they be called, and despisers of good and evil. But they are the reapers and rejoicers.

Fellow-creators, Zarathustra seeketh; fellow-reapers and fellow-rejoicers, Zarathustra seeketh: what hath he to do with herds and herdsmen and corpses!

And thou, my first companion, rest in peace! Well have I buried thee in thy hollow tree; well have I hid thee from the wolves.

But I part from thee; the time hath arrived. 'Twixt rosy dawn and rosy dawn there came unto me a new truth.

I am not to be a herdsman, I am not to be a grave-digger. Not any more will I discourse unto the people; for the last time have I spoken unto the dead.

With the creators, the reapers, and the rejoicers will I associate: the rainbow will I show them, and all the stairs to the Superman.

To the lone-dwellers will I sing my song, and to the twain-dwellers; and unto him who hath still ears for the unheard, will I make the heart heavy with my happiness.

I make for my goal, I follow my course; over the loitering and tardy will I leap. Thus let my on-going be their down-going!

10.

This had Zarathustra said to his heart when the sun stood at noontide. Then he looked inquiringly aloft,—for he heard above him the sharp call of a bird. And behold! An eagle swept through the air in wide circles, and on it hung a serpent, not like a prey, but like a friend: for it kept itself coiled round the eagle's neck.

"They are mine animals," said Zarathustra, and rejoiced in his heart.

"The proudest animal under the sun, and the wisest animal under the sun,—they have come out to reconnoitre.

They want to know whether Zarathustra still liveth. Verily, do I still live?

More dangerous have I found it among men than among animals; in dangerous paths goeth Zarathustra. Let mine animals lead me!"

When Zarathustra had said this, he remembered the words of the saint in the forest. Then he sighed and spake thus to his heart:

"Would that I were wiser! Would that I were wise from the very heart, like my serpent!

But I am asking the impossible. Therefore do I ask my pride to go always with my wisdom!

And if my wisdom should some day forsake me:—alas! it loveth to fly away!—may my pride then fly with my folly!"

Thus began Zarathustra's down-going.

THE FLIES IN THE MARKET-PLACE

Flee, my friend, into thy solitude! I see thee deafened with the noise of the great men, and stung all over with the stings of the little ones.

Admirably do forest and rock know how to be silent with thee. Resemble again the tree which thou lovest, the broad-branched one—silently and attentively it o'erhangeth the sea.

Where solitude endeth, there beginneth the market-place; and where the market-place beginneth, there beginneth also the noise of the great actors, and the buzzing of the poison-flies.

In the world even the best things are worthless without those who represent them: those representers, the people call great men.

Little do the people understand what is great—that is to say, the creating agency. But they have a taste for all representers and actors of great things.

Around the devisers of new values revolveth the world:—invisibly it revolveth. But around the actors revolve the people and the glory: such is the course of things.

Spirit, hath the actor, but little conscience of the spirit. He believeth always in that wherewith he maketh believe most strongly—in HIMSELF!

To-morrow he hath a new belief, and the day after, one still newer. Sharp perceptions hath he, like the people, and changeable humours.

To upset—that meaneth with him to prove. To drive mad—that meaneth with him to convince. And blood is counted by him as the best of all arguments.

A truth which only glideth into fine ears, he calleth falsehood and trumpery. Verily, he believeth only in Gods that make a great noise in the world!

Full of clattering buffoons is the market-place,—and the people glory in their great men! These are for them the masters of the hour.

But the hour presseth them; so they press thee. And also from thee they want Yea or Nay. Alas! thou wouldst set thy chair betwixt For and Against?

On account of those absolute and impatient ones, be not jealous, thou lover of truth! Never yet did truth cling to the arm of an absolute one.

On account of those abrupt ones, return into thy security: only in the market-place is one assailed by Yea? or Nay?

Slow is the experience of all deep fountains: long have they to wait until they know WHAT hath fallen into their depths.

Away from the market-place and from fame taketh place all that is great: away from the market-place and from fame have ever dwelt the devisers of new values.

Flee, my friend, into thy solitude: I see thee stung all over by the poisonous flies. Flee thither, where a rough, strong breeze bloweth!

Flee into thy solitude! Thou hast lived too closely to the small and the pitiable. Flee from their invisible vengeance! Towards thee they have nothing but vengeance.

Raise no longer an arm against them! Innumerable are they, and it is not thy lot to be a fly-flap.

Innumerable are the small and pitiable ones; and of many a proud structure, rain-drops and weeds have been the ruin.

Thou art not stone; but already hast thou become hollow by the numerous drops. Thou wilt yet break and burst by the numerous drops.

Exhausted I see thee, by poisonous flies; bleeding I see thee, and torn at a hundred spots; and thy pride will not even upbraid.

Blood they would have from thee in all innocence; blood their bloodless souls crave for—and they sting, therefore, in all innocence.

But thou, profound one, thou sufferest too profoundly even from small wounds; and ere thou hadst recovered, the same poison-worm crawled over thy hand.

Too proud art thou to kill these sweet-tooths. But take care lest it be thy fate to suffer all their poisonous injustice!

They buzz around thee also with their praise: obtrusiveness, is their praise. They want to be close to thy skin and thy blood.

They flatter thee, as one flattereth a God or devil; they whimper before thee, as before a God or devil. What doth it come to! Flatterers are they, and whimperers, and nothing more.

Often, also, do they show themselves to thee as amiable ones. But that hath ever been the prudence of the cowardly. Yea! the cowardly are wise!

They think much about thee with their circumscribed souls—thou art always suspected by them! Whatever is much thought about is at last thought suspicious.

They punish thee for all thy virtues. They pardon thee in their inmost hearts only—for thine errors.

Because thou art gentle and of upright character, thou sayest: "Blameless are they for their small existence." But their circumscribed souls think: "Blamable is all great existence."

Even when thou art gentle towards them, they still feel themselves despised by thee; and they repay thy beneficence with secret maleficence.

Thy silent pride is always counter to their taste; they rejoice if once thou be humble enough to be frivolous.

What we recognise in a man, we also irritate in him. Therefore be on your guard against the small ones!

In thy presence they feel themselves small, and their baseness gleameth and gloweth against thee in invisible vengeance.

Sawest thou not how often they became dumb when thou approachedst them, and how their energy left them like the smoke of an extinguishing fire?

Yea, my friend, the bad conscience art thou of thy neighbours; for they are unworthy of thee. Therefore they hate thee, and would fain suck thy blood.

Thy neighbours will always be poisonous flies; what is great in thee—that itself must make them more poisonous, and always more fly-like.

Flee, my friend, into thy solitude—and thither, where a rough strong breeze bloweth. It is not thy lot to be a fly-flap.—

Thus spake Zarathustra.

THE NEW IDOL

Somewhere there are still peoples and herds, but not with us, my brethren: here there are states.

A state? What is that? Well! open now your ears unto me, for now will I say unto you my word concerning the death of peoples.

A state, is called the coldest of all cold monsters. Coldly lieth it also; and this lie creepeth from its mouth: "I, the state, am the people."

It is a lie! Creators were they who created peoples, and hung a faith and a love over them: thus they served life.

Destroyers, are they who lay snares for many, and call it the state: they hang a sword and a hundred cravings over them.

Where there is still a people, there the state is not understood, but hated as the evil eye, and as sin against laws and customs.

This sign I give unto you: every people speaketh its language of good and evil: this its neighbour understandeth not. Its language hath it devised for itself in laws and customs.

But the state lieth in all languages of good and evil; and whatever it saith it lieth; and whatever it hath it hath stolen.

False is everything in it; with stolen teeth it biteth, the biting one. False are even its bowels.

Confusion of language of good and evil; this sign I give unto you as the sign of the state. Verily, the will to death, indicateth this sign! Verily, it beckoneth unto the preachers of death!

Many too many are born: for the superfluous ones was the state devised!

See just how it enticeth them to it, the many-too-many! How it swalloweth and cheweth and recheweth them!

"On earth there is nothing greater than I: it is I who am the regulating finger of God"—thus roareth the monster. And not only the long-eared and short-sighted fall upon their knees!

Ah! even in your ears, ye great souls, it whispereth its gloomy lies! Ah! it findeth out the rich hearts which willingly lavish themselves!

Yea, it findeth you out too, ye conquerors of the old God! Weary ye became of the conflict, and now your weariness serveth the new idol!

Heroes and honourable ones, it would fain set up around it, the new idol! Gladly it basketh in the sunshine of good consciences,—the cold monster!

Everything will it give YOU, if YE worship it, the new idol: thus it purchaseth the lustre of your virtue, and the glance of your proud eyes.

It seeketh to allure by means of you, the many-too-many! Yea, a hellish artifice hath here been devised, a death-horse jingling with the trappings of divine honours!

Yea, a dying for many hath here been devised, which glorifieth itself as life: verily, a hearty service unto all preachers of death!

The state, I call it, where all are poison-drinkers, the good and the bad: the state, where all lose themselves, the good and the bad: the state, where the slow suicide of all—is called "life."

Just see these superfluous ones! They steal the works of the inventors and the treasures of the wise. Culture, they call their theft—and everything becometh sickness and trouble unto them!

Just see these superfluous ones! Sick are they always; they vomit their bile and call it a newspaper. They devour one another, and cannot even digest themselves.

Just see these superfluous ones! Wealth they acquire and become poorer thereby. Power they seek for, and above all, the lever of power, much money—these impotent ones!

See them clamber, these nimble apes! They clamber over one another, and thus scuffle into the mud and the abyss.

Towards the throne they all strive: it is their madness—as if happiness sat on the throne! Ofttimes sitteth filth on the throne.—and ofttimes also the throne on filth.

Madmen they all seem to me, and clambering apes, and too eager. Badly smelleth their idol to me, the cold monster: badly they all smell to me, these idolaters.

My brethren, will ye suffocate in the fumes of their maws and appetites! Better break the windows and jump into the open air!

Do go out of the way of the bad odour! Withdraw from the idolatry of the superfluous!

Do go out of the way of the bad odour! Withdraw from the steam of these human sacrifices!

Open still remaineth the earth for great souls. Empty are still many sites for lone ones and twain ones, around which floateth the odour of tranquil seas.

Open still remaineth a free life for great souls. Verily, he who possesseth little is so much the less possessed: blessed be moderate poverty!

There, where the state ceaseth—there only commenceth the man who is not superfluous: there commenceth the song of the necessary ones, the single and irreplaceable melody.

There, where the state CEASETH—pray look thither, my brethren! Do ye not see it, the rainbow and the bridges of the Superman?—

Thus spake Zarathustra.

OF ETERNAL RECURRENCE

THE VISION AND THE ENIGMA

1.

When it got abroad among the sailors that Zarathustra was on board the ship—for a man who came from the Happy Isles had gone on board along with him,—there was great curiosity and expectation. But Zarathustra kept silent for two days, and was cold and deaf with sadness; so that he neither answered looks nor questions. On the evening of the second day, however, he again opened his ears, though he still kept silent: for there were many curious and dangerous things to be heard on board the ship, which came from afar, and was to go still further. Zarathustra, however, was fond of all those who make distant voyages, and dislike to live without danger. And behold! when listening, his own tongue was at last loosened, and the ice of his heart broke. Then did he begin to speak thus:

To you, the daring venturers and adventurers, and whoever hath embarked with cunning sails upon frightful seas,—

To you the enigma-intoxicated, the twilight-enjoyers, whose souls are allured by flutes to every treacherous gulf:

—For ye dislike to grope at a thread with cowardly hand; and where ye can DIVINE, there do ye hate to CALCULATE—

To you only do I tell the enigma that I SAW—the vision of the lonesomest one.—

Gloomily walked I lately in corpse-coloured twilight—gloomily and sternly, with compressed lips. Not only one sun had set for me.

A path which ascended daringly among boulders, an evil, lonesome path, which neither herb nor shrub any longer cheered, a mountain-path, crunched under the daring of my foot.

Mutely marching over the scornful clinking of pebbles, trampling the stone that let it slip: thus did my foot force its way upwards.

Upwards:—in spite of the spirit that drew it downwards, towards the abyss, the spirit of gravity, my devil and arch-enemy.

Upwards:—although it sat upon me, half-dwarf, half-mole; paralysed, paralysing; dripping lead in mine ear, and thoughts like drops of lead into my brain.

"O Zarathustra," it whispered scornfully, syllable by syllable, "thou stone of wisdom! Thou threwest thyself high, but every thrown stone must—fall!

O Zarathustra, thou stone of wisdom, thou sling-stone, thou star-destroyer! Thyself threwest thou so high,—but every thrown stone—must fall!

Condemned of thyself, and to thine own stoning: O Zarathustra, far indeed threwest thou thy stone—but upon THYSELF will it recoil!"

Then was the dwarf silent; and it lasted long. The silence, however, oppressed me; and to be thus in pairs, one is verily lonesomer than when alone!

I ascended, I ascended, I dreamt, I thought,—but everything oppressed me. A sick one did I resemble, whom bad torture wearieth, and a worse dream reawakeneth out of his first sleep.—

But there is something in me which I call courage: it hath hitherto slain for me every dejection. This courage at last bade me stand still and say: "Dwarf! Thou! Or I!"—

For courage is the best slayer,—courage which ATTACKETH: for in every attack there is sound of triumph.

Man, however, is the most courageous animal: thereby hath he overcome every animal. With sound of triumph hath he overcome every pain; human pain, however, is the sorest pain.

Courage slayeth also giddiness at abysses: and where doth man not stand at abysses! Is not seeing itself—seeing abysses?

Courage is the best slayer: courage slayeth also fellow-suffering. Fellow-suffering, however, is the deepest abyss: as deeply as man looketh into life, so deeply also doth he look into suffering.

Courage, however, is the best slayer, courage which attacketh: it slayeth even death itself; for it saith: "WAS THAT life? Well! Once more!"

In such speech, however, there is much sound of triumph. He who hath ears to hear, let him hear.—

2.

"Halt, dwarf!" said I. "Either I—or thou! I, however, am the stronger of the two:—thou knowest not mine abysmal thought! IT—couldst thou not endure!"

Then happened that which made me lighter: for the dwarf sprang from my shoulder, the prying sprite! And it squatted on a stone in front of me. There was however a gateway just where we halted.

"Look at this gateway! Dwarf!" I continued, "it hath two faces. Two roads come together here: these hath no one yet gone to the end of.

This long lane backwards: it continueth for an eternity. And that long lane forward—that is another eternity.

They are antithetical to one another, these roads; they directly abut on one another:—and it is here, at this gateway, that they come together. The name of the gateway is inscribed above: 'This Moment.'

But should one follow them further—and ever further and further on, thinkest thou, dwarf, that these roads would be eternally antithetical?"—

"Everything straight lieth," murmured the dwarf, contemptuously. "All truth is crooked; time itself is a circle."

"Thou spirit of gravity!" said I wrathfully, "do not take it too lightly! Or I shall let thee squat where thou squattest, Haltfoot,—and I carried thee HIGH!"

"Observe," continued I, "This Moment! From the gateway, This Moment, there runneth a long eternal lane BACKWARDS: behind us lieth an eternity.

Must not whatever CAN run its course of all things, have already run along that lane? Must not whatever CAN happen of all things have already happened, resulted, and gone by?

And if everything have already existed, what thinkest thou, dwarf, of This Moment? Must not this gateway also—have already existed?

And are not all things closely bound together in such wise that This Moment draweth all coming things after it? CONSEQUENTLY—itself also?

For whatever CAN run its course of all things, also in this long lane OUTWARD—MUST it once more run!—

And this slow spider which creepeth in the moonlight, and this moonlight itself, and thou and I in this gateway whispering together, whispering of eternal things—must we not all have already existed?

—And must we not return and run in that other lane out before us, that long weird lane—must we not eternally return?"—

Thus did I speak, and always more softly: for I was afraid of mine own thoughts, and arrear-thoughts. Then, suddenly did I hear a dog HOWL near me.

Had I ever heard a dog howl thus? My thoughts ran back. Yes! When I was a child, in my most distant childhood:

—Then did I hear a dog howl thus. And saw it also, with hair bristling, its head upwards, trembling in the stillest midnight, when even dogs believe in ghosts:

—So that it excited my commiseration. For just then went the full moon, silent as death, over the house; just then did it stand still, a glowing globe—at rest on the flat roof, as if on some one's property:—

Thereby had the dog been terrified: for dogs believe in thieves and ghosts. And when I again heard such howling, then did it excite my commiseration once more.

Where was now the dwarf? And the gateway? And the spider? And all the whispering? Had I dreamt? Had I awakened? 'Twixt rugged rocks did I suddenly stand alone, dreary in the dreariest moonlight.

BUT THERE LAY A MAN! And there! The dog leaping, bristling, whining—now did it see me coming—then did it howl again, then did it CRY:—had I ever heard a dog cry so for help?

And verily, what I saw, the like had I never seen. A young shepherd did I see, writhing, choking, quivering, with distorted countenance, and with a heavy black serpent hanging out of his mouth.

Had I ever seen so much loathing and pale horror on one countenance? He had perhaps gone to sleep? Then had the serpent crawled into his throat—there had it bitten itself fast.

My hand pulled at the serpent, and pulled:—in vain! I failed to pull the serpent out of his throat. Then there cried out of me: "Bite! Bite!

Its head off! Bite!"—so cried it out of me; my horror, my hatred, my loathing, my pity, all my good and my bad cried with one voice out of me.—

Ye daring ones around me! Ye venturers and adventurers, and whoever of you have embarked with cunning sails on unexplored seas! Ye enigma-enjoyers!

Solve unto me the enigma that I then beheld, interpret unto me the vision of the lonesomest one!

For it was a vision and a foresight:—WHAT did I then behold in parable? And WHO is it that must come some day?

WHO is the shepherd into whose throat the serpent thus crawled? WHO is the man into whose throat all the heaviest and blackest will thus crawl?

—The shepherd however bit as my cry had admonished him; he bit with a strong bite! Far away did he spit the head of the serpent—: and sprang up.—

No longer shepherd, no longer man—a transfigured being, a light-surrounded being, that LAUGHED! Never on earth laughed a man as HE laughed!

O my brethren, I heard a laughter which was no human laughter,—and now gnaweth a thirst at me, a longing that is never allayed.

My longing for that laughter gnaweth at me: oh, how can I still endure to live! And how could I endure to die at present!—

Thus spake Zarathustra.

THE CONVALESCENT

1.

One morning, not long after his return to his cave, Zarathustra sprang up from his couch like a madman, crying with a frightful voice, and acting as if some one still lay on the couch who did not wish to rise. Zarathustra's voice also resounded in such a manner that his animals came to him frightened, and out of all the neighbouring caves and lurking-places all the creatures slipped away—flying, fluttering, creeping or leaping, according to their variety of foot or wing. Zarathustra, however, spake these words:

Up, abysmal thought out of my depth! I am thy cock and morning dawn, thou overslept reptile: Up! Up! My voice shall soon crow thee awake!

Unbind the fetters of thine ears: listen! For I wish to hear thee! Up! Up! There is thunder enough to make the very graves listen!

And rub the sleep and all the dimness and blindness out of thine eyes! Hear me also with thine eyes: my voice is a medicine even for those born blind.

And once thou art awake, then shalt thou ever remain awake. It is not MY custom to awake great-grandmothers out of their sleep that I may bid them—sleep on!

Thou stirrest, stretchest thyself, wheezest? Up! Up! Not wheeze, shalt thou,—but speak unto me! Zarathustra calleth thee, Zarathustra the godless!

I, Zarathustra, the advocate of living, the advocate of suffering, the advocate of the circuit—thee do I call, my most abysmal thought!

Joy to me! Thou comest,—I hear thee! Mine abyss SPEAKETH, my lowest depth have

I turned over into the light!

Joy to me! Come hither! Give me thy hand—ha! let be! aha!—Disgust, disgust, disgust—alas to me!

2.

Hardly, however, had Zarathustra spoken these words, when he fell down as one dead, and remained long as one dead. When however he again came to himself, then was he pale and trembling, and remained lying; and for long he would neither eat nor drink. This condition continued for seven days; his animals, however, did not leave him day nor night, except that the eagle flew forth to fetch food. And what it fetched and foraged, it laid on Zarathustra's couch: so that Zarathustra at last lay among yellow and red berries, grapes, rosy apples, sweet-smelling herbage, and pine-cones. At his feet, however, two lambs were stretched, which the eagle had with difficulty carried off from their shepherds.

At last, after seven days, Zarathustra raised himself upon his couch, took a rosy apple in his hand, smelt it and found its smell pleasant. Then did his animals think the time had come to speak unto him.

"O Zarathustra," said they, "now hast thou lain thus for seven days with heavy eyes: wilt thou not set thyself again upon thy feet?

Step out of thy cave: the world waiteth for thee as a garden. The wind playeth with heavy fragrance which seeketh for thee; and all brooks would like to run after thee.

All things long for thee, since thou hast remained alone for seven days—step forth out of thy cave! All things want to be thy physicians!

Did perhaps a new knowledge come to thee, a bitter, grievous knowledge? Like leavened dough layest thou, thy soul arose and swelled beyond all its bounds.—"

—O mine animals, answered Zarathustra, talk on thus and let me listen! It refresheth me so to hear your talk: where there is talk, there is the world as a garden unto me.

How charming it is that there are words and tones; are not words and tones rainbows and seeming bridges 'twixt the eternally separated?

To each soul belongeth another world; to each soul is every other soul a back-world.

Among the most alike doth semblance deceive most delightfully: for the smallest gap is most difficult to bridge over.

For me—how could there be an outside-of-me? There is no outside! But this we forget on hearing tones; how delightful it is that we forget!

Have not names and tones been given unto things that man may refresh himself with them? It is a beautiful folly, speaking; therewith danceth man over everything.

How lovely is all speech and all falsehoods of tones! With tones danceth our love on variegated rainbows.—

—"O Zarathustra," said then his animals, "to those who think like us, things all dance themselves: they come and hold out the hand and laugh and flee—and return.

Everything goeth, everything returneth; eternally rolleth the wheel of existence. Everything dieth, everything blossometh forth again; eternally runneth on the year of existence.

Everything breaketh, everything is integrated anew; eternally buildeth itself the same house of existence. All things separate, all things again greet one another; eternally true to itself remaineth the ring of existence.

Every moment beginneth existence, around every 'Here' rolleth the ball 'There.' The middle is everywhere. Crooked is the path of eternity."—

—O ye wags and barrel-organs! answered Zarathustra, and smiled once more, how well do ye know what had to be fulfilled in seven days:—

—And how that monster crept into my throat and choked me! But I bit off its head and spat it away from me.

And ye—ye have made a lyre-lay out of it? Now, however, do I lie here, still exhausted with that biting and spitting-away, still sick with mine own salvation.

AND YE LOOKED ON AT IT ALL? O mine animals, are ye also cruel? Did ye like to look at my great pain as men do? For man is the cruellest animal.

At tragedies, bull-fights, and crucifixions hath he hitherto been happiest on earth; and when he invented his hell, behold, that was his heaven on earth.

When the great man crieth—: immediately runneth the little man thither, and his tongue hangeth out of his mouth for very lusting. He, however, calleth it his "pity."

The little man, especially the poet—how passionately doth he accuse life in words! Hearken to him, but do not fail to hear the delight which is in all accusation!

Such accusers of life—them life overcometh with a glance of the eye. "Thou lovest me?" saith the insolent one; "wait a little, as yet have I no time for thee."

Towards himself man is the cruellest animal; and in all who call themselves "sinners" and "bearers of the cross" and "penitents," do not overlook the voluptuousness in their plaints and accusations!

And I myself—do I thereby want to be man's accuser? Ah, mine animals, this only have I learned hitherto, that for man his baddest is necessary for his best,—

—That all that is baddest is the best POWER, and the hardest stone for the highest creator; and that man must become better AND badder:—

Not to THIS torture-stake was I tied, that I know man is bad,—but I cried, as no one hath yet cried:

"Ah, that his baddest is so very small! Ah, that his best is so very small!"

The great disgust at man—IT strangled me and had crept into my throat: and what the soothsayer had presaged: "All is alike, nothing is worth while, knowledge strangleth."

A long twilight limped on before me, a fatally weary, fatally intoxicated sadness, which spake with yawning mouth.

"Eternally he returneth, the man of whom thou art weary, the small man"—so yawned my sadness, and dragged its foot and could not go to sleep.

A cavern, became the human earth to me; its breast caved in; everything living became to me human dust and bones and mouldering past.

My sighing sat on all human graves, and could no longer arise: my sighing and questioning croaked and choked, and gnawed and nagged day and night:

—"Ah, man returneth eternally! The small man returneth eternally!"

Naked had I once seen both of them, the greatest man and the smallest man: all too like one another—all too human, even the greatest man!

All too small, even the greatest man!—that was my disgust at man! And the eternal return also of the smallest man!—that was my disgust at all existence!

Ah, Disgust! Disgust! Disgust!—Thus spake Zarathustra, and sighed and shuddered; for he remembered his sickness. Then did his animals prevent him from speaking further.

"Do not speak further, thou convalescent!"—so answered his animals, "but go out where the world waiteth for thee like a garden.

Go out unto the roses, the bees, and the flocks of doves! Especially, however, unto the singing birds, to learn SINGING from them!

For singing is for the convalescent; the sound ones may talk. And when the sound also want songs, then want they other songs than the convalescent."

—"O ye wags and barrel-organs, do be silent!" answered Zarathustra, and smiled at his animals. "How well ye know what consolation I devised for myself in seven days!

That I have to sing once more—THAT consolation did I devise for myself, and THIS convalescence: would ye also make another lyre-lay thereof?"

—"Do not talk further," answered his animals once more; "rather, thou convalescent, prepare for thyself first a lyre, a new lyre!

For behold, O Zarathustra! For thy new lays there are needed new lyres.

Sing and bubble over, O Zarathustra, heal thy soul with new lays: that thou mayest bear thy great fate, which hath not yet been any one's fate!

For thine animals know it well, O Zarathustra, who thou art and must become: behold, THOU ART THE TEACHER OF THE ETERNAL RETURN,—that is now THY fate!

That thou must be the first to teach this teaching—how could this great fate not be thy greatest danger and infirmity!

Behold, we know what thou teachest: that all things eternally return, and ourselves with them, and that we have already existed times without number, and all things with us.

Thou teachest that there is a great year of Becoming, a prodigy of a great year; it must, like a sand-glass, ever turn up anew, that it may anew run down and run out:—

—So that all those years are like one another in the greatest and also in the smallest, so that we ourselves, in every great year, are like ourselves in the greatest and also in the smallest.

And if thou wouldst now die, O Zarathustra, behold, we know also how thou wouldst then speak to thyself:—but thine animals beseech thee not to die yet!

Thou wouldst speak, and without trembling, buoyant rather with bliss, for a great weight and worry would be taken from thee, thou patientest one!—

'Now do I die and disappear,' wouldst thou say, 'and in a moment I am nothing. Souls are as mortal as bodies.

But the plexus of causes returneth in which I am intertwined,—it will again create me! I myself pertain to the causes of the eternal return.

I come again with this sun, with this earth, with this eagle, with this serpent—NOT to a new life, or a better life, or a similar life:

—I come again eternally to this identical and selfsame life, in its greatest and its smallest, to teach again the eternal return of all things,—

—To speak again the word of the great noontide of earth and man, to announce again to man the Superman.

I have spoken my word. I break down by my word: so willeth mine eternal fate—as announcer do I succumb!

The hour hath now come for the down-goer to bless himself. Thus—ENDETH Zarathustra's down-going.'"—

When the animals had spoken these words they were silent and waited, so that Zarathustra might say something to them: but Zarathustra did not hear that they were silent. On the contrary, he lay quietly with closed eyes like a person sleeping, although he did not sleep; for he communed just then with his soul. The serpent, however, and the eagle, when they found him silent in such wise, respected the great stillness around him, and prudently retired.

Part VI: Wagner And Cultural *Nihilism*

NIETZSCHE CONTRA WAGNER

WHEREIN I ADMIRE WAGNER.

I believe that artists very often do not know what they are best able to do. They are much too vain. Their minds are directed to something prouder than merely to appear like little plants, which, with freshness, rareness, and beauty, know how to sprout from their soil with real perfection. The ultimate goodness of their own garden and vineyard is superciliously under-estimated by them, and their love and their insight are not of the same quality. Here is a musician who is a greater master than anyone else in the discovering of tones, peculiar to suffering, oppressed, and tormented souls, who can endow even dumb misery with speech. Nobody can approach him in the colours of late autumn, in the indescribably touching joy of a last, a very last, and all too short gladness; he knows of a chord which expresses those secret and weird midnight hours of the soul, when cause and effect seem to have fallen asunder, and at every moment something may spring out of nonentity. He is happiest of all when creating from out the nethermost depths of human happiness, and, so to speak, from out man's empty bumper, in which the bitterest and most repulsive drops have mingled with the sweetest for good or evil at last. He knows that weary shuffling along of the soul which is no longer able either to spring or to fly, nay, which is no longer able to walk; he has the modest glance of concealed suffering, of understanding without comfort, of leave-taking without word or sign; verily as the Orpheus of all secret misery he is greater than anyone, and many a thing was introduced into art for the first time by him, which hitherto had not been given expression, had not even been thought worthy of art—the cynical revolts, for instance, of which only the greatest sufferer is capable, also many a small and quite microscopical feature of the soul, as it were the scales of its amphibious nature—yes indeed, he is the master of everything very small. But this he refuses to be! His tastes are much more in love with vast walls and with daring frescoes! ... He does not see that his spirit has another desire and bent—a totally different outlook—that it prefers to squat peacefully in the corners of broken-down houses: concealed in this way, and hidden even from himself, he paints his really great masterpieces, all of which are very short, often only one bar in length—there, only, does he become quite good, great and perfect, perhaps there alone.—Wagner is one who has suffered much—and this elevates him above other musicians.—I admire Wagner wherever he sets himself to music.—

WHEREIN I RAISE OBJECTIONS.

With all this I do not wish to imply that I regard this music as healthy, and least of all in those places where it speaks of Wagner himself. My objections to Wagner's music are physiological objections. Why should I therefore begin by clothing them in æsthetic formulæ? Æsthetic is indeed nothing more than applied physiology.—The fact I bring forward, my "petit fait vrai" is that I can no longer breathe with ease when this music begins to have its effect upon me; that my foot immediately begins to feel indignant at it and rebels: for what it needs is time, dance, march: even the young German Kaiser could not march to Wagner's Imperial March,—what my foot demands in the first place from music is that ecstasy which lies in good walking, stepping and dancing.

But do not my stomach, my heart, my circulation also protest? Are not my intestines also troubled? And do I not become hoarse unawares? ... in order to listen to Wagner I require Géraudel's Pastilles.... And then I ask myself, what is it that my whole body must have from music in general? for there is no such thing as a soul.... I believe it must have relief: as if all animal functions were accelerated by means of light, bold, unfettered, self-reliant rhythms; as if brazen and leaden life could lose its weight by means of delicate and smooth melodies. My melancholy would fain rest its head in the haunts and abysses of perfection: for this reason I need music. But Wagner makes one ill—What do I care about the theatre? What do I care about the spasms of its moral ecstasies in which the mob—and who is not the mob to-day?—rejoices? What do I care about the whole pantomimic hocus-pocus of the actor? You are beginning to see that I am essentially anti-theatrical at heart. For the stage, this mob art par excellence, my soul has that deepest scorn felt by every artist to-day. With a stage success a man sinks to such an extent in my esteem as to drop out of sight; failure in this quarter makes me prick my ears, makes me begin to pay attention. But this was not so with Wagner; next to the Wagner who created the most unique music that has ever existed there was the Wagner who was essentially a man of the stage, an actor, the most enthusiastic mimomaniac that has perhaps existed on earth, even as a musician. And let it be said en passant that if Wagner's theory was "drama is the object, music is only a means"—his practice was from beginning to end, the attitude is the end, drama and even music can never be anything else than means." Music as the manner of accentuating, of strengthening, and deepening dramatic poses and all things which please the senses of the actor; and Wagnerian drama only an opportunity for a host of interesting attitudes!—Alongside of all other instincts he had the dictatorial instinct of a great actor in everything: and, as I have already said, as a musician also.—On one occasion, and not without trouble, I made this clear to a Wagnerite pur sang,— clearness and a Wagnerite! I won't say another word. There were reasons for adding; "For heaven's sake, be a little more true unto yourself! We are not in Bayreuth now. In Bayreuth people are only upright in the mass; the individual lies, he even lies to himself. One leaves oneself at home when one goes to Bayreuth, one gives up all right to one's own tongue and choice, to one's own taste and even to one's own courage, one knows these things no longer as one is wont to have them and practise them before God and the world and between one's own four walls. In the theatre no one brings the finest senses of his art with him, and least of all the artist who works for the theatre,—for here loneliness is lacking; everything perfect does not suffer a witness.... In the theatre one becomes mob, herd, woman, Pharisee, electing cattle, patron, idiot—Wagnerite: there, the most personal conscience is bound to submit to the levelling charm of the great multitude, there the neighbour rules, there one becomes a neighbour."

WAGNER AS A DANGER.

1.

The aim after which more modern music is striving, which is now given the strong but obscure name of "unending melody," can be clearly understood by comparing it to one's feelings on entering the sea. Gradually one loses one's footing and one ultimately abandons oneself to the mercy or fury of the elements: one has to swim. In

the solemn, or fiery, swinging movement, first slow and then quick, of old music—
one had to do something quite different; one had to dance. The measure which was
required for this and the control of certain balanced degrees of time and energy, forced
the soul of the listener to continual sobriety of thought.—Upon the counterplay of the
cooler currents of air which came from this sobriety, and from the warmer breath of
enthusiasm, the charm of all good music rested—Richard Wagner wanted another
kind of movement,—he overthrew the physiological first principle of all music before
his time. It was no longer a matter of walking or dancing,—we must swim, we must
hover.... This perhaps decides the whole matter. "Unending melody" really wants to
break all the symmetry of time and strength; it actually scorns these things—Its wealth
of invention resides precisely in what to an older ear sounds like rhythmic paradox and
abuse. From the imitation or the prevalence of such a taste there would arise a danger
for music—so great that we can imagine none greater—the complete degeneration of
the feeling for rhythm, chaos in the place of rhythm.... The danger reaches its climax
when such music cleaves ever more closely to naturalistic play-acting and pantomime,
which governed by no laws of form, aïm at effect and nothing more.... Expressiveness
at all costs and music a servant, a slave to attitudes—this is the end....

2.

What? would it really be the first virtue of a performance (as performing musical artists
now seem to believe), under all circumstances to attain to a haut-relief which cannot
be surpassed? If this were applied to Mozart, for instance, would it not be a real sin
against Mozart's spirit,—Mozart's cheerful, enthusiastic, delightful and loving spirit?
He who fortunately was no German, and whose seriousness is a charming and golden
seriousness and not by any means that of a German clodhopper.... Not to speak of the
earnestness of the "marble statue." ... But you seem to think that all music is the music
of the "marble statue"? —that all music should, so to speak, spring out of the wall and
shake the listener to his very bowels? ... Only thus could music have any effect! But
on whom would the effect be made? Upon something on which a noble artist ought
never to deign to act,—upon the mob, upon the immature! upon the blasts! upon the
diseased! upon idiots! upon Wagnerites!...

A MUSIC WITHOUT A FUTURE.

Of all the arts which succeed in growing on the soil of a particular culture, music is the
last plant to appear; maybe because it is the one most dependent upon our innermost
feelings, and therefore the last to come to the surface—at a time when the culture to
which it belongs is in its autumn season and beginning to fade. It was only in the art of
the Dutch masters that the spirit of mediæval Christianity found its expression—, its
architecture of sound is the youngest, but genuine and legitimate, sister of the Gothic.
It was only in Handel's music that the best in Luther and in those like him found its
voice, the Judeo-heroic trait which gave the Reformation a touch of greatness—the
Old Testament, not the New, become music. It was left to Mozart, to pour out the
epoch of Louis XIV., and of the art of Racine and Claude Lorrain, in ringing gold; only
in Beethoven's and Rossini's music did the Eighteenth Century sing itself out—the
century of enthusiasm, broken ideals, and fleeting joy. All real and original music is a

swan song.—Even our last form of music, despite its prevalence and its will to prevail, has perhaps only a short time to live: for it sprouted from a soil which was in the throes of a rapid subsidence,—of a culture which will soon be submerged. A certain Catholicism of feeling, and a predilection for some ancient indigenous (so-called national) ideals and eccentricities, was its first condition. Wagner's appropriation of old sagas and songs, in which scholarly prejudice taught us to see something German par excellence—now we laugh at it all, the resurrection of these Scandinavian monsters with a thirst for ecstatic sensuality and spiritualisation—the whole of this taking and giving on Wagner's part, in the matter of subjects, characters, passions, and nerves, would also give unmistakable expression to the spirit of his music provided that this music, like any other, did not know how to speak about itself save ambiguously: for musica is a woman.... We must not let ourselves be misled concerning this state of things, by the fact that at this very moment we are living in a reaction, in the heart itself of a reaction. The age of international wars, of ultramontane martyrdom, in fact, the whole interlude-character which typifies the present condition of Europe, may indeed help an art like Wagner's to sudden glory, without, however, in the least ensuring its future prosperity. The Germans themselves have no future....

WE ANTIPODES.

Perhaps a few people, or at least my friends, will remember that I made my first plunge into life armed with some errors and some exaggerations, but that, in any case, I began with hope in my heart. In the philosophical pessimism of the nineteenth century, I recognised—who knows by what by-paths of personal experience—the symptom of a higher power of thought, a more triumphant plenitude of life, than had manifested itself hitherto in the philosophies of Hume, Kant and Hegel!—I regarded tragic knowledge as the most beautiful luxury of our culture, as its most precious, most noble, most dangerous kind of prodigality; but, nevertheless, in view of its overflowing wealth, as a justifiable luxury. In the same way, I began by interpreting Wagner's music as the expression of a Dionysian powerfulness of soul. In it I thought I heard the earthquake by means of which a primeval life-force, which had been constrained for ages, was seeking at last to burst its bonds, quite indifferent to how much of that which nowadays calls itself culture, would thereby be shaken to ruins. You see how I misinterpreted, you see also, what I bestowed upon Wagner and Schopenhauer—myself. Every art and every philosophy may be regarded either as a cure or as a stimulant to ascending or declining life: they always presuppose suffering and sufferers. But there are two kinds of sufferers:—those that suffer from overflowing vitality, who need Dionysian art and require a tragic insight into, and a tragic outlook upon, the phenomenon life,—and there are those who suffer from reduced vitality, and who crave for repose, quietness, calm seas, or else the intoxication, the spasm, the bewilderment which art and philosophy provide. Revenge upon life itself—this is the most voluptuous form of intoxication for such indigent souls!... Now Wagner responds quite as well as Schopenhauer to the twofold cravings of these people,—they both deny life, they both slander it but precisely on this account they are my antipodes.—The richest creature, brimming over with vitality,—the Dionysian God and man, may not only allow himself to gaze upon the horrible and the questionable; but he can also lend his hand to the terrible deed, and can indulge in all the luxury of destruction, disaggregation, and negation,—in him evil, purposelessness and ugliness, seem just as allowable as they are in nature—because of his bursting plenitude of creative and rejuvenating powers, which are able to convert every desert into a luxurious land of plenty. Conversely, it is the greatest sufferer and pauper in vitality, who is most in need of mildness, peace and goodness—that which to-day is called humaneness—in thought as well as in action, and possibly of a God whose speciality is to be a God of the sick, a Saviour, and also of logic or the abstract intelligibility of existence even for idiots (—the typical "free-spirits," like the idealists, and "beautiful souls," are décadents—); in short, of a warm, danger-tight, and narrow confinement, between optimistic horizons which would allow of stultification.... And thus very gradually, I began to understand Epicurus, the opposite of a Dionysian Greek; and also the Christian who in fact is only a kind of Epicurean, and who, with his belief that "faith saves," carries the principle of Hedonism as far as possible—far beyond all intellectual honesty.... If I am ahead of all other psychologists in anything, it is in this fact that my eyes are more keen for tracing those most difficult and most captious of all deductions, in which the largest number of mistakes have been made,—the deduction which makes one infer something concerning the author from his work, something concerning the doer from his deed, something concerning the idealist from the need which produced this ideal, and something concerning the imperious craving which stands at the back of all thinking and valuing.—In regard to all artists of what kind soever, I shall now avail myself of this radical distinction: does the creative power in this case arise from a loathing of life, or from an excessive plenitude of life? In Goethe, for instance, an overflow of vitality was creative, in Flaubert—hate: Flaubert, a new edition of Pascal, but as an artist with this instinctive belief at heart: "Flaubert est toujours haïssable, l'homme n'est rien, l'œuvre est tout...." He tortured himself when he wrote, just as Pascal tortured himself when he thought—the feelings of both were inclined to be "non-egoistic." ... "Disinterestedness"—the principle of decadence, the will to nonentity in art as well as in morality.

WHERE WAGNER IS AT HOME.

Even at the present day, France is still the refuge of the most intellectual and refined culture in Europe, it remains the high school of taste: but one must know where to find this France of taste. The North-German Gazette, for instance, or who-ever expresses his sentiments in that paper, thinks that the French are "barbarians,"—as for me, if I had to find the blackest spot on earth, where slaves still required to be liberated, I should turn in the direction of Northern Germany.... But those who form part of that select France take very good care to conceal themselves: they are a small body of men, and there may be some among them who do not stand on very firm legs—a few may be fatalists, hypochondriacs, invalids; others may be enervated, and artificial,—such are those who would fain be artistic,—but all the loftiness and delicacy which still remains to this world, is in their possession. In this France of intellect, which is also the France of pessimism, Schopenhauer is already much more at home than he ever was in Germany; his principal work has already been translated twice, and the second time so excellently that now I prefer to read Schopenhauer in French (—he was an accident among Germans, just as I am—the Germans have no fingers wherewith to grasp us; they haven't any fingers at all,—but only claws). And I do not mention Heine—l'adorable Heine, as they say in Paris—who long since has passed into the flesh and blood of the more profound and more soulful of French lyricists. How could the horned cattle of Germany know how to deal with the délicatesses of such a nature!—And as to Richard Wagner, it is obvious, it is even glaringly obvious, that Paris is the very soil for him: the more French music adapts itself to the needs of l'âme moderne, the more Wagnerian it will become,—it is far enough advanced in this direction already.—In this respect one should not allow one's self to be misled by Wagner himself—it was simply disgraceful on Wagner's part to scoff at Paris, as he did, in its agony in **1871**.... In spite of it all, in Germany Wagner is only a misapprehension: who could be more incapable of understanding anything about Wagner than the Kaiser, for instance?—To everybody familiar with the movement of European culture, this fact, however, is certain, that French romanticism and Richard Wagner are most intimately related. All dominated by literature, up to their very eyes and ears—the first European artists with a universal literary culture,—most of them writers, poets, mediators and minglers of the senses and the arts, all fanatics in expression, great discoverers in the realm of the sublime as also of the ugly and the gruesome, and still greater discoverers in passion, in working for effect, in the art of dressing their windows,—all possessing talent far above their genius,—virtuosos to their backbone, knowing of secret passages to all that seduces, lures, constrains or overthrows; born enemies of logic and of straight lines, thirsting after the exotic, the strange and the monstrous, and all opiates for the senses and the understanding. On the whole, a daring dare-devil, magnificently violent, soaring and high-springing crew of artists, who first had to teach their own century—-it is the century of the mob—what the concept "artist" meant. But they were ill....

WAGNER AS THE APOSTLE OF CHASTITY.

1.

Is this the German way?
Comes this low bleating forth from German hearts?
Should Teutons, sin repenting, lash themselves,
Or spread their palms with priestly unctuousness,
Exalt their feelings with the censer's fumes,
And cower and quake and bend the trembling knee,
And with a sickly sweetness plead a prayer?
Then ogle nuns, and ring the Ave-bell,
And thus with morbid fervour out-do heaven?
Is this the German way?
Beware, yet are you free, yet your own Lords.
What yonder lures is Rome, Rome's faith sung without words.

2.

There is no necessary contrast between sensuality and chastity; every good marriage, every genuine love affair is above this contrast; but in those cases where the contrast exists, it is very far from being necessarily a tragic one. This, at least, ought to hold good of all well-constituted and good-spirited mortals, who are not in the least inclined to reckon their unstable equilibrium between angel and petite bête, without further ado, among the objections to existence, the more refined and more intelligent like Hafis and Goethe, even regarded it as an additional attraction. It is precisely contradictions of this kind which lure us to life.... On the other hand, it must be obvious, that when Circe's unfortunate animals are induced to worship chastity, all they see and worship therein, is their opposite—oh! and with what tragic groaning and fervour, may well be imagined—that same painful and thoroughly superfluous opposition which, towards the end of his life, Richard Wagner undoubtedly wished to set to music and to put on the stage, And to what purpose? we may reasonably ask.

3.

And yet this other question can certainly not be circumvented: what business had he actually with that manly (alas! so unmanly) "bucolic simplicity," that poor devil and son of nature—Parsifal, whom he ultimately makes a catholic by such insidious means—what?—was Wagner in earnest with Parsifal? For, that he was laughed at, I cannot deny, any more than Gottfried Keller can.... We should like to believe that "Parsifal" was meant as a piece of idle gaiety, as the closing act and satyric drama, with which Wagner the tragedian wished to take leave of us, of himself, and above all of tragedy, in a way which befitted him and his dignity, that is to say, with an extravagant, lofty and most malicious parody of tragedy itself, of all the past and terrible earnestness and sorrow of this world, of the most ridiculous form of the unnaturalness of the ascetic ideal, at last overcome. For Parsifal is the subject par excellence for a comic opera.... Is Wagner's "Parsifal" his secret laugh of superiority at himself, the triumph of his last and most exalted state of artistic freedom, of artistic transcendence—is it Wagner able to laugh at himself? Once again we only wish it were so; for what could Parsifal be if he were meant seriously? Is it necessary in his case to say (as I have heard people say) that "Parsifal" is "the product of the mad hatred of knowledge, intellect, and sensuality?" a curse upon the senses and the mind in one breath and in one fit of hatred? an act of apostasy and a return to Christianly sick and obscurantist ideals? And finally even a denial of self, a deletion of self, on the part of an artist who theretofore had worked with all the power of his will in favour of the opposite cause, the spiritualisation and sensualisation of his art? And not only of his art, but also of his life? Let us remember how enthusiastically Wagner at one time walked in the footsteps of the philosopher Feuerbach. Feuerbach's words "healthy sensuality" struck Wagner in the thirties and forties very much as they struck many other Germans— they called themselves the young Germans—that is to say, as words of salvation. Did he ultimately change his mind on this point? It would seem that he had at least had the desire of changing his doctrine towards the end.... Had the hatred of life become dominant in him as in Flaubert? For "Parsifal" is a work of rancour, of revenge, of the most secret concoction of poisons with which to make an end of the first conditions of life; it is a bad work. The preaching of chastity remains an incitement to unnaturalness: I despise anybody who does not regard "Parsifal" as an outrage upon morality.—

HOW I GOT RID OF WAGNER.

1.

Already in the summer of **1876**, when the first festival at Bayreuth was at its height, I took leave of Wagner in my soul. I cannot endure anything double-faced. Since Wagner had returned to Germany, he had condescended step by step to everything that I despise—even to anti-Semitism. ... As a matter of fact, it was then high time to bid him farewell: but the proof of this came only too soon. Richard Wagner, ostensibly the most triumphant creature alive; as a matter of fact, though, a cranky and desperate décadent, suddenly fell helpless and broken on his knees before the Christian cross.... Was there no German at that time who had the eyes to see, and the sympathy in his soul to feel, the ghastly nature of this spectacle? Was I the only one who suffered from it?—Enough, the unexpected event, like a flash of lightning, made me see only too clearly what kind of a place it was that I had just left,—and it also made me shudder as a man shudders who unawares has just escaped a great danger. As I continued my journey alone, I trembled. Not long after this I was ill, more than ill—I was tired;—tired of the continual disappointments over everything which remained for us modern men to be enthusiastic about, of the energy, industry, hope, youth, and love that are squandered everywhere; tired out of loathing for the whole world of idealistic lying and conscience-softening, which, once again, in the case of Wagner, had scored a victory over a man who was of the bravest; and last but not least, tired by the sadness of a ruthless suspicion—that I was now condemned to be ever more and more suspicious, ever more and more contemptuous, ever more and more deeply alone than I had been theretofore. For I had no one save Richard Wagner.... I was always condemned to the society of Germans....

2.

Henceforward alone and cruelly distrustful of myself, I then took up sides—not without anger—against myself and for all that which hurt me and fell hard upon me: and thus I found the road to that courageous pessimism which is the opposite of all idealistic falsehood, and which, as it seems to me, is also the road to me—to my mission.... That hidden and dominating thing, for which for long ages we have had no name, until ultimately it comes forth as our mission,—this tyrant in us wreaks a terrible revenge upon us for every attempt we make either to evade him or to escape him, for every one of our experiments in the way of befriending people to whom we do not belong, for every active occupation, however estimable, which may make us diverge from our principal object:—aye, and even for every virtue which would fain protect us from the rigour of our most intimate sense of responsibility. Illness is always the answer, whenever we venture to doubt our right to our mission, whenever we begin to make things too easy for ourselves. Curious and terrible at the same time! It is for our relaxation that we have to pay most dearly! And should we wish after all to return to health, we then have no choice: we are compelled to burden ourselves more heavily than we had been burdened before....

THE PSYCHOLOGIST SPEAKS.

1.

The oftener a psychologist—a born, an unavoidable psychologist and soul-diviner—turns his attention to the more select cases and individuals, the greater becomes his danger of being suffocated by sympathy: he needs greater hardness and cheerfulness than any other man. For the corruption, the ruination of higher men, is in fact the rule: it is terrible to have such a rule always before our eyes. The manifold torments of the psychologist who has discovered this ruination, who discovers once, and then discovers almost repeatedly throughout all history, this universal inner "hopelessness" of higher men, this eternal "too late!" in every sense—may perhaps one day be the cause of his "going to the dogs "himself. In almost every psychologist we may see a tell-tale predilection in favour of intercourse with commonplace and well-ordered men: and this betrays how constantly he requires healing, that he needs a sort of flight and forgetfulness, away from what his insight and incisiveness—from what his "business"—has laid upon his conscience. A horror of his memory is typical of him. He is easily silenced by the judgment of others; he hears with unmoved countenance how people honour, admire, love, and glorify, where he has opened his eyes and seen—or he even conceals his silence by expressly agreeing with some obvious opinion. Perhaps the paradox of his situation becomes so dreadful that, precisely where he has learnt great sympathy, together with great contempt, the educated have on their part learnt great reverence. And who knows but in all great instances, just this alone happened: that the multitude worshipped a God, and that the "God" was only a poor sacrificial animal! Success has always been the greatest liar—and the "work" itself, the deed, is a success too; the great statesman, the conqueror, the discoverer, are disguised in their creations until they can no longer be recognised; the "work" of the artist, of the philosopher, only invents him who has created it, who is reputed to have created it; the "great men," as they are reverenced, are poor little fictions composed afterwards; in the world of historical values counterfeit coinage prevails.

2.

Those great poets, for example, such as Byron, Musset, Poe, Leopardi, Kleist, Gogol (I do not dare to mention much greater names, but I imply them), as they now appear, and were perhaps obliged to be: men of the moment, sensuous, absurd, versatile, light-minded and quick to trust and to distrust; with souls in which usually some flaw has to be concealed; often taking revenge with their works for an internal blemish, often seeking forgetfulness in their soaring from a too accurate memory, idealists out of proximity to the mud:—what a torment these great artists are and the so-called higher men in general, to him who has once found them out! We are all special pleaders in the cause of mediocrity. It is conceivable that it is just from woman—who is clair-voyant in the world of suffering, and, alas! also unfortunately eager to help and save to an extent far beyond her powers—that they have learnt so readily those outbreaks of boundless sympathy which the multitude, above all the reverent multitude, overwhelms with prying and self-gratifying interpretations. This sympathising invariably deceives itself as to its power; woman would like to believe that love can do everything—it is the superstition peculiar to her. Alas, he who knows the heart finds out how poor, helpless, pretentious, and blundering even the best and deepest love is—how much more readily it destroys than saves....

3.

The intellectual loathing and haughtiness of every man who has suffered deeply—the extent to which a man can suffer, almost determines the order of rank—the chilling uncertainty with which he is thoroughly imbued and coloured, that by virtue of his suffering he knows more than the shrewdest and wisest can ever know, that he has been familiar with, and "at home" in many distant terrible worlds of which "you know nothing!"—this silent intellectual haughtiness, this pride of the elect of knowledge, of the "initiated," of the almost sacrificed, finds all forms of disguise necessary to protect itself from contact with gushing and sympathising hands, and in general from all that is not its equal in suffering. Profound suffering makes noble; it separates.—One of the most refined forms of disguise is Epicurism, along with a certain ostentatious boldness of taste which takes suffering lightly, and puts itself on the defensive against all that is sorrowful and profound. There are "cheerful men" who make use of good spirits, because they are misunderstood on account of them—they wish to be misunderstood. There are "scientific minds" who make use of science, because it gives a cheerful appearance, and because love of science leads people to conclude that a person is shallow—they wish to mislead to a false conclusion. There are free insolent spirits which would fain conceal and deny that they are at bottom broken, incurable hearts— this is Hamlet's case: and then folly itself can be the mask of an unfortunate and alas! all too dead-certain knowledge.

EPILOGUE

I have often asked myself whether I am not much more deeply indebted to the hardest years of my life than to any others. According to the voice of my innermost nature, everything necessary, seen from above and in the light of a superior economy, is also useful in itself—not only should one bear it, one should love it.... Amor fati: this is the very core of my being.—And as to my prolonged illness, do I not owe much more to it than I owe to my health? To it I owe a higher kind of health, a sort of health which grows stronger under everything that does not actually kill it!—To it, I owe even my philosophy.... Only great suffering is the ultimate emancipator of spirit; for it teaches one that vast suspiciousness which makes an X out of every U, a genuine and proper X, i.e., the antepenultimate letter: Only great suffering; that great suffering, under which we seem to be over a fire of greenwood, the suffering that takes its time—forces us philosophers to descend into our nethermost depths, and to let go of all trustfulness, all good-nature, all whittling-down, all mildness, all mediocrity,—on which things we had formerly staked our humanity. I doubt whether such suffering improves a man; but I know that it makes him deeper.... Supposing we learn to set our pride, our scorn, our strength of will against it, and thus resemble the Indian who, however cruelly he may be tortured, considers himself revenged on his tormentor by the bitterness of his own tongue. Supposing we withdraw from pain into nonentity, into the deaf, dumb, and rigid sphere of self-surrender, self-forgetfulness, self-effacement: one is another person when one leaves these protracted and dangerous exercises in the art of self-mastery; one has one note of interrogation the more, and above all one has the will henceforward to ask more, deeper, sterner, harder, more wicked, and more silent questions, than anyone has ever asked on earth before.... Trust in life has vanished; life itself has become a problem. —But let no one think that one has therefore become a spirit of gloom or a blind owl! Even love of life is still possible,—but it is a different kind of love.... It is the love for a woman whom we doubt....

2.

The rarest of all things is this: to have after all another taste—a second taste. Out of such abysses, out of the abyss of great suspicion as well, a man returns as though born again, he has a new skin, he is more susceptible, more full of wickedness; he has a finer taste for joyfulness; he has a more sensitive tongue for all good things; his senses are more cheerful; he has acquired a second, more dangerous, innocence in gladness; he is more childish too, and a hundred times more cunning than ever he had been before.

Oh, how much more repulsive pleasure now is to him, that coarse, heavy, buff-coloured pleasure, which is understood by our pleasure-seekers, our "cultured people," our wealthy folk and our rulers! With how much more irony we now listen to the hubbub as of a country fair, with which the "cultured" man and the man about town allow themselves to be forced through art, literature, music, and with the help of intoxicating liquor, to "intellectual enjoyments." How the stage-cry of passion now stings our ears; how strange to our taste the whole romantic riot and sensuous bustle, which the cultured mob are so fond of, together with its aspirations to the sublime, to the exalted and the distorted, have become. No: if we convalescents require an art at all, it is another art-a mocking, nimble, volatile, divinely undisturbed, divinely artificial art, which blazes up like pure flame into a cloudless sky! But above all, an art for artists, only for artists! We are, after all, more conversant with that which is in the highest degree necessary— cheerfulness, every kind of cheerfulness, my friends!... We men of knowledge, now know something only too well: oh how well we have learnt by this time, to forget, not to know, as artists!... As to our future: we shall scarcely be found on the track of those Egyptian youths who break into temples at night, who embrace statues, and would fain unveil, strip, and set in broad daylight, everything which there are excellent reasons to keep concealed.[1] No, we are disgusted with this bad taste, this will to truth, this search after truth "at all costs": this madness of adolescence, "the love of truth"; we are now too experienced, too serious, too joyful, too scorched, too profound for that.... We no longer believe that truth remains truth when it is unveiled,—we have lived enough to understand this.... To-day it seems to us good form not to strip everything naked, not to be present at all things, not to desire to "know" all. "Tout comprendre c'est tout mépriser." ... "Is it true," a little girl once asked her mother, "that the beloved Father is everywhere?—I think it quite improper,"—a hint to philosophers.... The shame with which Nature has concealed herself behind riddles and enigmas should be held in higher esteem. Perhaps truth is a woman who has reasons for not revealing her reasons? ... Perhaps her name, to use a Greek word is Baubo?—Oh these Greeks, they understood, the art of living! For this it is needful to halt bravely at the surface, at the fold, at the skin, to worship appearance, and to believe in forms, tones, words, and the whole Olympus of appearance! These Greeks were superficial—from profundity. ... And are we not returning to precisely the same thing, we dare-devils of intellect who have scaled the highest and most dangerous pinnacles of present thought, in order to look around us from that height, in order to look down from that height? Are we not precisely in this respect—Greeks? Worshippers of form, of tones, of words? Precisely on that account—artists?

[1]An allusion to Schiller's poem: "Das verschleierte Bild zu Sais."—Tr.

Get Your Free E-book!

Scan the QR code below to instantly access the e-book **'The Nihilist's Dictionary: Nietzsche's Most Confusing Concepts Decoded'**, absolutely free

https://bonus.grapevinebooks.com/nihilistdictionary

Made in the USA
Monee, IL
07 July 2026

56550116R00104